The Analysis of Financial Statements

THE ANALYSIS OF FINANCIAL STATEMENTS

Leopold A. Bernstein, Ph.D., C.P.A.

Professor of Accounting
Bernard M. Baruch College
The City University of New York

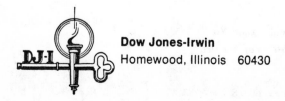

Dow Jones-Irwin
Homewood, Illinois   60430

An expanded version of this text is published by Richard D. Irwin, Inc. under the title *Financial Statement Analysis: Theory, Application, and Interpretation,* revised edition.

ISBN 0-87094-164-X
Library of Congress Catalog Card No. 78-55533
Printed in the United States of America

1 2 3 4 5 6 7 8 9 0 K 5 4 3 2 1 0 9 8

PREFACE

This book should prove of value to all those who need a thorough understanding of the uses to which financial statements are put as well as to those who must know how to use them intelligently and effectively. This encompasses accountants, security analysts, lending officers, credit analysts, managers, and investors and others who must make decisions on the basis of financial data. They will learn how knowledge of the accounting framework is integrated with the best tools and techniques that are available for the analysis and interpretations of financial statements.

Investing, lending, and other financial decisions require the ability to forecast—to foresee. Alfred North Whitehead assured us that foresight can be taught when he wrote: "Foresight depends upon understanding. In practical affairs it is a habit. But the habit of foreseeing is elicited by the habit of understanding. To a large extent, understanding can now be acquired by a conscious effort and it can be taught. Thus the training of foresight is by the medium of understanding."

The keynote of this work, thus, is understanding. It focuses on understanding the data which are analyzed as well as the methods by which they are analyzed and interpreted.

April 1978   *Leopold A. Bernstein*

CONTENTS

native methods of inventory management. Current liabilities: *Differences in the "nature" of current liabilities. Days purchases in accounts payable ratio. The capacity to borrow.* Interpretation of the current ratio: *Examination of trend. Interpretation of changes over time. Possibilities of manipulation. The use of "rules of thumb" standard. The net trade cycle. Valid working capital standards. The importance of sales. Common-size analysis of current assets composition. The liquidity index.* Acid-test ratio. Other measures of short-term liquidity: *Funds flow ratios. Cash flow related measures. Projecting changes in conditions or policies.*

Overview of cash flow and funds flow pattern. Short-term cash forecasts: *Importance of sales estimates. Pro forma financial statements as an aid to forecasting. Techniques of short-term cash forecasting. Differences between short-term and long-term forecasts.* Analysis of statements of changes in financial position: *First illustration of statement of changes in financial position analysis. Second illustration of statement of changes in financial position analysis.* Evaluation of the statement of changes in financial position. Projection of statements of changes in financial position: *The impact of adversity. The funds flow adequacy ratio. Funds reinvestment ratio.* Conclusion.

Key elements in the evaluation of long-term solvency. Importance of capital structure. Accounting principles: *Deferred credits. Long-term leases. Liabilities for pensions. Unconsolidated subsidiaries. Provisions, reserves and contingent liabilities. Minority interests. Convertible debt. Preferred stock. Effect of intangible assets. The significance of capital structure.* Reasons for employment of debt: *The concept of financial leverage. The effect of tax deductibility of interest. Other advantages of leverage. Measuring the effect of financial leverage. Financial leverage index. Measuring the effect of capital structure on long-term solvency. Long-term projections—usefulness and limitations.* Capital structure analysis—common-size statements. Capital structure ratios: *Equity capital/total liabilities. Equity capital/long-term debt. Short-term debt. Equity capital at market value. Interpretation of capital structure measures.* Measures of assets distribution. Measures of earnings coverage. Earnings available to meet fixed charges. Fixed charges to be included: *1. Interest on long-term debt. 2. Interest implicit in lease obligations. 3. Capitalized interest. 4. Other elements to be included in fixed charges. 5. Principal repayment requirements. 6. Other fixed charges. 7. Guarantees to pay fixed charges.* Illustration of earnings-coverage ratio calculations. Times-interest-earned ratio: *Ratio of earning to fixed charges. Coverage of ratios to senior bonds. Fixed-charges-coverage ratio—the SEC standard. Fixed-charges-coverage ratios—expanded concept of fixed charges. Noninterest portion of capitalized rents ($110,000). Noncancellable raw* *material purchase commitments. Recognition of benefits stemming from fixed charges. Computation of coverage ratio—expanded concept of fixed charges. Pro forma computations of coverage ratios. Funds flow coverage of fixed charges. Other useful tests of funds flow relationships. Stability of "flow of funds from operations."* Earnings coverage of preferred dividends. Evaluation of earnings-coverage ratios: *Importance of earnings variability. Importance of method of computation and of underlying assumptions. Example of minimum standard of coverage.* Appendix A: The rating of debt obligations. Appendix B: Ratios as predictors of business failure.

Diverse views of performance. Criteria of performance evaluation. Importance of return on investment (ROI). Major objectives in the use of ROI: *An indicator of managerial effectiveness. A method of projecting earnings. Internal decision and control tool.* Basic elements of ROI: *Defining the investment base.* Book versus market values in the investment base: *Difference between investor's cost and enterprise investment base. Averaging the investment base. Relating income to the investment base. Illustration of ROI computations. Analysis and interpretation of ROI.* Analysis of asset utilization: *Evaluation of individual turnover ratios. Use of averages. Other factors to be considered in return on asset evaluation. Equity growth rate. Return on shareholders' equity. Equity turnover. Measuring the financial leverage index. Analysis of financial leverage effects.*

The significance of income statement analysis. The major objectives of income analysis: *What is the relevant net income of the enterprise?* Analysis of components of the income statement: *Accounting principles used and their implication. Tools of income statement analysis.* The analysis of sales and revenues: *Major sources of revenue.* Financial reporting by diversified enterprises: *Reasons for the need for data by significant enterprise segments. Disclosure of "line of business" data. Income statement data. Balance sheet data. Research studies. Statement of Financial Accounting Standards 14. SEC reporting requirements. Implications for analysis. Stability and trend of revenues.* Management's discussion and analysis of the summary of earnings: *Implications for analysis. Methods of revenue recognition and measurement.*

Analysis of cost of sales. Gross profit: *Factors in the analysis of gross profit.* Analysis of changes in gross margin. Example of analysis of change in gross margin: *Interpretation of changes in gross margin.* Break-even analysis: *Concepts underlying break-even analysis. Equation approach.*

Graphic presentation. Contribution margin approach. Pocket calculator problem—additional considerations. Break-even techniques—problem areas and limitations. Break-even analysis—uses and their implications. Analytical implications of break-even analysis. The significance of the variable cost percentage. The significance of the fixed-cost level. The importance of the contribution margin. Additional considerations in the analysis of cost of sales. Depreciation. Amortization of special tools and similar costs. Maintenance and repairs costs. Other costs and expenses—general: *Selling expenses. Future directed marketing costs.* General, administration, financial, and other expenses: *Financial costs. "Other" expenses.* Other income. Income taxes. The operating ratio. Net income ratio: *Statement accounting for variation in net income.*

Objectives of earnings evaluation. Evaluation of earnings level and its quality. The concept of earnings quality: *Evaluation of discretionary and future-directed costs. Maintenance and repairs. Advertising. Research and development costs. Other future-directed costs.* Balance sheet analysis as a check on the validity and quality of reported earnings: *Importance of carrying amounts of assets. Importance of provisions and liabilities. Balance sheet analysis and the quality of earnings. Effect of valuation of specific assets on the validity and quality of reported income. The effect of external factors on the quality of earnings.* Evaluation of earnings stability and trend: *Determining the trend of income over the years.* Extraordinary gains and losses: *Significance of accounting treatment and presentation. Analysis and evaluation.* Earnings forecasting: *SEC disclosure requirements—aid to forecasting. Elements in earnings forecasts. Publication of financial forecasts. Estimating earning power. Monitoring performance and results.* Interim financial statements: *Year-end adjustments. Seasonality. APB Opinion No. 28.: SEC interim reporting requirements. Implications for analysis.*

The methodology of financial statement analysis. Significance of the "building block" approach to financial analysis. The earmarks of good financial analysis. Special industry or environmental characteristics. Illustration of comprehensive analysis of financial statements—Marine Supply Corporation: *Introduction. Financial statements. Additional information. Analysis of short-term liquidity. Analysis of funds flow. Analysis of capital structure and long-term solvency. Analysis of return on investment. Analysis of asset utilization. Analysis of operating performance. Summary and conclusions.* Uses of financial statement analysis.

Major provisions of *APB Opinion No. 15.: Simple capital structure. Computation of weighted average of common shares outstanding.* Complex capital structure: *Primary EPS. Fully diluted EPS. Requirements for additional disclosures in conjunction with the presentation of EPS data. Elections at the time EPS opinion became effective.* Comprehensive illustration of computation of EPS. Implications for analysis: *Statement accounting for changes in earnings per share*

1

TOOLS AND TECHNIQUES OF FINANCIAL STATEMENT ANALYSIS—AN OVERVIEW

Basic approaches to financial statement analysis

Not everyone who analyzes financial statements will want the same information from the same statement. Objectives differ from one group of analysts to another. The equity investor may want to know:

1. What has the company's operating performance been over the longer term and over the recent past? What does this record hold for future earnings prospects?
2. Has the company's earnings record been one of growth, stability, or decline? Does it display significant variability?
3. What is the company's current financial condition? What factors are likely to affect it in the near future?
4. What is the company's capital structure? What risks and rewards does it hold for the investor?
5. How does this company compare on the above counts with other companies in its industry?

The banker who is approached with a short-term loan request may look to the financial statements for answers to questions such as the following:

1. What are the underlying reasons for the company's needs for funds? Are these needs truly short term, and if so, will they be self-liquidating?

1

2. From what sources is the company likely to get funds for the payment of interest and the repayment of principal?

3. How has management handled its needs for short-term and long-term funds in the past? What does this portend for the future?

An important first step in any decision-making process is to identify the most significant, pertinent, and critical questions which have a bearing on the decision. Financial statement analysis does not, of course, provide answers to all such questions. However, each of the questions exemplified above can, to a significant extent, be answered by such analysis. Financial statement analysis utilizes a variety of approaches and techniques among which are the following.

Reconstruction of business transactions. Basic to the analyst's work is an ability to reconstruct the business transactions which are summarized in the financial statements. That requires an understanding of the *reality* underlying such business transactions as well as a knowledge of the *accounting entries* used to record it properly within the accounting framework.

The analyst must also know what information is not generally available in financial statements so that he may attempt to secure it. In addition to information such as commitments, lines of credit, and order backlogs, the analyst will also generally not find the *details* of changes in many important accounts. Thus, for example, a short-term bank loan account or a loan to officers account may show little or no change in year-end balances but may, in fact, have had significant interim balances which were liquidated during the year.

A knowledge of what information can be found in financial statements, where it is to be found and how to reconstruct transactions, including the making of reasonable assumptions, are important skills in the analysis of financial statements.

ILLUSTRATION 1. The analyst of the financial statements of Beta Company (see Appendix B to this chapter) wants to determine the actual amount of long-term debt paid off in 19X6. This involves the reconstruction and analysis of two accounts. To get all the pertinent information the analyst must refer to the balances of the long-term debt (current and noncurrent) accounts in the balance sheet, to footnote 8 as well as to the statement of changes in financial position.

Long-Term Debt—(Noncurrent)

Transfer to the current L.T.D. account (derived balancing figure)	124.1	Beginning balance	1,137.2
Ending balance	1,054.3	Long term borrowing (per statement of changes in financial position)	41.2
	1,178.4		1,178.4

Long-Term Debt—(Current)

→ Long-term debt paid off		Beginning balance	119.2
(balancing amount)	121.1	Transfer from L.T.D.—	
Ending balance	122.2	Noncurrent	124.1
	243.3		243.3

Direct measurements.   Some factors and relationships can be measured directly. For example, the relationship between the debt and the equity of an entity is a direct measurement. Both the amount of debt and that of equity can be measured in absolute terms (i.e., in dollars) and their relationship computed therefrom.

Indirect evidence.   Financial statement analysis can provide indirect evidence bearing on important questions. Thus, the analysis of past statements of changes in financial position can offer evidence as to the financial habits of a management team. Moreover, the analysis of operating statements will yield evidence regarding management's ability to cope with fluctuations in the level of the firm's business activity. While such indirect evidence and evaluation are often not precise or quantifiable, the data derived therefore nevertheless possess importance because the effects of almost all managerial decisions, or the lack of them, are reflected in the entity's financial statements.

Predictive functions.   Almost all decision questions, including those in the examples above, are oriented towards the future. Thus, an important measure of the usefulness of financial statement analysis tools and techniques is their ability to assist in the prediction of expected future conditions and results.

Comparison.   This is a very important analytical process. It is based on the elementary proposition that in financial analysis no number standing by itself can be meaningful, and that it gains meaning only when related to some other comparable quantity. By means of comparison, financial analysis is useful in performing important evaluative, as well as attention-directing and control, functions. Thus, it focuses on exceptions and variations, and saves the analyst the need to evaluate the normal and the expected. Moreover, by means of comparison, selection among alternative choices is accomplished.

Comparison may be performed by using:

1. A company's own experience over the years (i.e., internally derived data);
2. External data, such as industry statistics; or
3. Compiled yardsticks, including standards, budgets, and forecasts.

Historical company data can usually be readily obtained and most readily adjusted for inconsistencies.

Uses of external data. Useful comparison may also be made with external data. The advantages of external data are: (1) they are normally objective and independent; (2) they are derived from similar operations, thus performing the function of a standard of comparison; and (3) if current, they reflect events occurring during an identical period having as a consequence similar business and economic conditions in common.

External information must, however, be used with great care and discrimination. Knowledge of the basis and method of compilation, the period covered, and the source of the information will facilitate a decision of whether the information is at all comparable. At times, sufficient detail may be available to adjust data so as to render them comparable. In any event, a decision on a proper standard of comparison must be made by choosing from those available. Differences between situations compared must be noted. Such differences may be in accounting practices or specific company policies. It must also be borne in mind that the past is seldom an unqualified guide to the future.

SOURCES OF INFORMATION

For basic data on an enterprise and for comparative data of comparable entities in its industry, published financial statements provide the best and most readily available source.

Appendix A to this chapter presents a listing of Sources of Information on Financial and Operating Ratios of various industries as well as sample presentations from these sources. These data, while representing valuable sources for comparison, must be used with care and with as complete a knowledge of the basis of their compilation as is possible to obtain. A realistic and sometimes superior alternative for the analyst is to use as a basis of comparison the financial statements of one or more comparable companies in the same industry. In this way, one can usually have a better command over and comprehension of the data entering into the comparison base.

Annual reports to shareholders contain an ever-expanding amount of information required by either generally accepted accounting principles or by specific SEC requirements.[1]

In addition, company filings with the SEC, such as Registration

---

[1] For example, rule 14c-3 of the Securities Exchange Act of 1934 specifies that annual reports furnished to stockholders in connection with the annual meeting of stockholders include the following information: "certified" comparative financial statements, a 5-year summary of operations, a management's analysis of the summary of operations, a brief description of the company's business, a 5-year line of business breakdown, identification of the company's directors and executive officers and their principal occupation, and a statement of the market price range and dividends paid on voting securities for each quarterly period during the past 2 fiscal years.

Statements[2] pursuant to the Securities Act of 1933, supplemental and periodic reports which are required to be filed (such as Forms 8-K, 10-K[3], 10-Q, 14-K and 16-K), or proxy statements contain a wealth of information of interest to the analyst.

THE PRINCIPAL TOOLS OF ANALYSIS

In the analysis of financial statements, the analyst has available a variety of tools from which he can choose those best suited to his specific purpose. The following principal tools of analysis will be discussed in this chapter:

1. Comparative financial statements
   a. Year-to-year changes
2. Index-number trend series
3. Common-size financial statements
   a. Structural analysis
4. Ratio analysis
5. Specialized analyses
   a. Cash forecasts
   b. Analysis of changes in financial position
   c. Statement of variation in gross margin
   d. Break-even analysis

The application of these tools as well as other aspects of analysis will be illustrated by means of the financial statements of the Beta Company presented in Appendix B. Further examples of tabulations of analytical measures can be found in Chapter 9.

Comparative financial statements

The comparison of financial statements is accomplished by setting up balance sheets, income statements, or statements of changes in financial position, side by side and reviewing the changes which have occurred in individual categories therein from year to year and over the years.

The most important factor revealed by comparative financial statements is *trend*. The comparison of financial statements over a number of years will also reveal the direction, velocity, and the amplitude of

---

[2] SEC Regulation S-X which specifies the form and content of financial statements filed with the Commission contains numerous requirements for specific disclosures.

[3] A survey conducted in 1976, using the National Automated Accounting Research System Data Base, which aimed to identify the additional significant information that can be found in SEC annual reports (forms 10-K) when compared to annual reports to stockholders, found these to represent disclosures of compensating balances, income taxes and stock option, pension and profit sharing plans.

trend. Further analysis can be undertaken to compare the trends in related items. For example, a year-to-year increase in sales of 10 percent accompanied by an increase in freight-out costs of 20 percent requires an investigation and explanation of the reasons for the difference. Similarly, an increase of accounts receivable of 15 percent during the same period would also warrant an investigation into the reasons for the difference in the rate of increase of sales as against that of receivables.

Year-to-year change. A comparison of financial statements over two to three years can be undertaken by computing the *year-to-year change* in absolute amounts and in terms of percentage changes. Longer term comparisons are best undertaken by means of *index-number trend series.*

Year-to-year comparisons of financial statements are illustrated in Appendix B. When a two- or three-year comparison is attempted, such presentations are manageable and can be understood by the reader. They have the advantage of presenting changes in terms of absolute dollar amounts as well as in percentages. Both have to be considered because the dollar size of the different bases on which percentage changes are computed may yield large percentage changes which are out of proportion to their real significance. For example, in the same financial statements, a 50 percent change from a base figure of $1,000 is far less significant than the same percentage change from a base of $100,000. Thus, reference to the dollar amounts involved is always necessary in order to retain the proper perspective and to reach valid conclusions regarding the relative significance of the changes disclosed by this type of analysis.

The computation of year-to-year changes is a simple matter. However, a few clarifying rules should be borne in mind. When a negative amount appears in the base year and a positive amount in the following year, or vice versa, no percentage change can be meaningfully computed. When an item has a value in a base year and none in the following period, the decrease is 100 percent. Where there is no figure for the base year, no percentage change can be computed. The following summary will illustrate this:

			Change increase (decrease)	
Item	19X1 $	19X2 $	Amount $	%
Net income (loss)	(4,500)	1,500	6,000	—
Tax expense	2,000	(1,000)	(3,000)	—
Notes payable	—	8,000	8,000	—
Notes receivable	10,000	—	(10,000)	(100)

Comparative financial statements can also be presented in such a way that the cumulative total for the period for each item under study and the average for that period are shown.

The value of comparing yearly amounts with an average covering a number of years is that unusual factors in any one year are highlighted. Averages smooth out erratic or unusual fluctuations in data.

Index-number trend series

When a comparison of financial statements covering more than three years is undertaken, the year-to-year method of comparison may become too cumbersome. The best way to effect such longer term trend comparisons is by means of index numbers. Such a comparative statement for the Beta Company is illustrated in Appendix B.

The computation of a series of index numbers requires the choice of a base year which will, for all items, have an index amount of 100. Since such a base year represents a frame of reference for all comparisons, it is best to choose a year which, in a business conditions sense, is as typical or normal as possible. If the earliest year in the series compared cannot fulfill this function, another year is chosen. In our example of the Beta Company comparative statements, the year 19X3, rather than the first year in the series, was chosen.

As is the case with the computation of year-to-year percentage changes, certain changes, such as those from negative to positive amounts, cannot be expressed by means of index numbers. All index numbers are computed by reference to the base year.

ILLUSTRATION 2.   Assume that in the base year 19XA cash has a balance of $12,000. Based on an index number of 100 for 19XA, if the cash balance in the following year (19XB) is $18,000, then the index number will be

$$\frac{18,000}{12,000} \times 100 = 150$$

In 19XC if the cash balance is $9,000, the index will stand at 75 arrived at as follows:

$$\frac{9,000}{12,000} \times 100 \left(\frac{\text{Balance in Current Year}}{\text{Balance in Base Year}} \times 100 \right)$$

It should be noted that when using index numbers, percentage changes cannot be read off directly except by reference to the base year. Thus, the change of the cash balance between 19XA and 19XB is 50 percent (index 150 − index 100), and this can be read off directly from the index numbers. The change from 19XB to 19XC, however, is not 75 percent (150–75), as a direct comparison may suggest, but rather 50 percent (i.e., 9,000/18,000), which involves computing the 19XB to 19XC change by reference to the amount at 19XB. The percentage change can, however, be computed by use of the index numbers only, for example, 75/150 = .5 or a change of 50 percent.

In planning an index-number trend comparison, it is not necessary to include in it all the items in the financial statements. Only the most significant items need be included in such a comparison.

Care should be exercised in the use of index-number trend comparisons because such comparisons have weaknesses as well as strengths. Thus, in trying to assess changes in the current financial condition, the analyst may use to advantage comparative statements of changes in financial position. On the other hand, the index-number trend comparison is very well suited to a comparison of the changes in the *composition* of working capital items over the years.

The interpretation of percentage changes as well as those of index-number trend series must be made with a full awareness of the effect which the inconsistent application of accounting principles over the years can have on such comparisons. Thus, where possible, such inconsistencies must be adjusted. In addition, the longer the period covered by the comparison, the more distortive are the effects of price level changes on such comparisons likely to be, and the analyst must be aware of such effects.

One important value of trend analysis is that it can convey to the analyst a better understanding of management's philosophies, policies, and motivations, conscious or otherwise, which have brought about the changes revealed over the years. The more diverse the economic environments covering the periods compared are, the better a picture can be obtained by the analyst of the ways in which the enterprise has weathered its adversities and taken advantage of its opportunities.

Common-size financial statements

In the analysis of financial statements it is often instructive to find out the proportion of a total group or subgroup which a single item within them represents. In a balance sheet, the assets as well as the liabilities and capital are each expressed as 100 percent and each item in these categories is expressed as a percentage of the respective totals. Similarly, in the income statement net sales are set at 100 percent, and every other item in the statement is expressed as a percent of net sales. Since the totals always add up to 100 percent, this community of size has resulted in these statements being referred to as "common size." Similarly, following the eye as it reviews the common-size statement, this analysis is referred to as "vertical" for the same reason that the trend analysis is often referred to as "horizontal" analysis.

Selected common size of Beta Company are presented in Appendix B.

Structural analysis. The analysis of common-size financial statements may best be described as an analysis of the internal structure of the financial statements. In the analysis of a balance sheet this structural analysis focuses on two major aspects:

1. What are the sources of capital of the enterprise, that is, what is the distribution of equities as between current liabilities, long-term liabilities, and equity capital?
2. Given the amount of capital from all sources, what is the distribution of assets (current, fixed, and other) in which it is invested? Stated differently, what is the mix of assets with which the enterprise has chosen to conduct its operations.

The common-size balance sheet analysis can, of course, be carried further and extended to an examination of what proportion of a subgroup, rather than the total, an item is. Thus, in assessing the liquidity of current assets, it may be of interest to know not only what proportion of total assets is invested in inventories but also what proportion of current assets is represented by this asset.

In the case of the income statement, common-size statement analysis is a very useful tool transcending perhaps in importance the analysis of the balance sheet by such means. This is so because the income statement lends itself very well to an analysis whereby each item in it is related to a central quantum, that is, sales. With some exceptions the level of each expense item is affected to some extent by the level of sales, and thus it is instructive to know what proportion of the sales dollar is absorbed by the various costs and expenses incurred by the enterprise.

Comparisons of common-size statements of a single enterprise over the years are valuable in that they show the changing proportions of components within groups of assets, liabilities, costs, and other financial statement categories. However, care must be exercised in interpreting such changes and the trend which they disclose. For example, the table below shows the amount of patents and total assets of an enterprise over three years:

	19X3	19X2	19X1
Patents	50,000	50,000	50,000
Total assets	1,000,000	750,000	500,000
Patents as a percentage of total assets	5%	6.67%	10%

While the amount of patents remained unchanged, the increase in total assets made this item a progressively smaller proportion of total assets. Since this proportion can change with either a change in the absolute amount of the item or a change in the total of the group of which it is a part, the interpretation of a common-size statement comparison requires an examination of the actual figures and the basis on which they are computed.

Common-size statements are very well suited to intercompany comparison because the financial statements of a variety of companies can be recast into the uniform common-size format regardless of the size of individual accounts. While common-size statements do not reflect the relative sizes of the individual companies which are compared, the problem of actual comparability between them is a matter to be resolved by the analyst's judgment.

Comparison of the common-size statements of companies within an industry or with common-size composite statistics of that industry can alert the analyst's attention to variations in account structure or distribution, the reasons for which should be explored and understood. A comparison of selected common-size statement items of the Marine Supply Corporation with similar industry statistics is presented in Exhibit 9–8 (in Chapter 9).

Ratio analysis

Ratios are among the best known and most widely used tools of financial analysis. At the same time their function is often misunderstood, and consequently their significance may easily be overrated.

A ratio expresses the mathematical relationship between one quantity and another. The ratio of 200 to 100 is expressed as 2 : 1 or as 2. While the computation of a ratio involves a simple arithmetical operation, its interpretation is a far more complex matter.

To begin with, to be significant the ratio must express a relationship that has significance. Thus, there is a clear, direct, and understandable relationship between the sales price of an item on one hand and its cost on the other. As a result, the ratio of cost of goods sold to sales is a significant one. On the other hand, there is no a priori or understandable relationship between freight costs incurred and the marketable securities held by an enterprise; and hence, a ratio of one to the other must be deemed to be of no significance.

Ratios are tools of analysis which, in most cases, provide the analyst with clues and symptoms of underlying conditions. Ratios, properly interpreted, can also point the way to areas requiring further investigation and inquiry. The analysis of a ratio can disclose relationships as well as bases of comparison which reveal conditions and trends that cannot be detected by an inspection of the individual components of the ratio.

Since ratios, like other tools of analysis, are future oriented, the analyst must be able to adjust the factors present in a relationship to their probable shape and size in the future. He must also understand the factors which will influence such ratios in the future. Thus, in the final analysis, the usefulness of ratios is wholly dependent on their intelligent and skillful interpretation. This is, by far, the most difficult aspect of ratio analysis. Let us, by way of example, consider the interpretation of a ratio derived from an area outside that of the business world:

In comparing the ratio of gas consumption to mileage driven, A claims to have a superior performance, that is, 28 mpg compared to B's 20 mpg. Assuming that they drove identical cars, the following are factors which affect gas consumption and which will have to be considered before one can properly interpret the ratios and judge whose performance is better:

1. Weight of load driven.
2. Type of terrain (flat versus hilly).
3. City or country driving.
4. Kind of gasoline used.
5. Speed at which cars were driven.

Numerous as the factors which influence gas consumption are, the evaluation of the gas consumption ratio is, nevertheless, a simpler process than the evaluation of most ratios derived from business variables. The reason for this is that the interrelationships of business variables and the factors which affect them are multifaceted and very complex. In addition to the internal operating conditions which affect the ratios of an enterprise, the analyst must be aware of the factors, such as general business conditions, industry position, management policies, as well as accounting principles, which can affect them.

Ratios should always be interpreted with great care since factors affecting the numerator may correlate with those affecting the denominator. Thus, for example, it is possible to improve the ratio of operating expenses to sales by reducing costs which act to stimulate sales. If the cost reduction consequently results in a loss of sales or share of market such a seeming improvement in profitability may, in fact, have an overall detrimental effect on the future prospects of the enterprise and must be interpreted accordingly.

It should also be recognized that many ratios have important variables in common with other ratios thus tending to make them vary and be influenced by the same factors. Consequently, there is no need to use all available ratios in order to diagnose a given condition.

Ratios, like most other relationships in financial analysis, are not significant in themselves and can be interpreted only by comparison with (1) past ratios of the same enterprise, or (2) some predetermined standard, or (3) ratios of other companies in the industry. The range of a ratio over time is also significant as is the trend of a given ratio over time.

A great many ratios can be developed from the multitude of items included in an enterprises' financial statements. Some ratios have general application in financial analysis, while others have specific uses in certain circumstances or in specific industries. Listed below are some of the most significant ratios which have general applicability to most business situations. They are grouped by major objectives of financial analysis:

Major categories of ratios	Method of computation	Beta Corporation ratio for 19X6 (see Appendix B)
Short-term liquidity ratios:		
Current ratio	$\dfrac{\text{Current assets}}{\text{Current liabilities}} = \dfrac{1,019.4}{513.7}$	1.98:1
Acid test	$\dfrac{\text{Cash + Cash equivalents + Receivables}}{\text{Current liabilities}}$ $= \dfrac{41.5 + 284.8 + 307.7 + 37.8}{513.7} =$	1.31:1
Days sales in receivables (collection period)	$\dfrac{\text{Accounts receivables}}{\text{Credit sales} \div 360} = \dfrac{307.7}{3,540.6 \div 360} =$	31 days
Inventory turnover	$\dfrac{\text{Cost of goods sold}}{\text{Average inventory during period}}$ $= \dfrac{2,513.8}{(343.7 + 347.6)/2} =$	7.27
Capital structure and long-term solvency ratios:		
Net worth to total debt	$\dfrac{\text{Net worth}}{\text{Total debt}} = \dfrac{1,826.5}{3,639.6 - 1,826.5} =$	1:1
Net worth to long-term debt	$\dfrac{\text{Net worth}}{\text{Long-term debt}} = \dfrac{1,826.5}{1,054.3 + 212 + 33.1}$	1.41:1
Net worth to fixed assets	$\dfrac{\text{Net worth}}{\text{Fixed assets}} = \dfrac{1,826.5}{2,382.3} =$	.77:1
Times interest earned	$\dfrac{\text{Income before interest and taxes}}{\text{Interest expenses}}$ $= \dfrac{379.5 + 92.4}{92.4} =$	5.11 times
Return on investment ratios:		
Return on total assets	$\dfrac{\text{Net income + Interest expense}(1 - \text{Tax Rate})}{\text{Average total assets}}$ $= \dfrac{253.6 + 92.4(1 - 0.332)}{(3,341 + 3,639.6)/2} =$	9%
Return on equity capital	$\dfrac{\text{Net income}}{\text{Average equity capital}} = \dfrac{253.6}{(1,501.6 + 1,826.5)/2} =$	15%

Major categories of ratios	Method of computation	Beta Corporation ratio for 19X6 (see Appendix B)
Operating performance ratios:		
Gross margin ratio	$\dfrac{\text{Gross profit (margin)}}{\text{Sales}} = \dfrac{3{,}540.6 - 2{,}513.8}{3{,}540.6} =$	29%
Operating profits to sales	$\dfrac{\text{Operating profit}}{\text{Sales}} = \dfrac{379.5 + 92.40}{3{,}540.6} =$	13.3%
Pretax income to sales	$\dfrac{\text{Pretax income}}{\text{Sales}} = \dfrac{379.5}{3{,}540.6} =$	10.7%
Net income to sales	$\dfrac{\text{Net income}}{\text{Sales}} = \dfrac{253.6}{3{,}540.6} =$	7.2%
Asset-utilization ratios:		
Sales to cash	$\dfrac{\text{Sales}}{\text{Cash}} = \dfrac{3{,}540.6}{41.5} =$	85.3:1
Sales to accounts receivables	$\dfrac{\text{Sales}}{\text{Accounts receivable}} = \dfrac{3{,}540.6}{307.7} =$	**11.5:1**
Sales to inventories	$\dfrac{\text{Sales}}{\text{Inventories}} = \dfrac{3{,}540.6}{347.6} =$	10.2:1
Sales to working capital	$\dfrac{\text{Sales}}{\text{Working capital}} = \dfrac{3{,}540.6}{1{,}019.4 - 513.7} =$	7:1
Sales to fixed assets	$\dfrac{\text{Sales}}{\text{Fixed assets}} = \dfrac{3{,}540.6}{2{,}382.3} =$	1.5:1
Sales to other assets	$\dfrac{\text{Sales}}{\text{Other assets}} = \dfrac{3{,}540.6}{237.9} =$	14.9:1
Sales to total assets	$\dfrac{\text{Sales}}{\text{Total assets}} = \dfrac{3{,}540.6}{3{,}639.6} =$	.97:1
Market measures:		
Price/Earnings ratio	$\dfrac{\text{Market price}}{\text{Earnings per share}} = \dfrac{67^*}{5.60} =$	11.98
Dividend yield	$\dfrac{\text{Dividends per share}}{\text{Market price per share}} = \dfrac{2}{67^*} =$	2.98%
Dividend payout ratio	$\dfrac{\text{Dividends declared}}{\text{Net income}} = \dfrac{91.4}{253.6} =$	36.04%

* Average for last quarter of 19X6.

Each of the above five major objectives of financial statement analysis will be examined in subsequent chapters; and therein the computation, use, and interpretation of the ratios listed under each category as well as other ratios will be examined in detail and thoroughly discussed. The listing includes the respective ratios for 19X6 of the Beta Company (see Appendix B).

TESTING THE UNDERSTANDING OF RELATIONSHIPS

The following is an example of an exercise designed to test the reader's understanding of various intra- and interstatement ratios and relationships.

ILLUSTRATION 3.   Given the following information we are to complete the balance sheet below:

```
Cash
Accounts Receivable
Inventory .........................    $50
Building
Land
Current Liabilities
Common Stock
Retained Earnings .................   $100
```

Assets − Liabilities = $600.

Stockholders Equity = 3 times debt.

The carrying amount of Land is ⅔ of that of the building.

Acid test ratio = 1.25.

Inventory turnover based on Cost of Goods Sold is 15.

Gross Profit is 44% of the Cost of Goods Sold.

There are 20 days sales in Accounts Receivable.

The determination of the balance sheet which follows is based on the steps described below:

Cash	$190	Current Liabilities	200
Accounts Receivable	60	Common Stock	500
Inventory	50	Retained Earnings	100
Buildings	300		800
Land	200		
	800		

STEP 1

Assets − Liabilities = 600

Stockholders equity = 600

Retained Earnings = 100 (as given)

Common Stock   = 500

STEP 2

Equity = 3 × debt

3 × current liabilities (which are the total debt) = $600

Add current liabilities   200

So total assets equal $800

STEP 3

Acid test = 1.25

$$\frac{\text{Cash} + \text{Accounts Receivable}}{200} = 1.25$$

hence

Cash + Accounts Receivable = $250

STEP 4

Inventory + Buildings + Land   = $550 [i.e., Total Assets − (Cash + A/R)]

Buildings and Land = 500

Land = ⅔ of building; thus, if x = carrying amount of building
$$x + \tfrac{2}{3}x = 500 \qquad x = \underline{\underline{300}} \text{ (building)}$$

Land = \$500 − \$300 = $\underline{\underline{\$200}}$

STEP 5

$$\frac{\text{Cost of Goods Sold (CGS)}}{\text{Inventory}} = \text{Inventory Turnover; } \frac{\text{CGS}}{50} = 15$$

Cost of Goods Sold = $\underline{\underline{\$750}}$ Gross Profit 44% of 750 = $\underline{\underline{\$330}}$

STEP 6

Cost of Good Sold + Gross Profit (\$750 + \$330) = Sales = \$1080

Amount of Sales per day $\dfrac{\$1080}{360} = \$3$

Accounts Receivable = 20 days sales = 20 × \$3 = 60
Cash = \$250 − Accounts Receivable (\$60) = $\underline{\underline{\$190}}$

Specialized tools of analysis

In addition to the multipurpose tools of financial statement analysis which we discussed above, such as trend indices, common-size statements, and ratios, the analyst has at his disposal a variety of special-purpose tools. These tools focus on specific financial statements or segments of such statements or they can address themselves specifically to the operating conditions of a particular industry, for example, occupancy-capacity analysis in the hotel, hospital, or airline industries. These special purpose tools of analysis include cash forecasts, analyses of changes in financial position, statements of variation in gross margin, and break-even analyses.

BUILDING BLOCKS OF FINANCIAL STATEMENT ANALYSIS

Whatever approach to financial statement analysis the analyst takes and whatever methods he uses he will always have to examine one or more of the important aspects of an enterprise's financial condition and results of its operations. All such aspects, with perhaps the exception of the most specialized ones, can be found in one of the following six categories:

1. Short-term liquidity.
2. Funds flow.
3. Capital structure and long-term solvency.
4. Return on investment.
5. Operating performance.
6. Assets utilization.

Each of the above categories and the tools used in measuring them will be discussed in greater depth in Chapters 2 to 9. In this way the financial analysis required by any conceivable set of objectives may be structured by examining any or all of the above areas in any sequence and with any degree of relative emphasis called for by circumstances. Thus these six areas of inquiry and investigation can be considered as building blocks of financial statement analysis.

COMPUTER ASSISTED FINANCIAL ANALYSIS

The major emphasis throughout this work is on the application of thoughtful and logical analysis upon carefully evaluated and verified data. Financial statement analysis does, however, involve a significant amount of work of a computational nature as well as numerous logical steps which can be preplanned and programmed. It is in these areas that the financial analyst can utilize computers to great advantage.

The modern electronic computer has a remarkable facility for performing complex computations with great speed. Moreover, it can perform these computations, comparisons, and other logical steps for long periods of time without exhaustion and, once properly programmed, will do them without error. In today's environment, when business complexity has outstripped our ability to grasp it and when our ability to generate information has outrun our ability to utilize it, the computer can render vital assistance.

The intelligent use of the computer's formidable capabilities in financial analysis depends, however, on thorough understanding of the limitations to which this powerful tool is subject. Thus, the computer lacks the ability to make intuitive judgments or to gain insights, capabilities which are essential to a competent and imaginative financial analysis.

There is nothing that the computer can do which a competent analyst armed with a calculator cannot do. On the other hand, the speed and the capabilities of modern computers are such that to accomplish what they can do would require so many hours of work as to render most such efforts uneconomical or unfeasible. Computers have thus automated some of the statistical and analytical steps which were previously done manually.

The stored data bases on which computer assisted security analysis often relies do not include all the information which is needed to adjust accounting data in order to render it comparable or in order to make it conform to the analyst's specific needs. This is particularly true for the following reasons:

1. The data banks generally lack information on accounting policies and principles employed by a given enterprise. This information is essential to an interpretation of the data and to its comparison to other data.

2. Footnotes and other explanatory or restrictive information usually found in individual enterprise reports containing the financial statements are also generally not available in any meaningfull detail.
3. Lack of retroactive adjustments, because the necessary data are often not available.
4. Errors and omissions may occur when large masses of financial data are processed on a uniform basis for purposes of inclusion in the data base.
5. The aggregation of dissimilar or noncomparable data results in a loss of vital distinctions and thus reduces its meaning and its value for analysis.

Given an understanding of the capabilities as well as the limitations to which the computer is subject, the following are the more significant uses which can be made of this important tool in the broad area of financial analysis:

1. Data storage, retrieval, and computational ability

A machine-accessible comprehensive data base is essential to the use of the computer in most phases of security and credit analysis. The ability of the computer to store vast amounts of data and to afford access to them is one of its important capabilities. Another is the ability to sift these data, to manipulate them mathematically and to select from among them in accordance with set criteria, as well as to constantly update and modify them. Moreover, the ability of computers to perform computations (of ratios etc.) is almost unlimited.

A large commercially available data base comprising financial information on many hundreds of corporations covering twenty or more years is available from COMPUSTAT, a service of Standard & Poor's Corporation. Many other specialized data bases and time-sharing services are available from various sources and those include the AICPA time-sharing program library.

2. Screening large masses of data

The computer can be used to screen for specified criteria as a means of selecting investment opportunities and for other purposes. A variation of these techniques consists of "filtering" data in accordance with a set of preselected criteria (e.g., certain sales levels, returns, growth rates, financial characteristics, etc.)

3. A research tool

It can be used as a research tool for uncovering characteristics of and relationships between data on companies, industries, the market behavior and the economy.

4. Specialized financial analyses

The computer can be an input tool for financial analysis in credit extension and security analysis.

A. *Financial analysis in credit extension*

  (1) Storage of facts for comparison and decision making.
  (2) Projection of enterprise cash requirements under a variety of assumptions.
  (3) Projection of financial statements under a variety of assumptions showing the impact of changes on key variables. Known as *sensitivity analysis,* this technique allows the user to explore the effect of systematically changing a given variable repeatedly by a predetermined amount.
  (4) The introduction of probabilistic inputs. The data can be inserted as probability distributions, either normally shaped or skewed, or random probability distributions otherwise known as "Monte Carlo trials."

B. *Security analysis*

  (1) Calculations based on past data.
  (2) Trend computations.
     —Simple
     —Regression analysis
  (3) Predictive models.
  (4) Projections and forecasts.
  (5) Sensitivity analysis.
  (6) Complex probabilistic analysis.

Given an understanding of the capabilities of the modern electronic computer, as well as the limitations to which it is subject, the financial analyst will find in it an important tool which promises to grow in importance as new applications to which it can be put are perfected in the future.

ANALYTICAL REVIEW OF ACCOUNTING PRINCIPLES—PURPOSES AND FOCUS

In the chapters which follow we shall present a review of accounting standards used in the preparation of financial statements. The purpose of this review is to examine the variety of standards which can be applied to similar transactions and circumstances, as well as the latitude which is possible in the interpretation and application of these standards in practice. Thus, the focus is on an understanding of accounting standards as well as on an appreciation of the impact which the application of these standards may have on the reported financial condition and results of operations of an enterprise. Such possible impact must be appreciated and understood before any intelligent analysis can be undertaken or any useful and meaningful comparison is made.

Example of importance of accounting assumptions, standards, and determinations: Illustration of a simple investment decision

The importance of standards and assumptions in accounting determinations can perhaps be best illustrated and understood within the framework of an exceedingly simple example of a business situation. Let us assume that the owner of an apartment building has found an interested buyer. How should the price be set? How should the buyer gain confidence in the soundness and profitability of such investment at a given price?

The first question is the method to be followed in arriving at a fair value of the building. While many approaches are possible, such as comparable current values, reproduction costs; and so forth, let us settle here on the most widely accepted method for the valuation of income-producing properties as well as other investments: the capitalization of earnings. If earning power is the major consideration, then the focus must be on the income statement. The prospective buyer is given the following income statement:

184 EAGLE STREET APARTMENT HOUSE
Income Statement
For the Year Ending December 31, 19X9

Rental revenue		$46,000
Garage rentals		2,440
Other income from washer and dryer concession		300
Total revenue		$48,740
Expenses:		
Real estate taxes	$4,900	
Mortgage interest	2,100	
Electricity and gas	840	
Water	720	
Superintendent's salary	1,600	
Insurance	680	
Repairs and maintenance	2,400	13,240
Income before depreciation		$35,500
Depreciation		9,000
Net income		$26,500

The first questions the prospective buyer will want to ask himself about the foregoing income statement are these:

1. Can I rely on the fairness of presentation of the income statement?
2. What adjustments have to be made so as to obtain a net income figure which can be used with confidence in arriving at a proper purchase price?

In our society the most common way of gaining assurance about the fairness of presentation of financial statements is to rely on the opinion of an independent certified public accountant. This professional is assumed to perform a skilful audit and to satisfy himself that the financial statements do accurately portray the results of operations and the financial position, in accordance with principles which are generally accepted as proper and useful in the particular context in which they are applied. Such an auditor is also presumed to understand that someone like our prospective buyer will rely on his opinion in reaching a decision on whether to buy and at what price.

Our prospective buyer's second question is far more complex. The auditor's opinion relates to the income statement as representing fairly the net income for the year ended December 31, 19X9. That in no way means that this is *the* relevant figure to use in arriving at a valuation of the apartment building. Nor would an auditor ever claim that his opinion is directed at the relevance of financial statement figures to any particular decision. Let us then examine what information our buyer will need and what assumptions he will have to make in order that he may arrive at a figure of net income which can be used in setting the value of the apartment building.

Rental income. Does the $46,000 figure represent 100 percent occupancy during the year? If so, should an allowance be made for possible vacancies? What are rental trends in the area? What would rents be in five years? In 10 years? Are demand factors for apartments in the area going to stay stable, improve, or deteriorate? The aim, of course, is to come nearest to that figure of yearly rental income which approximates a level which, on the average, can be expected to prevail over the forseeable future. Prior years' data will be useful in judging this.

Real estate taxes. Here the trend of taxes over the years is an important factor. That in turn depends on the character of the taxing community and revenue and expense trends within it.

Mortgage interest. This expense is relevant to the buyer only if he assumes the existing mortgage. Otherwise the interest cost which will be incurred as a result of new financing will have to be substituted.

Utilities.   These expenses must be scrutinized with a view to ascertaining whether they are at a representative level of what can be expected to prevail.

Superintendent's salary.   Is the pay adequate to secure acceptable services? Can the services of superintendent be retained?

Insurance.   Are all forseeable risks insured for? Is the coverage adequate?

Repairs and maintenance.   These expenses must be examined over a number of years in order to determine an average or representative level. Is the level of expenses such that it affords proper maintenance of the property or is the expense account "starved" so as to show a higher net income?

Depreciation.   This figure is not likely to be relevant to the buyer's decision unless his cost approximates that of the seller. If the cost to the buyer differs, then depreciation will have to be computed on that cost using a proper method of depreciation over the useful life of the building, so as to recover the buyer's original cost.

The buyer must also ascertain whether any expenses which he will be properly expected to incur are omitted from the above income statement. Additional considerations concern the method of financing this acquisition and other costs related thereto.

It should be understood that most of the above questions will have to be asked and properly answered even if the auditor issues an unqualified opinion on the financial statements. Thus, for example, while "generally accepted accounting principles" require that insurance expense include accruals for the full year, they are not concerned with the adequacy of insurance coverage or of the maintenance policy, or the superintendent's pay, or with expected, as opposed to actual, revenues or expense levels.

If one views the many complex questions and problems that arise in the attempt to analyze this very simple income statement for decision-making purposes, one can begin to grasp the complexities involved in the analysis of the financial statements of a sizable, modern business enterprise.

It is clear that essential to an intelligent analysis of such statements is an appreciation of what financial statements do portray as well as what they do not or cannot portray. As we have seen, there are items which properly belong in such statements and there are items which, because of an inability to quantify them or to determine them objectively, cannot be included.

Those items which properly belong in the financial statements should be presented therein in accordance with principles of accounting which enjoy general acceptance. The wide variety of standards which are "acceptable" as well as the even greater variety in the ways in which they can be applied in practice make it imperative that the user of financial statements be fully aware of these possibilities and their implications. The following chapters will explore this important area.

The example of the apartment house buyer illustrates the obvious fact that despite their limitations, financial statements and presentations are indispensible to the decision-making process. While the potential buyer could not use the income statement without obtaining more information and making further assumptions and adjustments, he would not have had any basis for his decision without it. Had he not received one, he would have had to make one up without utilization of the objectivity and the benefit of the experience of actual transactions over a period of time. Thus, in most cases, the interpretation of historical financial statements represents the essential first step in the decision-making process.

APPENDIX A

SOURCES OF INFORMATION ON FINANCIAL AND OPERATING RATIOS

A good way to achieve familiarity with the wide variety of published financial and operating ratios available is to classify them by the type of source that collects or compiles them. The specific sources given under each category are intended to exemplify the type of material available. These are by no means complete lists:

Professional and commercial organizations

Dun and Bradstreet, Inc., Business Economics Division, 99 Church Street, New York, N.Y. 10007

Key Business Ratios. Important Operating and Financial Ratios in 71 Manufacturing Lines, 32 Wholesale Lines and 22 Retail Lines and published in *Dun's Review* of Modern Industry. Five year summaries are also published. The data is presented in three ranges: lower quartile, median, and upper quartile.

Cost-of-Doing Business Series. Typical operating ratios for 185 lines of business, showing national averages. They represent a percentage of business receipts reported by a representative sample of the total of all Federal tax returns.

Moody's Investor Service, New York, N.Y.

Moody's Manuals contain financial and operating ratios on individual companies covered.

National Cash Register Company. *Expenses in Retail Businesses*. Biennial.
Operating ratios for 36 lines of retail business, as taken from trade associ-
ations and other sources including many from *Barometer of Small
Business*
Robert Morris Associates. *Annual Statement Studies*.
Financial and operating ratios for about 300 lines of business—
manufacturers, wholesalers, retailers, services and contractors—based on
information obtained from member banks of RMA. Data is broken down
by company size. Part 4 gives "Additional Profit and Loss Data."
Standard & Poor Corporation
Industry Surveys in two parts: (1) Basic Analysis and (2) Current Analysis
contains many industry and individual company ratios.
Almanac of Business and Industrial Financial Ratios, by Leo Troy. Prentice-
Hall, Inc., Englewood Cliffs, N.J.
A compilation of corporate performance ratios (operating and financial). The
significance of these ratios is explained. All industries are covered in the
study, each industry is subdivided by asset size.

The federal government

Small Business Administration
Publications containing industry statistics:
Small Marketers Aids.
Small Business Management Series.
Business Service Bulletins.

U.S. Department of Commerce
Census of Business—Wholesale Trade—Summary Statistics. Monthly
Wholesale Trade Report. Ratio of operating expenses to sales.
Department of the Treasury
Statistics of Income, Corporation Income Tax Returns. Operating Statistics
based on income tax returns.
Federal Trade Commission—Securities and Exchange Commission.
Quarterly Financial Report for Manufacturing, Mining and Trade Corpo-
rations. Contains operating ratios and balance sheet ratios as well as the
balance sheet in ratio format.

Sources of specific industry ratios

Bank Operating Statistics. Federal Deposit Insurance Corporation. Annual.
Institute of Real Estate Management. Experience Exchange Committee. *A
Statistical Compilation and Analysis of Actual (year) Income and Expenses
Experienced in Apartment, Condominium and Cooperative Building Oper-
ation*. Annual.
Discount Merchandiser. *The True Look of the Discount Industry*. June issue
each year. Includes operating ratios.

The Lilly Digest. Eli Lilly and Company. Annual.

National Electrical Contractors Association. *Operation Overhead.* Annual.

National Farm & Power Equipment Dealers Association. *Cost of Doing Business Study.* Annual.

Journal of Commercial Bank Lending. "Analysis of Year End Composite Ratios of Instalment Sales Finance and Small Loan Companies."

Harris, Kerr, Forster & Company. *Trends in the Hotel-Motel Business.* Annual.

Ohio Lumber and Building Product Dealers Association. *Survey of Operating Profits.* Compiled by Battelle and Battelle. Annual.

American Meat Institute. *Financial Facts about the Meat Packing Industry.* Includes operating ratios.

Chase Manhattan Bank. *Financial Analysis of a Group of Petroleum Companies.* Annual.

National Office Products Association. *Survey of Operating Results of NOPA Dealers.* Annual.

American Paint and Wallcoverings Dealer. *Report on Annual Survey.*

Printing Industries of America. *Ratios for Use of Printing Management.* Annual.

Restaurants, Country Clubs, City Clubs: Reports on Operations. Laventhol Krekstein Horwath & Horwath. Annual.

National Association of Textile and Apparel Wholesalers. *Performance Analysis of NATAW Members.* Annual.

Bibliographies

Robert Morris Associates. *Sources of Composite Financial Data—A Bibliography.* 3d ed. N.Y., 1971. 28 pp.

An annotated list of sources, with an index by specific industry at front.

Sanzo, Richard. *Ratio Analysis for Small Business.* 3d ed. Washington, D.C., 1970. 65 p. (U.S. Small Business Administration, Small Business Management Series, No. 20).

"Sources of Ratio Studies": p. 22–35, lists the industries covered by basic sources such as D & B, Robert Morris Associates; also the names of trade associations which have published ratio studies. Published financial and operating ratios are also occasionally listed in the monthly *Marketing Information Guide.*

EXAMPLE A-1

Dun & Bradstreet—Key Business Ratios (cost of doing business ratios—corporations)

Industry	Total number of returns filed	Cost of goods sold %	Gross margin %	Compensation of officers %	Rent paid on business property %	Repairs %	Bad debts %	Interest paid %	Taxes paid %	Amortization depreciation depletion %	Advertising %	Pension other employee benefit plans %
								Selected operating expenses				
All industrial groups	1,658,820	70.77	29.23	1.94	1.38	.85	.38	3.31	2.98	3.55	1.13	1.12
Contract construction	127,670	82.97	17.03	3.33	.53	.57	.19	.72	1.92	1.90	.20	.71
Building construction	42,597	89.34	10.66	2.38	.35	.20	.10	.76	1.20	.95	.20	.39
General contractors, except building construction	12,627	80.74	19.26	2.25	.62	1.36	.20	.96	2.10	3.94	.12	.77
Special trade contractors	72,446	76.95	23.05	5.14	.68	.49	.29	.52	2.65	1.69	.26	1.05
Retailers & wholesalers	524,586	77.44	22.56	1.86	1.42	.31	.22	.75	1.40	.92	1.02	.35
Retailers	351,819	72.55	27.45	1.88	2.08	.38	.24	.81	1.60	1.09	1.51	.37
Building materials, hardware & farm equipment	31,715	75.65	24.35	3.23	.99	.34	.48	.79	1.64	1.04	.79	.37

Note: The above operating ratios for 185 lines of business have been derived to provide a guide as to the average amount spent by corporations for these items. They represent a percentage of business receipts as reported by a representative sample of the total of all federal income tax returns filed for 1969–70.

EXAMPLE A-2
Robert Morris Associates statement studies

	Not elsewhere classified—Construction sand & gravel*					Not elsewhere classified—Crude petroleum & natural gas mining†				
	Under $250M	$250M & less than $1MM	$1MM & less than $10MM	$10MM & less than $50MM	All sizes	Under $250M	$250M & less than $1MM	$1MM & less than $10MM	$10MM & less than $50MM	All size
Asset size										
Number of statements		24	15		46		16	42	35	97
Assets										
Cash		5.5%	3.4%		3.0%		7.3%	4.9%	5.3%	5.3%
Marketable securities		1.6	.7		2.3		7.7	1.2	2.5	2.3
Receivables net		16.9	17.2		16.0		15.9	14.9	12.9	13.3
Inventory net		4.8	6.5		4.4		7.5	8.0	6.8	7.0
All other current		2.0	1.6		1.0		4.9	3.7	3.4	3.5
Total current		30.7	29.3		26.7		43.3	32.7	30.9	31.3
Fixed assets net		59.5	50.9		61.9		45.5	54.9	62.2	60.8
All other noncurrent		9.8	19.8		11.4		11.2	12.4	6.9	7.9
Total		100.0%	100.0%		100.0%		100.0%	100.0%	100.0%	100.0%
Liabilities										
Due to banks—short term		6.6%	7.7%		4.3%		5.6%	8.5%	3.2%	4.1%
Due to trade		8.2	10.0		8.5		10.9	14.5	15.3	15.1
Income taxes		1.7	1.9		1.2		2.5	2.0	1.8	1.8
Current maturities LT debt		6.2	5.1		3.1		2.8	6.2	5.1	5.3
All other current		7.8	5.9		5.8		5.8	5.7	2.9	3.4
Total current debt		30.6	30.5		23.0		27.7	36.9	28.3	29.8
Noncurrent debt, unsub		17.0	19.6		12.2		20.5	22.9	20.3	20.7

Total unsubordinated debt	47.6	50.1	35.2	48.2	59.8	48.6	50.5
Subordinated debt	1.4	1.1	.7	1.7	1.3	1.4	1.4
Tangible net worth	51.1	48.8	64.1	50.1	38.8	50.0	48.1
Total	100.0%	100.0%	100.0%	100.0%	100.0%	100.0%	100.0%

Income data

Net sales	100.0%	100.0%	100.0%	100.0%	100.0%	100.0%	100.0%
Cost of sales	63.0	77.9	75.2	30.6	52.4	51.4	56.3
Gross profit	37.0	22.1	24.8	69.4	47.6	48.6	43.7
All other expense net	30.7	19.7	19.3	49.5	31.1	28.9	26.8
Profit before taxes	6.3	2.4	5.5	20.0	16.5	19.7	16.9

Ratios

Quick	1.2%	1.2%	1.2%	2.1%	.8%	1.2%	1.1%
	.8	.8	.8	.8	.6	.7	.7
	.4	.3	.4	.5	.3	.5	.4
Current	1.4	1.5	1.5	2.3	1.1	1.5	1.5
	1.1	1.2	1.1	1.2	.9	1.1	1.0
	.5	.6	.6	.9	.6	.8	.8
Fixed/Worth	.9	.6	.8	.5	.7	1.0	.8
	1.2	1.0	1.2	1.1	1.3	1.3	1.2
	2.2	1.8	1.9	2.2	2.4	1.6	2.1
Debt/Worth	.6	.4	.5	.6	.5	.4	.5
	1.4	1.0	1.1	1.7	1.9	1.0	1.3
	2.3	2.3	2.1	2.4	4.0	1.9	2.5
Unsub. debt/Capital funds	.5	.4	.4	.3	.5	.4	.4
	1.2	.8	.9	1.7	1.4	.9	1.2
	2.1	2.3	2.0	2.4	4.0	1.9	2.5

* 14 statements ended on or about June 30, 1974. 32 statements ended on or about December 31, 1974.
† 51 statements ended on or about June 30, 1974. 46 statements ended on or about December 31, 1974.

EXHIBIT B–1

APPENDIX B

BETA COMPANY*
Consolidated Balance Sheet
(in millions of dollars)

Assets	December 31	
	19X6	19X5
Current Assets:		
Cash (Note 1)	$ 41.5	$ 47.2
Temporary investments	284.8	192.6
Accounts and notes receivable	307.7	322.1
Inventories (Note 2)	347.6	343.7
Deferred income taxes (Note 3)	37.8	30.7
Total Current Assets	$1,019.4	$ 936.3
Property:		
Plants and Properties (Note 4)	$2,463.4	$2,187.3
Pulp and paper	562.0	496.0
Oil and gas	547.1	531.7
Other	3,572.5	3,215.0

Liabilities and Share Owners' Equity	December 31	
	19X6	19X5
Current Liabilities:		
Notes payable and current maturities		
of long-term debt	$ 138.2	$ 133.0
Accounts payable	200.9	189.2
Accrued liabilities	146.1	145.4
Accrued income taxes	28.5	30.5
Total Current Liabilities	$ 513.7	$ 498.1
Long-term debt (Note 8)	$1,054.3	$1,137.2
Deferred income taxes (Note 3)	212.0	161.8
Reserves and deferred liabilities	33.1	42.3
Commitments and contingent liabilities		
(Notes 16 & 17)		
Share owners' equity (Note 9)		
Serial preferred stock, $1 par value	—	—

Less: Accumulated depreciation and depletion	1,624.6	1,471.7
Total Plants and Properties	1,947.9	1,743.3
Timberlands—net (Note 5)		
Owner in fee	398.8	388.8
Capitalized timber harvesting rights	35.6	48.6
Total timberlands	434.4	437.4
Total Property	$2,382.3	$2,180.7
Other Assets:		
Investments—at cost (Note 6)	$ 45.0	$ 45.4
Investments in affiliates—at equity	59.2	43.2
Notes and land contracts receivable	20.9	28.0
Cost in excess of assigned value of businesses acquired—net (Note 7)	52.6	49.1
Environmental construction funds held by trustees	18.7	27.6
Deferred charges and other assets	41.5	30.7
Total Other Assets	237.9	224.0
Total Assets	$3,639.6	$3,341.0

Cumulative $4 preferred stock, no par value	5.0	5.4
Common stock, $2.50 par value	118.5	112.5
Capital from conversion of 5% preferred stock	40.4	40.4
Capital surplus	582.7	427.4
Retained earnings	1,104.4	942.2
	1,851.0	1,527.9
Less: Common shares held in treasury, at cost	24.5	26.3
Total Share Owners' Equity	1,826.5	1,501.6
Total Liabilities and Share Owners' Equity	$3,639.6	$3,341.0

* A land resources management enterprise engaged in the production of paper, pulp, packaging and wood products as well as in the exploration for oil and other natural resources.

BETA COMPANY
Consolidated Statement of Changes in Financial Position
For the Five Years Ended December 31, 19X6
(in millions)

	19X6	19X5	19X4	19X3	19X2
Source of funds:					
Net earnings	$253.6	$218.0	$262.6	$159.8	$102.7
Expenses not requiring outlays of working capital:					
Depreciation	129.0	118.6	108.5	104.2	98.2
Depletion of oil and gas properties.......................	50.5	45.1	—	—	—
Cost of timber harvested	33.3	28.8	26.6	17.7	14.3
Deferred income taxes— noncurrent	43.0	49.1	17.5	28.8	18.5
Funds provided from operations	509.4	459.6	415.2	310.5	233.7
Issuance of common stock	159.5	2.1	.1	—	.1
Issuance of long-term debt	41.2	191.2	170.7	40.7	38.9
Reduction of long-term investments	.4	47.9	24.6	(73.8)	6.1
Sales of properties......................	5.3	2.8	4.1	38.6	3.5
Other sources—net	(5.6)	12.4	(3.9)	1.4	12.6
	710.2	716.0	610.8	317.4	294.9
Application of funds:					
Acquisition of General Crude Oil Company:					
Properties acquired...................	—	482.6	—	—	—
Long-term portion of debt issued and assumed	—	(288.1)	—	—	—
Other, net	—	5.0	—	—	—
Working capital required by the acquisition	—	199.5	—	—	—
Cash dividends paid	91.4	88.6	77.4	77.9	67.3
Invested in plants and properties	398.4	365.2	196.4	106.0	109.5
Invested in timberlands	37.5	95.7	216.3	35.6	13.6
Reduction of long-term debt	124.1	69.4	26.0	36.3	24.8
Purchase of treasury stock	.2	.4	.5	20.8	—
Environmental construction funds held by trustees	(8.9)	(.1)	13.8	3.1	(.1)
	642.7	818.7	530.4	279.7	215.1
Increase (decrease) in working capital	$ 67.5	($102.7)	$ 80.4	$ 37.7	$ 79.8
Changes in working capital:					
Increases (decreases) in current assets:					
Cash	($ 5.7)	$ 13.2	$ 19.0	$ 1.0	($ 11.6)
Temporary investments	92.2	(104.3)	90.2	60.5	145.3
Accounts and notes receivable	(14.4)	(11.7)	58.7	7.7	10.8
Inventories	3.9	19.3	96.5	(2.7)	(47.7)
Deferred income taxes	7.1	2.7	14.7	(2.8)	8.5
	83.1	(80.8)	279.1	63.7	105.3
(Increases) decreases in current liabilities:					
Notes payable and current maturities of long-term debt	(5.2)	(47.1)	(45.7)	(9.9)	18.3
Accounts payable and accrued liabilities	(12.4)	(86.8)	(43.2)	(12.9)	(34.6)
Accrued income taxes	2.0	112.0	(109.8)	(3.2)	(9.2)
	(15.6)	(21.9)	(198.7)	(26.0)	(25.5)
Increase (decrease) in working capital	$ 67.5	($102.7)	$ 80.4	$ 37.7	$ 79.8

EXHIBIT B-3

BETA COMPANY
Consolidated Statement of Earnings and Retained Earnings
(in millions of dollars except per-share amounts)

	Years ended December 31		Increase (decrease)	
	19X6	*19X5*	*Amount*	*%*
Income:				
Net sales	$3,540.6	$3,080.8	459.8	14.9
Other income, net (Note 11)...............	40.9	29.2	11.7	40.1
Total Income........................	3,581.5	3,110.0	471.5	15.2
Costs and expenses:				
Cost of products sold	2,513.8	2,134.0	379.8	17.8
Distribution expenses......................	191.6	172.2	19.4	11.3
Selling and administrative expenses	191.4	156.6	34.8	22.2
Depreciation	129.0	118.6	10.4	8.8
Depletion of oil and gas properties	50.5	45.1	5.4	12.0
Cost of timber harvested	33.3	28.8	4.5	15.6
Interest	92.4	83.4	9.0	10.8
Total Costs and Expenses	3,202.0	2,738.7	463.3	16.9
Earnings before income taxes	379.5	371.3	8.2	2.2
Provision for income taxes (Note 3)	125.9	153.3	(27.4)	(17.9)
Net Earnings	253.6	218.0	35.6	16.3
Retained earnings—beginning of year	942.2	812.8	129.4	15.9
	1,195.8	1,030.8	165.0	16.0

Cash dividends	*19X6*	*19X5*			
	(per share)				
$4.00 preferred stock	$4.00	$4.00	.2	.2	0	0
Common Stock	$2.00	$2.00	91.2	88.4	2.8	3.2

Retained Earnings—end of year			$1,104.4	$ 942.2	162.2	17.2
Earnings Per Common Share			$ 5.60	$ 4.93	.67	13.6

Statement of significant accounting policies

Consolidation—The consolidated financial statements include the accounts of the company and its subsidiaries, except for a wholly-owned financial services subsidiary and, in 19X6, a real estate subsidiary in process of liquidation which are accounted for by the equity method. All significant intercompany items and transactions have been eliminated. Investments in affiliated companies, owned 20 percent or more, are accounted for by the equity method, and accordingly, the company's share of affiliates' net income has been included in the consolidated results of operations. Cost in excess of assigned value of businesses acquired is being amortized over a period of forty years.

Foreign currency translation—Cash and amounts receivable or payable that are denominated in local currency are translated at the rates of exchange in effect at the end of the respective periods (current rate). All other balance sheet accounts are translated using the rates of exchange in effect at the time of the transactions (historic rate). Depreciation expense is translated at the rates of exchange in effect when the related assets were acquired, and substantially all other income and expense accounts are translated at the rates in effect during each month. The net effects of gains or losses on foreign exchange are included in other income.

Inventories are stated at the lower of cost or market. Inventory costs include raw material, labor, and manufacturing overhead except for certain costs, principally depreciation. Cost of raw materials, paper and pulp products, lumber, and certain operating supplies is generally determined on the last-in, first-out basis. During periods of rising prices, this method results in charging increased inventory production costs to operations on a current basis and tends to eliminate inflationary gains on inventory balances from current operating results. If the first-in, first-out method had been utilized, it would have had the effect of increasing inventory balances by approximately $108 million and $94 million at December 31, 19X6 and 19X5, respectively. Other inventories are stated on the first-in, first-out or average cost basis.

Plants and properties are stated at cost. With regard to the company's oil and gas properties, the company follows the "full-cost" method of accounting under which all direct costs incurred in the acquisition, exploration, and development of oil and gas properties are capitalized and amortized on a company-wide composite method over the productive life of the producing properties.

Depreciation is computed principally on a straight-line method for financial reporting purposes and on accelerated methods for tax purposes, based upon estimated useful lives. Depreciation rates, for financial reporting purposes, are as follows: building 2.5 percent; machinery and equipment 5 percent to 25 percent; woods equipment 10 percent to 16 percent.

Depletion of oil and gas properties is determined on the basis of the percentage of the oil and gas revenues during the period to the total estimated future gross revenues from proven reserves.

Timberlands, including capitalized timber harvesting rights, are stated at cost, less cost of timber harvested. The portion of the cost of timberlands attributed to standing timber is charged against income as timber is cut, at rates determined annually, based on the relationship of unamortized timber costs to the estimated volume of recoverable timber. The costs of roads, park developments, and other land improvements are capitalized and amortized over their economic life.

The company capitalizes those timber cutting contracts where the gross price to be paid is fixed.

Income taxes—Deferred income taxes are provided for timing differences between financial and tax reporting. The investment tax credit is recognized currently in earnings.

The company provides deferred taxes on the income of its Domestic International Sales Corporation (DISC).

The company does not provide taxes on undistributed earnings that are considered permanently reinvested in the business outside the United States.

Research and development costs—The Company is committed to an ongoing research program which is primarily conducted at its four research centers in the United States and Canada. Such costs amounted to $20.1 million and $16.5 million in the years 19X6 and 19X5, respectively, and have been charged to operations as incurred.

Earnings per common share have been computed on the basis of the average number of shares outstanding—19X6-45.2 million; 19X5-44.2 million.

Notes to consolidated financial statements

Note 1.   Lines of credit—The Company maintains bank lines of credit ($232 million at December 31, 19X6) with certain U.S. and foreign banks. There have been no borrowings under these lines during 19X5 or 19X6 and, while the Company maintains deposits with some of these banks equal to approximately 10 percent of such lines, it is free to withdraw these deposits at any time.

Note 2.   Inventories by major category include:

(in millions)	19X6	19X5
Raw materials	$120.0	$118.1
Finished paper and pulp products	95.5	92.8
Finished lumber and plywood products	25.4	26.3
Operating supplies	96.4	95.1
Other	10.3	11.4
Total	$347.6	$343.7

Note 3.   Income taxes—The components of the provision for income taxes are:

(In millions)	19X6	19X5
Current:		
United States		
Federal	$ 45.5	$ 57.5
State	12.5	8.4
Outside U.S.	32.0	41.0
	90.0	106.9
Deferred:		
U.S. Federal	37.7	40.9
Outside U.S.	(1.8)	5.5
	35.9	46.4
Total	$125.9	$153.3

The principal items giving rise to deferred income taxes are:

(In millions)	19X6	19X5
Drilling and exploration costs, expensed for tax purposes	$17.9	$13.6
Depreciation	16.6	11.9
Discontinued operations	4.4	.1
DISC................................	2.5	8.8
Foreign exchange losses	(1.3)	(.1)
Other, net	(4.2)	12.1
	$35.9	$46.4

The principal components of the company's income tax rate are as follows:

	19X6	19X5
Ordinary U.S. income tax rate	48.0%	48.0%
Reduction resulting from:		
Income taxed at capital gains rate ...	5.5	3.7
Investment tax credit[1]	8.4	3.7
Other, net	.9	(.7)
Effective income tax rate	33.2%	41.3%

[1] Includes, in 19X6, an additional 1% investment tax credit (ITC) related to an Employee Stock Ownership Plan adopted by the Company in 19X6. This additional ITC ($2.9 million) has also been reflected in the accompanying income statement as compensation expense. Total ITC was: 19X6—$31.9 million; 19X5—$13.6 million.

Note 4. Plants and properties by major classification, and related accumulated depreciation and depletion reserves, at December 31, 19X6 were as follows:

(In millions)	Cost	Accumulated depreciation depletion	Net
Pulp and paper facilities:			
Mills..........................	$2,089.3	$1,125.7	$ 963.6
Packaging plants	374.1	171.2	202.9
	2,463.4	1,296.9	1,166.5
Oil and gas properties	562.0	94.5	467.5
Other properties:			
Wood products facilities	136.5	72.0	64.5
Woods equipment	206.0	103.6	102.4
Other	204.6	57.6	147.0
	547.1	233.2	313.9
Total	$3,572.5	$1,624.6	$1,947.9

Note 5. Timberlands—At December 31, 19X6, timberlands owned in fee consisted of 7.2 million acres in the United States with a book value of $391.6 million and 1.3 million acres in Canada with a book value of $7.2 million.

Capitalized timber harvesting rights consist principally of those timber cutting contracts in the United States where the gross price to be paid has been fixed.

The company has timber harvesting licensing arrangements on a total of 12.4 million acres in the Canadian provinces of Quebec and New Brunswick plus additional harvesting rights measured in wood volume in the province of Quebec.

Legislation was enacted in Quebec in 19X4 directed towards the eventual replacement of existing licensing arrangements by guarantees of timber supplies from public lands. These guarantees are in the form of grants of rights to cut standing timber sufficient to supply wood processing plants for as long as such plants carry on normal operations. Such grants are expected to be economically equivalent to the rights presently held.

Note 6. **Investments at cost,** include, at December 31, 19X6 and 19X5, $33.7 million representing the cost of 1,404,000 restricted shares of capital stock of C. R. Bard, Inc. Long-term debt of $53.3 million (4¼ percent Subordinated Debentures due 19X6) is exchangeable for the C. R. Bard, Inc. shares at a rate equivalent to $38 a share. The market price of C. R. Bard, Inc. shares was $14.63 per share on December 31, 19X6.

Note 7. **Notes and land contracts receivable** include $6.9 million and $9.2 million at December 31, 19X6 and 19X5, respectively, representing the long-term portion of a secured interest-bearing note of Donald L. Bren Company. The note is payable in substantially equal annual installments through 19Y0, and is secured by 132,828 shares of the common stock of the Beta Company. The company has a warrant to purchase 49 percent of the oustanding stock of the Bren Company at any time through June 30, 19Y0 at its then book value.

Note 8. **Long-term debt**—A summary of long-term debt follows:

(In millions)	19X6	19X5
5⅛% Notes—due 19X7-19Y6	$ 100.0	$ 110.0
5⅞% Notes—due 19X7-19Y6	20.0	22.0
6⅜% Notes—due 19X7-19Y8	120.0	130.0
8½% Notes—due 19X7-19Y2	275.6	323.3
9¼% Notes—due 19X7-19X8	69.1	103.9
8.85% Sinking fund debentures—due 19Y1-19Z5	150.0	150.0
8.85% Sinking fund debentures—due 19Y6-19Z9	150.0	150.0
4¼% Subordinated debentures—due 19Z6	53.3	53.3
Environmental bond issues	139.3[1]	112.1
Other	99.2	101.8
	$1,176.5	$1,256.4
Less—Current maturities	122.2	119.2
Total	$1,054.3[2]	$1,137.2

[1] Average interest rate of 6.5%.

[2] Total maturities over the next five years are as follows: 19X7—$122.2 million; 19X8—$113.5 million; 19X9—$77.8 million; 19Y0—$76.1 million; 19Y1—$78.4 million. Long-term debt at December 31, 19X6 includes local borrowings of Canadian and other subsidiaries outside the U.S. amounting to $73.1 million.

Note 9. **Capital stock**—A summary of capital stock at December 31, 19X6 follows:

	Shares[1]	
	$4 preferred stock	*Common stock*[2]
Authorized	400,000	72,000,000
Issued	230,579	47,381,674
In Treasury........	180,686	684,716
Outstanding	49,893	46,696,958

[1] In April 19X6, the share owners approved the creation of a new class of serial preferred stock ($1.00 par value 15,000,000 shares) and the elimination of preemptive rights of common stock.

[2] Shares issued and outstanding increased by 2,447,414 shares during 19X6, principally due to the sale of 2.25 million shares in August for approximately $150 million. As a result of such sale, $143.9 million has been credited to capital surplus.

Note 10.   Operations outside the United States—A summary of operations outside the U.S. (principally Canada) follows:

(In millions)	*19X6*
Sales[1]	$826.4
Working capital	249.8
Assets.......................	721.6
Undistributed earnings[2]	425.7

[1] Comparable sales for the year ended December 31, 19X5 were $780.6.

[2] Substantially all of these earnings have been permanently reinvested outside the U.S.

Note 11.   Other income, net—The major components of other income were as follows:

(In millions)	*19X6*	*19X5*
Interest income	$18.8	$17.6
Equity in earnings of affiliates	9.3	3.8
Sale of capital assets	5.5	1.7
Foreign exchange	(1.1)	(.6)
Miscellaneous....................	8.4	6.7
	$40.9	$29.2

Note 12.   Incentive plans—The company has a Profit Improvement Plan under which a maximum of 750,000 shares of treasury stock may be awarded. Under the plan, which terminates in 19Y0, contingent awards of shares of common stock, covering a three-year period, are granted by a committee composed of members of the Board of Directors who are not eligible for awards. Awards are earned in any year in which earnings per share, as defined, exceed the predetermined profit base. Through December 31, 19X6, 212,741 shares have been earned under the Plan, including 51,601 shares earned in 19X6 and

40,113 shares earned in 19X5. At December 31, 19X6, 52,276 shares have been contingently awarded for the year ending December 31, 19X7.

The company also has an Incentive Compensation Plan. Participants include those employees who are in a position to make substantial contributions to the management of the Company. Awards may be made in any year in which net earnings, as defined, exceed six percent of share owners' equity, but are limited to the lesser amount of eight percent of such excess or ten percent of the cash dividends declared on the outstanding common stock of the Company during the year. The awards may be in cash, payable immediately, or in treasury common shares, payable in the future.

Provision for the cost of the Company's two incentive plans amounted to $12.2 million and $8.5 million for the respective years of 19X6 and 19X5.

Note 13. Retirement plans—The company and its consolidated subsidiaries have several pension plans which provide retirement benefits to substantially all employees.

The company has amended its pension plans to conform to the provisions of the Employees Retirement Income Security Act which became effective on January 1, 19X6. The effect of such amendments on annual pension costs and the funding of such costs was not significant.

Annual pension costs, which reflect amortization of prior service costs over periods of up to 30 years, are funded currently by payments to the trustees of the various plans. Pension costs were $57 million in 19X6 and $45 million in 19X5. At December 31, 19X6, unfunded prior service costs amounted to $189 million, and it is estimated that the actuarially computed value of vested benefits exceeded the value of fund assets by approximately $76 million.

Note 14. Interim financial results (unaudited)

19X6	Sales	Net earnings	Earnings per common share
	($ in millions except per-share amounts)		
First	$ 866.8	$ 63.6	$1.43
Second	906.1	83.5	1.88
Third	884.0	58.8	1.29
Fourth	883.7	47.7	1.02
Year	$3,540.6	$253.6	$5.60[1]

[1] Total 19X6 per-share amount does not equal the sum of the individual quarters because of the effect on average shares outstanding of the sale of 2.25 million shares in August 19X6.

Note 15. Effects of inflation—(unaudited) During recent years, the overall rate of cost inflation has accelerated faster than the rate of productivity improvement in the company's operations. As a result, price increases have been necessary to achieve and maintain profit margins at acceptable levels. The company believes that over the next several years additional price increases, together with aggressive cost reduction and technological improvements, will be required to provide the profit margins necessary to justify new investment in the Company's principal businesses. In addition, future investment decisions will depend upon sound federal income tax policies and realistic environmental regulations.

The Company's Form 10-K, filed with the Securities and Exchange Commission, includes certain quantitative information with respect to the estimated replacement cost of inventories and plant and equipment at December 31, 19X6, and the related estimated effect of such costs on the cost of products sold, depreciation expense, and cost of timber harvested for the year then ended. A copy of Beta's Form 10-K is available upon request.

Note 16. Commitments—Rent expense, principally relating to vessels and data processing equipment, was $33 million in 19X6 and $31 million in 19X5. At December 31, 19X6, rental commitments under existing leases were $22 million, $21 million, $20 million, $15 million, and $9 million for the five years ending 19X1, $27 million for the 19X2–19X6 period, and $10 million thereafter.

The Company has many purchase commitments involving such matters as timber supply contracts, material supply contracts, and construction contracts.

EXHIBIT B–4
Report of independent public accountants

To the Share Owners of Beta Company:

We have examined the consolidated balance sheet of Beta Company and consolidated subsidiaries as of December 31, 19X6 and 19X5, and the related consolidated statements of earnings and retained earnings and changes in financial position for the years then ended. Our examination was made in accordance with generally accepted auditing standards, and accordingly included such tests of the accounting records and such other auditing procedures as we considered necessary in the circumstances. The financial statements of Canadian Beta Company included in the consolidated financial statements (constituting approximately 15% of total consolidated assets and 20% of total consolidated sales for both 19X6 and 19X5) were examined by other independent public accountants whose report thereon has been furnished to us and our opinion expressed herein, insofar as it relates to the amounts included for Canadian Beta Company, is based solely upon such report.

In our opinion, based upon our examination and the report of other independent public accountants, the accompanying consolidated financial statements present fairly the consolidated financial position of Beta Company and consolidated subsidiaries as of December 31, 19X6 and 19X5, and the results of their operations and the changes in their financial position for the years then ended, in conformity with generally accepted accounting principles consistently applied during the periods.

New York, N.Y.,
February 8, 19X7

Good, Better & Co.

EXHIBIT B–5

BETA COMPANY

Summary of Earnings	Trend analysis (index numbers)					Common size analysis				
	19X6	19X5	19X4	19X3†	19X2	19X6	19X5	19X4	19X3	19X2
Income:										
Net sales	153.0	133.1	131.5	100	90.5	100	100	100	100	100
Other income, net	100.0	70.7	129.3	100	51.2	1.2	.9	1.7	1.8	1.0
Total Income	152.1	132.1	131.4	100	89.8	101.2	100.9	101.7	101.8	101.0
Costs and expenses:										
Cost of products sold	151.4	128.5	128.1	100	91.1	71.0	69.3	70.0	71.8	72.3
Distribution expenses	123.1	110.3	119.2	100	100.6	5.4	5.6	6.1	6.7	7.5
Selling and administrative expenses	148.1	121.7	110.9	100	103.1	5.4	5.1	4.7	5.6	6.4
Depreciation	124.0	114.4	103.8	100	94.2	3.6	3.9	3.6	4.5	4.7
Depletion of oil and gas properties	113.3	100†	—	—	—	1.4	1.5	.9	—	—
Cost of timber harvested	183.3	161.1	150.0	100	77.8	.9	.9	—	.8	.7
Interest	224.4	202.4	109.8	100	92.7	2.6	2.7	1.5	1.8	1.8
Total Costs and Expenses	151.8	129.9	125.0	100	92.7	90.4	88.9	86.7	91.1	93.4
Earnings before income taxes	154.5	150.8	186.2	100	65.0	10.8	12.0	15.0	10.7	7.6
Provision for income taxes	146.5	177.9	226.7	100	66.3	3.6	5.0	6.4	3.7	2.7
Earnings before extraordinary items	158.8	136.3	164.4	100	64.4	7.2	7.0	8.6	7.0	4.9
Extraordinary items, net	—	—	—	100	—	—	—	—	—	—
Net Earnings	158.8	136.3	164.4	100	64.4	7.2	7.0	8.6	7.0	4.9
Cash Dividends	116.7	114.1	98.7	100	85.9	2.6	2.9	2.5	3.4	3.2
Financial Position*										
Current assets	138.1	126.8	137.8	100	91.3	28.0	28.0	37.3	33.6	32.5
Plants and properties—net	197.0	176.2	107.5	100	104.1	53.5	52.2	39.0	45.0	49.6
Timberlands—net	237.2	238.8	203.3	100	90.2	11.9	13.1	13.6	8.3	7.9
Other assets	83.0	78.1	96.2	100	71.9	6.6	6.7	10.1	13.1	10.0
Total Assets	165.6	152.0	124.2	100	94.4	100.0	100.0	100.0	100.0	100.0
Current liabilities	184.9	179.1	171.2	100	90.3	14.1	14.9	17.4	12.6	12.1
Long-term debt	180.8	195.0	124.7	100	99.1	29.0	34.0	26.6	26.5	27.8
Reserves and deferred liabilities	156.1	129.9	101.3	100	82.2	6.7	6.1	5.8	7.1	6.2
Total share owners' equity	154.8	127.3	115.8	100	94.7	50.2	45.0	50.2	53.8	53.9
Total liabilities and equity	165.6	152.0	124.2	100	94.4	100.0	100.0	100.0	100.0	100.0

* Reclassified from Form 10-K data.
† Base year.

EXHIBIT B-6

BETA COMPANY
Ten Year Financial Summary
(in millions of dollars except per-share amounts)

	19X6	19X5	19X4	19X3	19X2	19X1	19X0	19W9	19W8	19W7
Ten year summary of earnings										
Income:										
Net sales	$3,541	$3,081	$3,042	$2,314	$2,093	$1,970	$1,841	$1,777	$1,574	$1,421
Other income, net	41	29	53	41	21	17	17	22	19	13
Total Income	3,582	3,110	3,095	2,355	2,114	1,987	1,858	1,799	1,593	1,434
Costs and expenses:										
Cost of products sold	2,514	2,134	2,128	1,661	1,514	1,432	1,323	1,246	1,115	1,028
Distribution expenses	192	172	186	156	157	148	139	132	120	106
Selling and administrative expenses	191	157	143	129	133	149	139	120	96	86
Depreciation	129	119	108	104	98	97	89	79	78	74
Depletion of oil and gas properties	51	45	—	—	—	—	—	—	—	—
Cost of timber harvested	33	29	27	18	14	14	10	9	7	3
Interest	92	83	45	41	38	41	39	26	17	9
Total Costs and Expenses	3,202	2,739	2,637	2,109	1,954	1,881	1,739	1,612	1,433	1,306
Earnings before income taxes	380	371	458	246	160	106	119	187	160	128
Provision for income taxes	126	153	195	86	57	37	37	73	62	44
Earnings before extraordinary items	254	218	263	160	103	69	82	114	98	84
Extraordinary items, net	—	—	—	—	—	(15)	(39)	—	—	—
Net Earnings	$254	$218	$263	$160	$103	$54	$43	$114	$98	$84

	$ 91	$ 89	$ 77	$ 78	$ 67	$ 67	$ 67	$ 66	$ 61	$ 59
Cash Dividends										
Financial position										
Current assets	$1,019	$ 936	$1,017	$ 738	$ 674	$ 569	$ 607	$ 572	$ 538	$ 453
Current liabilities	514	498	476	278	251	226	277	313	225	214
Working capital	505	438	541	460	423	343	330	259	313	239
Plants and properties—net	1,948	1,743	1,063	989	1,030	1,060	1,060	978	869	798
Timberlands—net	434	437	372	183	165	166	171	154	153	156
Long-term debt	1,054	1,137	727	583	578	564	534	373	359	181
Reserves and deferred liabilities	245	204	159	157	129	160	138	79	58	42
Common share owners' equity	1,822	1,496	1,361	1,173	1,106	1,069	1,081	1,105	1,068	1,036
Per share of common stock										
Earnings before extraordinary items	$ 5.60	$ 4.93	$ 5.95	$ 3.60	$ 2.30	$ 1.53	$ 1.84	$ 2.54	$ 2.18	$ 1.90
Extraordinary items, net	—	—	—	—	—	(.33)	(.89)	—	—	—
Net earnings	5.60	4.93	5.95	3.60	2.30	1.20	.95	2.54	2.18	1.90
Cash dividends	2.00	2.00	1.75	1.75	1.50	1.50	1.50	1.50	1.38¾	1.35
Common share owners' equity	39.01	33.81	30.84	26.62	24.83	24.03	24.38	24.93	23.95	23.11
Market price range per share* HIGH	80	62	56	57	42	46	40	46	40	32
LOW	58	35	32	33	33	28	28	35	26	25

Stock price by quarter*

19X6

	Fourth	Third	Second	First
High	71	75	78	80
Low	63	64	69	58

19X5

	Fourth	Third	Second	First
High	60	62	55	44
Low	50	49	41	35

* High and low market price on Composite Tape to nearest dollar.

In the opinion of management, no losses are anticipated in the liquidation of these commitments.

Note 17. Litigation—During 19X6, the company was fined $50,000 pursuant to a plea of *nolo contendere* to a charge of violation of federal antitrust laws in the sale of folding cartons. The company is one of the defendants in a number of purported class actions which were filed during 19X6 and which seek treble damages for alleged antitrust violations in the sale of folding cartons and the sale of box board used in the manufacture of folding cartons. All of these cases are in preliminary stages and the court has not yet determined which, if any, of the cases may be maintained as class actions.

In this increasingly litigious society, the company is also a defendant in other cases involving, among other matters, land sales, environmental protection, alleged discrimination in employment practices, securities matters, and private antitrust damage claims involving the sale of plywood. If the plaintiffs should prevail in various of the foregoing cases as class actions, damages against the company could be substantial. The company is also involved in several grand jury investigations concerning compliance with the antitrust laws. While any litigation or investigation has an element of uncertainty, the company believes that the outcome of any lawsuit or claim which is pending or threatened, or all of them combined, will not have a materially adverse effect on its financial condition or results of operations.

QUESTIONS

1. As a potential investor in a common stock, what information would you seek? How do you get such information?
2. The president of your client company approached you, the financial officer of a local bank, for a substantial loan. What could you do?
3. What, in broad categories, are some of the approaches utilized by the financial analyst in diagnosing the financial health of a business?
4. How useful is a comparative financial analysis? How do you make useful comparison?
5. What are some of the precautions required of a financial analyst in his comparative analytical work?
6. Give four broad categories of analysis tools.
7. Is the trend of the past a good predictor of the future? Give reasons for your argument.
8. Which is the better indicator of significant change—the absolute amount of change or the change in percentage? Why?
9. What conditions would prevent the computation of a valid percentage change? Give an example.
10. What are some of the criteria to be used in picking out a base year in an index number comparative analysis?
11. What information can be obtained from trend analysis?
12. What is a common-size financial statement? How do you prepare one?

2

ANALYSIS OF SHORT-TERM LIQUIDITY

SIGNIFICANCE OF SHORT-TERM LIQUIDITY

The short-term liquidity of an enterprise is measured by the degree to which it can meet its short-term obligations. Liquidity implies the ready ability to convert assets into cash or to obtain cash. The short term is conventionally viewed as a time span up to a year, although it is sometimes also identified with the normal operating cycle of a business, that is, the time span encompassing the buying-producing-selling and collecting cycle of an enterprise.

The importance of short-term liquidity can best be gauged by examining the repercussions which stem from a lack of ability to meet short-term obligations.

Liquidity is a matter of degree. A lack of liquidity may mean that the enterprise is unable to avail itself of favorable discounts and is unable to take advantage of profitable business opportunities as they arise. At this stage a lack of liquidity implies a lack of freedom of choice as well as constraints on management's freedom of movement.

A more serious lack of liquidity means that the enterprise is unable to pay its current debts and obligations. This can lead to the forced sale of long-term investments and assets and, in its most severe form, to insolvency and bankruptcy.

To the owners of an enterprise a lack of liquidity can mean reduced profitability and opportunity or it may mean loss of control and partial or total loss of the capital investment. In the case of owners with unlimited liability, the loss can extend beyond the original investment.

To creditors of the enterprise a lack of liquidity can mean delay in collection of interest and principal due them or it can mean the partial or total loss of the amounts due them.

Customers as well as suppliers of goods and services to an enterprise can also be affected by its short-term financial condition. Such effects may take the form of inability of the enterprise to perform under contracts and the loss of supplier relationships.

From the above description of the significance of short-term liquidity it can be readily appreciated why the measures of such liquidity have been accorded great importance. For, if an enterprise cannot meet its current obligations as they become due, its continued existence becomes in doubt and that relegates all other measures of performance to secondary importance if not to irrelevance. The evaluation of short-term liquidity is concerned with the assessment of the financial risk of the enterprise.

While accounting determinations are made on the assumption of indefinite continuity of the enterprise, the financial analyst must always submit the validity of such assumption to the test of the enterprise's liquidity and solvency.

One of the most widely used measures of liquidity is working capital. In addition to its importance as a pool of liquid assets which provides a safety cushion to creditors, net working capital is also important because it provides a liquid reserve with which to meet contingencies and the ever present uncertainty regarding an enterprise's ability to balance the outflow of funds with an adequate inflow of funds.

WORKING CAPITAL

The basic concept of working capital is relatively simple. It is the excess of current assets over current liabilities. That excess is sometimes referred to as "net working capital" because some businessmen consider current assets as "working capital." A working capital deficiency exists when current liabilities exceed current assets.

The importance attached by credit grantors, investors, and others to working capital as a measure of liquidity and solvency has caused some enterprises, in the desire to present their current condition in the most favorable light, to stretch to the limit the definition of what constitutes a current asset and a current liability. For this reason the analyst must use his own judgment in evaluating the proper classification of items included in "working capital."

Current assets

Current assets include cash and other assets that are reasonably expected to be realized in cash or sold or consumed during the normal operating cycle of the business or within one year if the operating cycle is shorter than one year. Current liabilities include those expected to be satisfied by either the use of assets classified as current in the same balance sheet or the creation of other current liabilities, or those expected to be satisfied within a relatively short period of time, usually one year. (APB *Statement No. 4,* Par. 198.)

The general rule about the ability to convert current assets into cash within a year is subject to important qualifications. The most important qualification relates to the operating cycle. The operating cycle comprises the average time span intervening between the acquisition of materials and services entering the production or trading process to the final realization in cash of the proceeds from the sale of the enterprise's products. This time span can be quite extended in industries which require a long inventory holding period (e.g., tobacco, distillery, and lumber) or those which sell on the installment plan. Whenever no clearly defined operating cycle is evident, the arbitrary one-year rule prevails.

The most common categories of current assets are:

1. Cash.
2. Cash equivalents (i.e., temporary investments).
3. Accounts and notes receivable.
4. Inventories.
5. Prepaid expenses.

Cash is, of course, the ultimate measure of a current asset since current liabilities are paid off in cash. However, earmarked cash held for specific purposes, such as plant expansion, should not be considered as current. Compensating balances under bank loan agreements cannot, in most cases, be regarded as "free" cash. SEC *Accounting Series Release* (ASR) 148 requires the disclosure of compensating balance arrangements with the lending banks as well as the segregation of such balances.

Cash equivalents represent temporary investments of cash in excess of current requirements made for the purpose of earning a return on these funds.

The analyst must be alert to the valuation of such investments. Equity investments are now accounted for in accordance with SFAB *12*. Debt securities may still be carried above market if management views a decline as merely "temporary" in nature. Similarly, the "cash equivalent" nature of securities investments may sometimes be stretched quite far.

The mere ability to convert an asset to cash is not the sole determinant of its current nature. It is the intention and normal practice that governs. Intention is, however, not always enough. Thus, the cost of fixed assets which are intended for sale should be included in current assets only if the enterprise has a contractual commitment from a buyer to purchase the asset at a given price within the following year or the following operating cycle.

An example where the above principle was not followed is found in the 1970 annual report of International Industries. In this report the company carries as a current asset $37.8 million in "Real estate held for sale." A related footnote explains that "the company intends to sell this real estate during the ensuing operating cycle substantially at cost under sale and leaseback agreements, however, prevailing economic conditions may affect its ability to do so."

This is an obvious attempt to present a current position superior to the one the company can justifiably claim. Without the inclusion of real estate, the company's current ratio would have dropped to 1.1 (with working capital at about $3 million) as against a current ratio, based on reported figures, of 1.8 and a working capital of $40.3 million.

This reinforces the ever-recurring message in this text that the analyst cannot rely on adherence to rules or accepted principles of preparation of financial statements, but instead must exercise eternal vigilance in his use of ratios and all other analytical measures which are based on such statements. If anything, attempts by managements to stretch the rules in order to present a situation as better than it really is should serve as an added warning of potential trouble and risk.

Accounts receivable, net of provisions for uncollectible accounts, are current unless they represent receivables for sales, not in the ordinary course of business, which are due after one year. Installment receivables from customary sales usually fall within the operating cycle of the enterprise.

The analyst must be alert to the valuation as well as validity of receivables particularly in cases such as those where "sales" are made on consignment or subject to the right of return.

Receivables from affiliated companies or from officers and employees can be considered current only if they are collectible in the ordinary course of business within a year or, in the case of installment sales, within the operating cycle.

Inventories are considered current assets except in cases where they are in excess of current requirements. Such excess inventories, which should be shown as noncurrent, must be distinguished from inventories, such as tobacco, which require a long aging cycle. The variations in practice in this area are considerable, as the following illustrations will show, and should be carefully scrutinized by the analyst.

ILLUSTRATION 1.   National Fuel Gas Company (prospectus dated 7/23/69) shows a current as well as a noncurrent portion of gas stored underground and explains this as follows:

"Included in property, plant, and equipment as gas stored underground—noncurrent is $18,825,232 at April 30, 1969, the cost of the volume of gas required to maintain pressure levels for normal operating purposes at the low point of the storage cycle. The portion of gas in underground storage included in current assets does not exceed estimated withdrawals during the succeeding two years."

ILLUSTRATION 2.   Some trucking concerns include the tires on their trucks as current assets presumably on the theory that they will be used up during the normal operating cycle.

The analyst must pay particular attention to inventory valuation. Thus, for example, the inclusion of inventories at Lifo can result in a significant understatement of working capital.

Prepaid expenses are considered current, not because they can be converted into cash but rather because they represent advance payments for services and supplies which would otherwise require the current outlay of cash.

Current liabilities

Current liabilities are obligations which would, generally, require the use of current assets for their discharge or, alternatively, the creation of other current liabilities. The following are current liabilities most commonly found in practice:

1. Accounts payable.
2. Notes payable.
3. Short-term bank and other loans.
4. Tax and other expense accruals.
5. Current portion of long-term debt.

The foregoing current liability categories are usually clear and do not require further elaboration. However, as is the case with current assets, the analyst cannot assume that they will always be properly classified for his purposes. Thus, for example, current practice sanctions the presentation as noncurrent of current obligations which are expected to be refunded. The degree of assurance of the subsequent refunding is mostly an open question which in the case of adverse developments may well be resolved negatively as far as the enterprise is concerned.

SEC *ASR 148* has expanded significantly the disclosure requirements regarding short-term bank and commercial paper borrowing. SFAS 6 established criteria for the balance sheet classification of short-term obligations that are expected to be refinanced.

The analyst must also be alert to the possibility of presentations designed to present the working capital in a better light than warranted by circumstances.

ILLUSTRATION 3. Penn Central Company excluded the current maturities of long-term debt from the current liability category and included it in the "long-term debt" section of the balance sheet. In 1969, this treatment resulted in an excess of current assets over current liabilities of $21 million, whereas the inclusion of current debt maturities among current liabilities would have resulted in a working capital *deficit* of $207 million. (The subsequent financial collapse of this enterprise is now a well-known event.)

The analyst must also ascertain whether all obligations, regarding which there is a reasonably good probability that they will have to be met, have been included as current liabilities in computing an effective working capital figure. Two examples of such obligations follow:

1. The obligation of an enterprise for notes discounted with a bank where the bank has full recourse in the event the note is not paid when due is generally considered a contingent liability. However, the likelihood of the contingency materializing must be considered in the computation of working capital. The same principle applies in case of loan guarantees.
2. A contract for the construction or acquisition of long-term assets may call for substantial progress payments. Such obligations for payments are, for accounting purposes, considered as commitments rather than liabilities, and hence are not found among the latter. Nevertheless, when computing the excess of liquid assets over short-term obligations such commitments may have to be recognized.

Other problem areas in definition of current assets and liabilities

An area which presented a problem of classification but which has now been settled in favor of consistency is that of deferred tax accounting. Thus, if an asset (e.g., installment accounts receivable) is classified as current, the related deferred tax arising from differences in treatment between book and tax return must be similarly classified.

Many concerns which have fixed assets as the main "working assets," such as, for example, trucking concerns and some leasing companies, carry as current prospective receipts from billings out of which their current equipment purchase obligations must be met. Such treatments, or the absence of any distinction between current and noncurrent on the balance sheet, as is the case with real estate companies, is an attempt by such concerns to convey to the reader their "special" financing and operating conditions which make the current versus noncurrent distinction inapplicable and which have no parallel in the regular trading or industrial concern.

Some of these "special" circumstances may indeed be present, but they do not necessarily change the relationship existing between current obligations and the liquid funds available, or reasonably expected to become available, to meet them. It is to this relationship that the analyst, faced with the task of evaluating liquidity, must train his attention.

Working capital as a measure of liquidity

The popularity of working capital as a measure of liquidity and of short-term financial health is so widespread that it hardly needs documentation. Credit grantors compute the relationship between current assets and current liabilities; financial analysts measure the size of the working capital of enterprises they analyze; government agencies compute aggregates of working capital of corporations; and most published balance sheets distinguish between current and noncurrent assets and liabilities. Moreover, loan agreements and bond indentures often contain stipulations regarding the maintenance of minimum working capital levels.

The absolute amount of working capital has significance only when related to other variables such as sales, total assets, and so forth. It is at best of limited value for comparison purposes and for judging the adequacy of working capital. This can be illustrated as follows:

	Company A	Company B
Current assets	$300,000	$1,200,000
Current liabilities	100,000	1,000,000
Working capital	$200,000	$ 200,000

While both companies have an equal amount of working capital, a cursory comparison of the relationship of current assets to current liabilities suggests that Company A's current condition is superior to that of Company B.

CURRENT RATIO

The above conclusion is based on the ratio of current assets to current liabilities. It is 3:1 (300,000/100,000) for Company A and 1.2:1 (1,200,000/1,000,000) for Company B. It is this ratio that is accorded substantial importance in the assessment of an enterprise's current liquidity.

Some of the basic reasons for the widespread use of the current ratio as a measure of liquidity are obvious:

1. It measures the degree to which current assets cover current liabilities. The higher the amount of current assets in relation to current liabilities the more assurance exists that these liabilities can be paid out of such assets.
2. The excess of current assets over current liabilities provides a buffer against losses which may be incurred in the disposition or liquidation of the current assets other than cash. The more substantial such a buffer is, the better for creditors. Thus, the current ratio measures the margin of safety available to cover any possible shrinkage in the value of current assets.
3. It measures the reserve of liquid funds in excess of current obligations which is available as a margin of safety against uncertainty and the random shocks to which the flows of funds in an enterprise are subject. Random shocks, such as strikes, extraordinary losses, and other uncertainties can temporarily and unexpectedly stop or reduce the inflow of funds.

What is not so obvious, however, is the fact that the current ratio, as a measure of liquidity and short-term solvency, is subject to serious theoretical as well as practical shortcomings and limitations. Consequently, before we embark on a discussion of the uses of the current ratio and related measures of liquidity, these limitations must be thoroughly understood.

Limitations of the current ratio

The first step in our examination of the current ratio as a tool of liquidity and short-term solvency analysis is to examine the components which are normally included in the ratio shown in Exhibit 2–1.

EXHIBIT 2–1

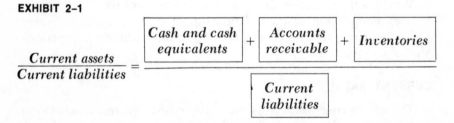

Disregarding, for purposes of this evaluation, prepaid expenses and similar unsubstantial items entering the computation of the current ratio, we are left with the above four major elements which comprise this ratio.

Now, if we define liquidity as the ability to balance required cash outflows with adequate inflows, including an allowance for unexpected interruptions of inflows or increases in outflows, we must ask: Does the relationship of these four elements at a given point in time—

1. Measure and predict the pattern of future fund flows?
2. Measure the adequacy of future fund inflows in relation to outflows.

Unfortunately, the answer to these questions is mostly negative. The current ratio is a static or "stock" concept of what resources are available at a given moment in time to meet the obligations at that moment. The existing reservoir of net funds does not have a logical or causative relationship to the future funds which will flow through it. And yet it is the future flows that are the subject of our greatest interest in the assessment of liquidity. These flows depend importantly on elements *not* included in the ratio itself, such as sales, profits, and changes in business conditions. To elaborate, let us examine more closely the four elements comprising the ratio.

Cash and Cash Equivalents The amount of cash held by a well-managed enterprise is in the nature of a precautionary reserve, intended to take care of short-term imbalances in cash flows. For example, in cases of a business downturn, sales may fall more rapidly than outlays for purchases and expenses. Since cash is a nonearning asset and cash equivalents are usually low-yielding securities, the investment in such assets is kept at a safe minimum. To conceive of this minimum balance as available for payment of current debts would require the dropping of the going-concern assumption underlying accounting statements. While the balance of cash has some relation to the existing level of activity, such a relationship is not very strong nor does it contain predictive implications regarding the future. In fact, some enterprises may use cash substitutes in the form of open lines of credit which, of course, do not enter at all into the computation of the current ratio.

The important link between cash and solvency in the minds of many is due to the well-known fact that a shortage of cash, more than any other factor, is the element which can clinch the insolvency of an enterprise.

Accounts Receivable The major determinant of the level of accounts receivable is sales. The size of accounts receivable in relation to sales is governed by terms of trade and credit policy. Changes in receivables will correspond to changes in sales though not necessarily on a directly proportional basis.

When we look at accounts receivable as a source of cash we must, except in the case of liquidation, recognize the revolving nature of the asset with the collection of one account replaced by the extension of fresh credit. Thus, the level of receivables per se is not an index to future net inflows of cash.

| *Inventory* | As is the case with accounts receivable, the main determinant of the size of inventories is the level of sales, or expected sales, rather than the level of current liabilities. Given that the level of sales is a measure of the level of demand then, scientific methods of inventory management (economic order quantities, safe stock levels, and reorder points) generally establish that inventory increments vary not in proportion to demand but vary rather with the *square root* of demand.

The relationship of inventories to sales is further accented by the fact that it is sales that is the one essential element which starts the conversion of inventories to cash. Moreover, the determination of future cash inflows through the sale of inventories is dependent on the profit margin which can be realized because inventories are generally stated at the lower of *cost* or market. The current ratio, while including inventories, gives no recognition to the sales level or to profit margin, both of which are important elements entering into the determination of future cash inflows.

| *Current Liabilities* | The level of current liabilities, the safety of which the current ratio is intended to measure, is also largely determined by the level of sales.

Current liabilities are a source of funds in the same sense that receivables and inventories tie up funds. Since purchases, which give rise to accounts payable, are a function of the level of activity (i.e., sales), these payables vary with sales. As long as sales remain constant or are rising, the payment of current liabilities is essentially a refunding operation. There again the components of the current ratio give little, if any, recognition to these elements and their effects on the future flow of funds. Nor do the current liabilities which enter into the computation of the current ratio include prospective outlays, such as commitments under construction contracts, loans, leases, or pensions, all of which affect the future outflow of funds.

Implications of the limitations to which the current ratio is subject

There are a number of conclusions which can be reached on the basis of the foregoing discussion:

1. Liquidity depends to some extent on cash or cash equivalents balances and to a much more significant extent on prospective cash flows.
2. There is no direct or established relationship between balances of working capital items and the pattern which future cash flows are likely to assume.
3. Managerial policies directed at optimizing the levels of receivables and inventories are oriented primarily towards efficient and profitable assets utilization and only secondarily at liquidity.[1]

Given these conclusions, which obviously limit the value of the current ratio as an index of liquidity, and given the static nature of this ratio and the fact that it is composed of items which affect liquidity in different ways, we may ask why this ratio enjoys such widespread use and in what way, if any, it can be used intelligently by the analyst.

The most probable reasons for the popularity of the current ratio are evidently the simplicity of its basic concept, the ease with which it can be computed, and the readiness with which data for it can be obtained. It may also derive its popularity from the credit grantor's, and especially the banker's, propensity to view credit situations as conditions of last resort. They may ask themselves: "What if there were a complete cessation of funds inflow? Would the current assets then be adequate to pay off the current liabilities?" The assumption of such extreme conditions is, of course, not always a useful way of measuring liquidity.

To what use can the intelligent analyst put the current ratio?

Let it first be said that the analyst who wishes to measure short-term liquidity and solvency will find cash flow projections and pro forma financial statements to be the most relevant and reliable tools to use. This involves obtaining information which is not readily available in published financial statements and it also involves the need for a great deal of estimation. This area of analysis will be discussed in the next chapter.

The current ratio as a valid tool of analysis

Should the analyst want to use the current ratio as a static measure of the ability of current assets to satisfy the current liabilities, he will be employing a different concept of liquidity from the one discussed above. In this context liquidity means the readiness and speed with which current assets can be converted to cash and the degree to which

---

[1] The nature of the business is also a factor. For example, Fair Lanes, a bowling lanes operator, does obviously not sell on credit and thus has no receivables. It also carries no inventories of any consequences. Consequently it has during most of its 50 year existence operated with a working capital deficiency. With almost all of its current assets in cash it has no problem meeting current obligations.

such conversion will result in shrinkage in the stated value of current assets.

It is not our purpose here to discredit the current ratio as a valid tool of analysis but rather to suggest that its legitimate area of application is far less wide than popularly believed.

Defenders of this, the oldest and best known of financial ratios, may say that they are aware of the multitude of limitations and inconsistencies of concept outlined above but that they will "allow" for them in the evaluation of the ratio. A careful examination of these limitations suggests that such process of "allowing" for such limitations is well nigh impossible.

The better and most valid way to use this ratio is to recognize its limitations and to restrict its use to the analytical job it can do, that is, measuring the ability of *present* current assets to discharge *existing* current liabilities and considering the excess, if any, as a liquid surplus available to meet imbalances in the flow of funds and other contingencies. This should be done with an awareness of the fact that the test envisages a situation of enterprise liquidation[2] whereas in the normal, going-concern situation current assets are of a revolving nature, for example, the collected receivable being replaced with a newly created one, while the current liabilities are essentially of a refunding nature, that is, the repayment of one is followed by the creation of another.

Given the analytical function of the current ratio, as outlined above, there are two basic elements which must be measured before the current ratio can form the basis for valid conclusions:

1. The quality of the current assets and the nature of the current liabilities which enter the determination of the ratio.
2. The rate of turnover of these assets and liabilities that is, the average time span needed to convert receivables and inventories into cash and the amount of time which can be taken for the payment of current liabilities.

To measure the above, a number of ratios and other tools have been devised, and these can enhance the use of the current ratio as an analytic tool.

Measures which supplement the current ratio

The most liquid of current assets is, of course, cash, which is the standard of liquidity itself. A close second to cash is "temporary in-

---

[2] It should be realized that the circumstances leading to bankruptcy or liquidation will have an effect on how much the amounts realized on asset dispositions will shrink. They will, for example, be likely to shrink more severely if the liquidation is caused by overall adverse industry conditions than if caused by specific difficulties such as poor management or inadequate capitalization.

vestments" which are usually highly marketable and relatively safe temporary repositories of cash. These are, in effect, considered as "cash equivalents" and usually earn a modest return.

Cash ratios.   The proportion which cash and cash equivalents constitute of the total current assets group is a measure of the degree of liquidity of this group of assets. It is measured by the cash ratio which is computed as follows:

$$\frac{\text{Cash} + \text{Cash Equivalents}}{\text{Total Current Assets}}$$

Evaluation.   The higher the ratio the more liquid is the current asset group. This, in turn, means that with respect to this cash and cash equivalents component there is a minimal danger of loss in value in cash of liquidation and that there is practically no waiting period for conversion of these assets into usable cash.

APB *Opinion No. 18* generally requires the carrying of investments, representing an interest of 20 percent or higher, at underlying equity. This is, of course, neither cost nor, necessarily, market value. While such substantial positions in the securities of another company are not usually considered cash equivalents, *should* they nevertheless be so considered, their market value would be the most appropriate figure to use in the computation of liquidity ratios.

As to the availability of cash, the analyst should bear in mind possible restrictions which may exist with respect to the use of cash balances. An example is the so-called "compensating balances" which banks, which extend credit, expect their customers to keep. While such balances can be used, the analyst must nevertheless assess the effect on a company's credit standing and credit availability, as well as on its banking connection, of a breach of the tacit agreement not to draw on the "compensating cash balance."

An additional ratio which measures cash adequacy should be mentioned. The cash to current liabilities ratio is computed as follows:

$$\frac{\text{Cash} + \text{Cash Equivalents}}{\text{Current Liabilities}}$$

It measures how much cash is available to pay current obligations. This is a severe test which ignores the refunding nature of current liabilities. It supplements the cash ratio discussed above in that it measures cash availability from a somewhat different point of view.

To view the cash ratio as a further extension of the acid test ratio (see below) would, except in extreme cases, constitute a test of short-term liquidity too severe to be meaningful. Nevertheless, the importance of cash as the ultimate form of liquidity should never be underestimated. The record of business failures provides many examples of insolvent companies, possessing sizable noncash assets, current and noncurrent, and no cash to pay debts or to operate with.

Measures of accounts receivable liquidity

In most enterprises which sell on credit, accounts and notes receivable are a significant part of working capital. In assessing the quality of working capital and of the current ratio, it is important to get some measure of the quality and the liquidity of the receivables.

Both the quality[3] and liquidity of accounts receivable are affected by their rate of turnover. By quality is meant the likelihood of collection without loss. An indicator of this likelihood is the degree to which receivables are within the terms of payment set by the enterprise. Experience has shown that the longer receivables remain outstanding beyond the date on which they are due, the lower is the probability of their collection in full. Turnover is an indicator of the age of the receivables, particularly when it is compared with an expected turnover rate which is determined by credit terms granted.

The measure of liquidity is concerned with the speed with which accounts receivables will, on average, be converted into cash. Here again turnover is among the best measures to use.

AVERAGE ACCOUNTS RECEIVABLE TURNOVER RATIO

The receivable turnover ratio is computed as follows:

$$\frac{\text{Net Sales on Credit}}{\text{Average Accounts Receivable}}$$

The quickest way for an external analyst to determine the average accounts receivable is to take the beginning receivables of the period, add the ending receivables, and divide the sum by two. The use of monthly or quarterly sales figures can lead to an even more accurate result. The more widely sales fluctuate, the more subject to distortion this ratio is, unless the receivables are properly averaged.

Notes receivable arising from normal sales should be included in the accounts receivable figure in computing the turnover ratio. Discounted notes receivable which are still outstanding should also be included in the accounts receivable total.

The sales figure used in computing the ratio should be that of credit sales only, because cash sales obviously do not generate receivables. Since published financial statements rarely disclose the division be-

---

[3] The validity of the collection claim is also one aspect of quality. Thus, the analyst must be alert to problems which can arise from "sales" on consignment or those with right of return.

tween cash and credit sales, the external analyst may have to compute the ratio under the assumption that cash sales are relatively insignificant. If they are not insignificant, then a degree of distortion may occur in the ratio. However, if the proportion of cash sales to total sales remains relatively constant, the year-to-year comparison of changes in the receivables turnover ratio may nevertheless be validly based.

The average receivables turnover figure indicates how many *times,* on average, the receivables revolve, that is, are generated and collected during the year.

For example, if sales are $1,200,000 and beginning receivables are $150,000 while year-end receivables are $250,000, then receivable turnover is computed as follows:

$$\frac{1,200,000}{(150,000 + 250,000) \div 2} = \frac{1,200,000}{200,000} = 6 \text{ times}$$

While the turnover figure furnishes a sense of the speed of collections and is valuable for comparison purposes, it is not directly comparable to the terms of trade which the enterprise normally extends. Such comparison is best made by converting the turnover into days of sales tied up in receivables.

Collection period for accounts receivable

This measure, also known as *days sales in accounts receivable* measures the number of days it takes, on average, to collect accounts (and notes) receivable. The number of days can be obtained by dividing the average accounts receivable turnover ratio discussed above into 360, the approximate round number of days in the year. Thus

$$\text{Collection Period} = \frac{360}{\text{Average Accounts Receivable Turnover}}$$

Using the figures of the preceding example, the collection period is:

$$\frac{360}{6} = 60 \text{ days}$$

An alternative computation is to first obtain the average daily sale and then divide the *ending gross* receivable balance by it.

$$\text{Accounts Receivable} \div \frac{\text{Sales}}{360}$$

The result will differ from the foregoing computation because the average accounts receivable turnover figure uses *average* accounts receivable, while this computation uses *ending* accounts receivable only; it thus focuses specifically on the latest accounts receivable balances. Using the figures from our example, the computation is:

$$\text{Average Daily Sales} = \frac{\text{Sales}}{360} = \frac{1,200,000}{360} = \$3,333$$

$$\frac{\text{Accounts Receivable}}{\text{Average Daily Sales}} = \frac{250,000}{3,333} = 75 \text{ days}$$

Note that if the collection period computation would have used ending receivables rather than *average* receivables turnover, the identical collection period, that is, 75 could have been obtained as follows:

$$\frac{\text{Sales}}{\text{Accounts Receivable (ending)}} = \frac{\$1,200,000}{\$250,000} = 4.8 \text{ times}$$

$$\frac{360}{\text{Receivable Turnover}} = \frac{360}{4.8} = 75 \text{ days}$$

The use of 360 days is arbitrary because while receivables are outstanding 360 days (used for computational convenience instead of 365), the sales days of the year usually number less than 300. However, consistent computation of the ratio will make for valid period to period comparisons.

Evaluation

Accounts receivable turnover rates or collection periods can be compared to industry averages (see Chapter 1) or to the credit terms granted by the enterprise.

When the collection period is compared with the terms of sale allowed by the enterprise, the degree to which customers are paying on time can be assessed. Thus, if the average terms of sale in the illustration used above are 40 days, then an average collection period of 75 days reflects either some or all of the following conditions:

1. A poor collection job.
2. Difficulty in obtaining prompt payment from customers in spite of diligent collection efforts.
3. Customers in financial difficulty.

The first conclusion calls for remedial managerial action, while the last two reflect particularly on both the quality and the liquidity of the accounts receivable.

An essential analytical first step is to determine whether the accounts receivable are representative of company sales activity. Significant receivables may, for example, be lodged in the captive finance company of the enterprise. In that case the bad debt provision may also relate to receivables not on company books.

It is always possible that an *average* figure is not representative of the receivables population it represents. Thus, it is possible that the 75-day average collection period does not represent an across-the-board payment tardiness on the part of customers but is rather caused by the excessive delinquency of one or two substantial customers.

The best way to investigate further an excessive collection period is to *age* the accounts receivable in such a way that the distribution of each account by the number of days past-due is clearly apparent. An aging schedule in a format such as given below will show whether the problem is widespread or concentrated:

Accounts receivable aging schedule:

	Days past due			
Accounts receivable	*0–30*	*31–60*	*61–90*	*Over 90*

The age distribution of the receivables will, of course, lead to better informed conclusions regarding the quality and the liquidity of the receivables as well as the kind of action which is necessary to remedy the situation. Another dimension of receivables classification is by quality ratings of credit agencies such as Dun & Bradstreet.

Notes receivable deserve the particular scrutiny of the analyst because while they are normally regarded as more negotiable than open accounts, they may be of poorer quality than regular receivables if they originated as an extension device for an unpaid account rather than at the inception of the original sale.

In assessing the quality of receivables the analyst should remember that a significant conversion of receivables into cash, except for their use as collateral for borrowing, cannot be achieved without a cutback in sales volume. The sales policy aspect of the collection period evaluation must also be kept in mind. An enterprise may be willing to accept slow-paying customers who provide business which is, on an overall basis, profitable, that is, the profit on sale compensates for the extra use by the customer of the enterprise funds. This circumstance may modify the analyst's conclusions regarding the *quality* of the receivables but not those regarding their *liquidity*.

In addition to the consideration of profitability, an enterprise may extend more liberal credit in cases such as (1) the introduction of a new product, (2) a desire to make sales in order to utilize available excess capacity, or (3) special competitive conditions in the industry. Thus, the relationship between the level of receivables and that of sales and profits must always be borne in mind when evaluating the collection period. The trend of the collection period over time is always important in an assessment of the quality and the liquidity of the receivables.

Another trend which may be instructive to watch is that of the relationship between the provision for doubtful accounts and gross accounts receivable. The ratio is computed as follows:

$$\frac{\text{Provision for Doubtful Accounts}}{\text{Gross Accounts Receivable}}$$

An increase in this ratio over time may indicate management's conclusion that the collectibility of receivables has deteriorated. Conversely, a decrease of this ratio over time may lead to the opposite conclusion or may cause the analyst to reevaluate the adequacy of the provision for doubtful accounts.

Measures of accounts receivable turnover are, as we have seen in this section, important in the evaluation of liquidity. They are also important as measures of asset utilization, a subject which will be covered in Chapter 5.

MEASURES OF INVENTORY TURNOVER

Inventories represent in many cases a very substantial proportion of the current asset group. This is so for reasons that have little to do with an enterprise's objective of maintaining adequate levels of liquid funds. Reserves of liquid funds are seldom kept in the form of inventories. Inventories represent investments made for the purpose of obtaining a return. The return is derived from the expected profits which may result from sales. In most businesses a certain level of inventory must be kept in order to generate an adequate level of sales. If the inventory level is inadequate, the sales volume will fall to below the level otherwise attainable. Excessive inventories, on the other hand, expose the enterprise to expenses such as storage costs, insurance and taxes, as well as to risks of loss of value through obsolescence and physical deterioration. Moreover, excessive inventories tie up funds which can be used more profitably elsewhere.

Due to the risk involved in holding inventories as well as the fact that inventories are one step further removed from cash than receivables (they have to be sold before they are converted into receivables), inventories are normally considered the least liquid component of the current assets group. As is the case with most generalizations, this is not always true. Certain staple items, such as commodities, raw materials, standard sizes of structural steel, etc., enjoy broad and ready markets and can usually be sold with little effort, expense, or loss. On the other hand, fashion merchandise, specialized components, or perishable items can lose their value rapidly unless they are sold on a timely basis.

The evaluation of the current ratio, which includes inventories in its computation, must include a thorough evaluation of the quality as well as the liquidity of these assets. Here again, measures of turnover are the best overall tools available for such an evaluation.

Inventory turnover ratio

The inventory turnover ratio measures the average rate of speed with which inventories move through and out of the enterprise.

Computation. The computation of the average inventory turnover is as follows:

$$\frac{\text{Cost of Goods Sold}}{\text{Average Inventory}}$$

Consistency of valuation requires that the cost of goods sold be used because, as is the case with inventories, it is stated principally at *cost*. Sales, on the other hand, normally include a profit. Although the cost of goods sold figure is now disclosed in most published income statements, the external analyst is still occasionally confronted with an unavailability of such a figure. In such a case the sales figure must be substituted. While this results in a theoretically less valid turnover ratio, it can still be used for comparison and trend development purposes, especially if used consistently and when sharp changes in profit margins are not present.

The average inventory figure is most readily obtained as follows:

$$\frac{\text{Opening Inventory} + \text{Closing Inventory}}{2}$$

Further refinement in the averaging process can be achieved, where possible and necessary, by adding up the monthly inventory figures and dividing the total by 12.

Before a turnover ratio is computed the analyst must carefully examine the composition of the inventory figure and make adjustments, such as those from Lifo to Fifo, etc.

Days to sell inventory

Another measure of inventory turnover which is also useful in assessing purchasing policy is the required number of *days to sell inventory*. The computation which follows, i.e.

$$\frac{360 \text{ days}}{\text{Average Inventory Turnover}}$$

measures the number of days it takes to sell the average inventory in a given year and, an alternative computation

$$\frac{\text{Ending Inventory}}{\text{Cost of Average Day's Sales}}$$

measures the number of days which are required to sell off the ending inventory, assuming the given rate of sales where the

$$\text{Cost of an Average Day's Sales} = \frac{\text{Cost of Goods Sold}}{360}$$

Example of computations

Sales	1,800,000
Cost of goods sold	1,200,000
Beginning inventory	200,000
Ending inventory	400,000

$$\text{Inventory Turnover} = \frac{1,200,000}{(200,000 + 400,000) \div 2} = \frac{1,200,000}{300,000} = 4 \text{ times}$$

$$\text{Number of Days to Sell Average Inventory} = \frac{360}{4} = 90 \text{ days}$$

Alternatively the computation based on ending inventory is as follows:

Step 1:

$$\frac{\text{Cost of Goods Sold}}{360} = \frac{1,200,000}{360} = 3,333 \text{ (cost of average day's sales)}$$

Step 2:

$$\frac{\text{Ending Inventory}}{\text{Cost of Average Day's Sales}} = \frac{400,000}{3,333} = 120 \text{ days}$$

Interpretation of inventory turnover ratios. The current ratio computation views its current asset components as sources of funds which can, as a means of last resort, be used to pay off the current liabilities. Viewed this way, the inventory turnover ratios give us a measure of the quality as well as of the liquidity of the inventory component of the current assets.

The quality of inventory is a measure of the enterprise's ability to use it and dispose of it without loss. When this is envisaged under conditions of forced liquidation, then recovery of cost is the objective. In the normal course of business the inventory will, of course, be sold at a profit. Viewed from this point of view, the normal profit margin realized by the enterprise assumes importance because the funds which will be obtained, and which would theoretically be available for payment of current liabilities, will include the profit in addition to the recovery of cost. In both cases costs of sale will reduce the net proceeds.

In practice a going concern cannot use its investment in inventory for the payment of current liabilities because any drastic reduction in normal inventory levels will surely cut into the sales volume.

A rate of turnover which is slower than that experienced histori-
cally, or which is below that normal in the industry, would lead to the
preliminary conclusion that it includes items which are slow moving
because they are obsolete, in weak demand, or otherwise unsaleable.
Such conditions do, of course, cast doubt on the feasibility of recover-
ing the cost of such items.

Further investigation may reveal that the slowdown in inventory
turnover is due to a buildup of inventory in accordance with a future
contractual commitment, in anticipation of a price rise, in anticipation
of a strike or shortage, or for any number of other reasons which must
be probed into further.

A better evaluation of inventory turnover can be obtained from the
computation of separate turnover rates for the major components of
inventory such as (1) raw materials, (2) work in process, and (3) finished goods. Departmental or divisional turnover rates can similarly
lead to more useful conclusions regarding inventory quality. One
should never lose sight of the fact that the total inventory turnover ratio
is an aggregate of widely varying turnover rates of individual
components.

The biggest problem facing the external analyst who tries to compute inventory turnover ratios by individual components is obtaining
the necessary detailed data. This is, at present, rarely provided in
published financial statements.

The turnover ratio is, of course, also a gauge of liquidity in that it
conveys a measure of the speed with which inventory can be converted into cash. In this connection a useful additional measure is the
conversion period of inventories.

Conversion period of inventories. This computation adds the collection period of receivables to the days needed to sell inventories in
order to arrive at the time interval needed to convert inventories into
cash.

Using figures developed in our examples of the respective ratios
above, we get

Days to sell inventory 90
Days to collect receivables 60
Total conversion period of inventories .... 150 days

It would thus normally take 150 days to sell inventory on credit and
to collect the receivable. This is a period identical to the *operating
cycle* which we discussed earlier in this chapter.

The effect of alternative methods of inventory management

In evaluating the inventory turnover ratio the analyst must be alert
to the influence which alternative accounting principles have on the

determination of the ratio's components. It is obvious that the use of the Lifo method of inventory valuation may render both the turnover ratios as well as the current ratio practically meaningless. Limited information is usually found in published financial statements which enables the analyst to adjust the unrealistically low Lifo inventory valuation occurring in times of rising price levels so as to render it useful for inclusion in turnover ratio or the current ratio. Even if two companies employ Lifo cost methods for their inventory valuation computation of their ratios, using such inventory figures may nevertheless not be comparable because their respective Lifo inventory pools (bases) may have been acquired in years of significantly different price levels. The inventory figure enters the numerator of the current ratio and also the denominator because the inventory method utilized affects the income tax liability.

The analyst must also bear in mind that companies using the so-called "natural year" may have at their year-end an unrepresentatively low inventory level and that this may increase the turnover ratio to unrealistically high levels.

Prepaid expenses are expenditures made for benefits which are expected to be received in the future. Since most such benefits are recievable within a year or within an enterprise's operating cycle they will conserve the outlay of current funds.

Usually, the amounts included in this category are relatively small compared to the size of the other current assets, and consequently no extensive discussion of their treatment is needed here. However, the analyst must be aware of the tendency of managements of enterprises with weak current positions to include in prepaid expenses deferred charges and other items of dubious liquidity. Such items must consequently be excluded from the computation of working capital and of the current ratio.

CURRENT LIABILITIES

In the computation of working capital and of the current ratio, current liabilities are important for two related reasons:

1. A basic objective of measuring the excess of current assets over current liabilities is to determine whether the latter are covered by current assets and what margin of safety is provided by the excess of such assets over current liabilities.
2. Current liabilities are deducted from current assets in arriving at the net working capital position.

In the computation of the current ratio, the point of view adopted toward current liabilities is *not* one of a continuing enterprise but rather of an enterprise in liquidation. This is so because in the normal course of operations, current liabilities are not paid off but are rather of a refunding nature. As long as the sales volume remains stable, purchases will also remain at a stable level, and that in turn will cause current liabilities to remain level. Increasing sales, in turn, will generally result in an increasing level of current liabilities. Thus, it can be generally stated that the trend and direction of sales is a good indication of the future level of current liabilities.

In assessing the quality of the current ratio, the nature of the current liabilities must be carefully examined.

Differences in the "nature" of current liabilities

Not all liabilities represent equally urgent and forceful calls for payment. At one extreme we find liabilities for taxes of all kinds which must be paid promptly regardless of current financial difficulties. The powers of collection of federal and local government authorities are as well known as they are powerful.

On the other hand, current liabilities to suppliers with whom the enterprise has a long standing relationship and who depend on, and value, the enterprise's business are of a very different degree of urgency. Postponement and renegotiation of such debts in times of financial stringency are both possible and are commonly found.

The "nature" of current liabilities in terms of our present discussion must be judged in the light of the degree of urgency of payment which attaches to them. It should be understood that if fund inflows from current revenues are viewed as sources of funds available for the payment of current liabilities, then labor costs and other current fund-requiring costs and expenses have a first call on sales revenues and that trade bills and other liabilities can be paid only after such recurring outlays have been met. This dynamic aspect of funds flow will be examined more closely in the chapter which follows.

The analyst must also be aware of unrecorded liabilities which may have a claim to current funds. Examples of these are purchase commitments and obligations under pensions and leases. Moreover, under long-term loan acceleration clauses, a failure to meet current installments of long-term debt may render the entire debt due and payable, that is, cause it to become current.

Days purchases in accounts payable ratio

A measure of the degree to which accounts payable represent current rather than overdue obligations can be obtained by calculating the *days purchases in accounts payable ratio*. This ratio is computed as follows:

$$\text{Accounts Payable} \div \frac{\text{Purchases}}{360}$$

The difficulty which the external analyst will encounter here is that normally purchases are not separately disclosed in published financial statements. A very rough approximation of the amount of purchases can be obtained by adjusting the cost of goods sold figure for depreciation and other nonfund requiring charges as well as for changes in inventories. However, the cost of goods sold figure may contain significant cash charges, and this may reduce the validity of a computation which contains such an approximation of purchases.

The capacity to borrow

An important aspect of an enterprise's liquidity which can be determined only after careful analysis and interpretation of its financial statements is its capacity to borrow. It can be a very significant off-balance sheet liquidity resource.

The capacity to borrow depends on numerous factors and is subject to rapid change. It depends on profitability, stability, relative size, industry position, asset composition and capital structure. It will depend, moreover, as such external factors as credit market conditions and trends.

The capacity to borrow is important as a source of funds in time of need for funds and is also important when an enterprise must roll over its short-term debt.

INTERPRETATION OF THE CURRENT RATIO

In the foregoing sections we have examined the means by which the quality and the liquidity of the individual components of the current ratio is measured. This evaluation is, of course, essential to an overall interpretation of the current ratio as an indicator of short-term liquidity and financial strength.

The analyst must, however, exercise great care if he wants to carry the interpretation of the current ratio beyond the conclusion that it represents an excess of current resources over current obligations as of a given point in time.

Examination of trend

An examination of the trend of the current ratio over time can be very instructive. Two tools of analysis which were discussed in Chapter 1 are useful here. One is *trend analysis,* where the components of working capital as well as the current ratio would be converted into an index to be compared over time. The other is *common-size analysis,* by means of which the *composition* of the current asset group is examined over time. A historical trend and common-size comparison over time, as well as an intra-industry comparison of such trends can also be instructive.

Interpretation of changes over time

Changes in the current ratio over time must, however, be interpreted with great care. They do not automatically imply changes in liquidity or operating results. Thus, for example, in a prosperous year an increased liability for taxes may result in a lowering of the current ratio. Conversely, during a business contraction, current liabilities may be paid off while there may be a concurrent involuntary accumulation of inventories and uncollected receivables causing the ratio to rise.

In times of business expansion, which may reflect operating successes, the enterprise may suffer from an expansion in working capital requirements, otherwise known as a "prosperity squeeze" with a resulting contraction of the current ratio. This can be seen in the following example:

	Year 1	Year 2
Current assets	$300,000	$600,000
Current liabilities	100,000	400,000
Working capital	$200,000	$200,000
Current ratio	3:1	1.5:1

As can be seen from the above example, a doubling of current assets, accompanied by a quadrupling of current liabilities and an unchanged amount of working capital will lead to a halving of the current ratio. This is the effect of business expansion unaccompanied by an added capital investment. Inflation can have a similar effect on a business enterprise in that it will lead to a substantial increase in all current items categories.

Possibilities of manipulation

The analyst must be aware of the possibilities of year-end manipulation of the current ratio, otherwise known as "window dressing."

For example, towards the close of the fiscal year the collection of receivables may be pressed more vigorously, advances to officers may be called in for temporary repayment, and inventory may be reduced to below normal levels. Proceeds from these steps can then be used to pay off current liabilities. The effect on the current ratio of the reduction of current liabilities through the use of current assets can be seen in the following example:

	Payoff of $50,000 in liabilities	
	Before	After
Current asets	$200,000	$150,000
Current liabilities	100,000	50,000
Current ratio	2:1	3:1

The accounting profession, sensing the propensity of managements to offset liabilities against assets, has strengthened its prohibitions against offsets by restricting them strictly to situations where the legal right to offset exists.

To the extent possible, the analyst should go beyond year-end measures and should try to obtain as many interim readings of the current ratio as possible, not only in order to guard against the practice of "window dressing" described above but also in order to gauge the seasonal changes to which the ratio is exposed. The effect of a strong current ratio in December on an assessment of current financial condition may be considerably tempered if it is discovered that at its seasonal peak in July the enterprise is dangerously close to a serious credit squeeze.

The use of "rules of thumb" standards

A popular belief that has gained considerable currency is that the current ratio can be evaluated by means of "rules of thumb." Thus, it is believed that if the current ratio is 2 : 1 (or 200 percent), it is sound and anything below that norm is bad while the higher above that figure the current ratio is, the better.

This rule of thumb may reflect the lender's, and particularly the banker's, conservatism. The fact that it is down from the norm of 2.5 : 1 prevailing at the turn of the century may mean that improved financial reporting has reduced this size of the "cushion" which the banker and other creditors would consider as the minimum protection they need.

What the 2 : 1 standard means is that there are $2 of current assets available for each dollar of current liabilities or that the value of current assets can, on liquidation, shrink by 50 percent before it will be inadequate to cover the current liabilities. Of course, a current ratio much higher than 2 : 1, while implying a superior coverage of current liabilities, may also mean a wasteful accumulation of liquid resources which do not "carry their weight" by earning an appropriate return for the enterprise.

It should be evident by now that the evaluation of the current ratio in terms of rules of thumb is a technique of dubious validity. This is so for two major reasons:

2/Analysis of short-term liquidity 69

1. As we have learned in the preceding sections, the quality of the current assets, as well as the composition of the current liabilities which make up this ratio, are the most important determinants in an evaluation of the quality of the current ratio. Thus, two companies which have identical current ratios may nevertheless be in quite different current financial condition due to variations in the quality of the working capital components.
2. The need of an enterprise for working capital varies with industry conditions as well as with the length of its own particular *net trade cycle.*

The net trade cycle

An enterprise's need for working capital depends importantly on the relative size of its required inventory investment as well as on the relationship between the credit terms it receives from its suppliers as against those it must extend to its customers.

ILLUSTRATION 4.   Assume a company shows the following data at the end of 19X1:

Sales for 19X1	$360,000
Receivables	40,000
Inventories	50,000
Accounts payable	20,000

The following tabulation measures the company's cash cycle in terms of days:

$$\text{Sales per day } \frac{\$360,000}{360} = \quad \$1,000$$

Number of days sales in:

Accounts receivable	40 days
Inventories	50
Total trade cycle	90 days
Less: Accounts payable	20
Net trade cycle	70 days

From the above we can see that the company is keeping 50 days of sales in inventory and that it receives only 20 sales days of trade credit while it must extend 40 sales days of credit to its customers. Obviously the higher the *net trade cycle* a company has the larger its investment in working capital is likely to be. Thus, in our above example, if the company could lower its investment in inventories by 10 sales days, it could lower its investment in working capital by $10,000. A similar result can be achieved by increasing the number of days sales in accounts payable by 10.

It should be noted that for the sake of simplicity and uniformity the net trade cycle computation uses number of *days sales* as a common factor. This does introduce, however, a degree of distortion because, while receivables can be related directly to sales, inventories are more logically related to cost of goods sold and accounts payable to purchases. This distortion will, however, not normally be large enough to invalidate the tool for analytical and comparison purposes and the degree of distortion will depend on factors such as the profit margin.

The working capital requirements of a supermarket with its high inventory turnover and low outstanding receivables are obviously lower than those of a tobacco company with its slow inventory turnover.

Valid working capital standards

Comparison with industry current ratios as well as analyses of working capital requirements such as the net trade cycle analysis described above can lead to far more valid conclusions regarding the adequacy of an enterprise's working capital than can a mechanical comparison of its current ratio to the 2 : 1 "rule of thumb" standard.

The importance of sales

In an assessment of the overall liquidity of current assets, the trend of sales is an important factor. Since it takes sales to convert inventory into receivables or cash, an uptrend in sales indicates that the conversion of inventories into more liquid assets will be easier to achieve than when sales remain constant. Declining sales, on the other hand, will retard the conversion of inventories into cash.

Common-size analysis of current assets composition

The composition of the current asset group, which can be analyzed by means of common-size statements, is another good indicator of relative working capital liquidity.

Consider, for example, the following comparative working capital composition:

	Year 1		Year 2	
	$	%	$	%
Current Assets:				
Cash	30,000	30	20,000	20
Accounts receivable	40,000	40	30,000	30
Inventories	30,000	30	50,000	50
Total Current Assets	100,000	100	100,000	100

From the simple illustration above it can be seen, even without the computation of common-size percentages, that the liquidity of the current asset group has deteriorated in year 2 by comparison with year 1. However, the use of common-size percentage comparisons will greatly facilitate the evaluation of comparative liquidity, regardless of the size of the dollar amounts involved.

The liquidity index

The measurement of the comparative liquidity of current assets can be further refined through the use of a *liquidity index*. The construction of this index (first suggested by A. H. Finney) can be illustrated as follows:

Using the working capital figures from the common-size computation above, and assuming that the conversion of inventories into accounts receivable takes 50 days on average and that the conversion of receivables into cash takes an average of 40 days, the index is computed as follows:

Year 1

	Amount	×	Days removed from cash	=	Product dollar-days
Cash	30,000		—		—
Accounts receivable	40,000		40		1,600,000
Inventories	30,000		90		2,700,000
Total	100,000 (a)				4,300,000 (b)

$$\text{Liquidity index} = \frac{b}{a} = \frac{4,300,000}{100,000} = \underline{\underline{43}}$$

Year 2

	Amount	×	Days removed from cash	=	Product dollar-days
Cash	20,000		—		—
Accounts receivable	30,000		40		1,200,000
Inventories	50,000		90		4,500,000
Total	100,000				5,700,000

$$\text{Liquidity index } \frac{5,700,000}{100,000} = \underline{\underline{57}}$$

The computation of the respective liquidity indices for the years 1 and 2 tells what we already knew instinctively in the case of this simple example, that is, that the liquidity has deteriorated in year 2 as compared to year 1.

The liquidity index must be interpreted with care. The index is in itself a figure without significance. It gains its significance only from a comparison between one index number and another as a gauge of the period to period change in liquidity or as a company to company comparison of relative liquidity. Increases in the index signify a deterioration in liquidity while decreases signify changes in the direction of improved liquidity. The index which is expressed in days is a weighing mechanism and its validity depends on the validity of the assumptions implicit in the weighing process.

An additional popular technique of current ratio interpretation is to submit it to a somewhat sterner test.

ACID-TEST RATIO

This test is the acid-test ratio, also known as the "quick ratio" because it is assumed to include the assets most quickly convertible into cash.

The acid-test ratio is computed as shown in Exhibit 2–2.

The omission of inventories from the acid-test ratio is based on the belief that they are the least liquid component of the current asset group. While this is generally so, we have seen in an earlier discussion in this chapter that this is not always true and that certain types of inventory can be more liquid than are slow-paying receivables. Another reason for the exclusion of inventories is the belief, quite often warranted, that the valuation of inventories normally requires a greater degree of judgment than is required for the valuation of the other current assets.

EXHIBIT 2–2

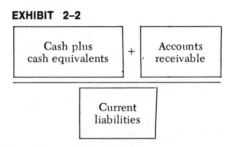

Since prepaid expenses are usually insignificant in relation to the other current assets, the acid test ratio is sometimes computed simply by omitting the inventories from the current asset figure.

The interpretation of the acid-test ratio is subject to most of the same considerations which were discussed regarding the interpretation of the current ratio. Moreover, the acid-test ratio represents an even sterner test of an enterprise's liquidity than does the current ratio, and the analyst must judge by himself what significance to his conclusions the total omission of inventories, as a source of current funds, is.

OTHER MEASURES OF SHORT-TERM LIQUIDITY

The static nature of the current ratio which measures the relationship of current assets to current liabilities, at a given moment in time, as well as the fact that this measure of liquidity fails to accord recognition to the great importance which funds or cash flows play in an enterprise's ability to meet its maturing obligations has lead to a search for more dynamic measures of liquidity.

Funds flow ratios

Funds flow ratios relate obligations to funds (working capital) generated by operations which are available to meet them. These resources do consequently not include funds from nonoperating sources such as borrowing or the sale of fixed assets.

One such ratio relates current liabilities to the funds from operations for the year:

$$\frac{\text{Funds Provided by Operations}}{\text{Current Liabilities}}$$

This is a measure of how many times current liabilities are covered by the funds flow of the year just elapsed. It is, of course, backward looking while current liabilities as of a certain date must be paid out of *future*, rather than past, funds flow. Nevertheless, in the absence of drastic changes in conditions, the latest yearly funds flow represents at least a good basis for an estimate of the next period's funds flow.

Importance of nonfund items in net income. Since the conversion of income into funds flow depends on the size of the net *nonfund* items included in it, a useful comparison measure is the relationship between the net nonfund items in income and net income. The computation of this ratio is as follows:

$$\frac{\text{Net Nonfund Items in Income}}{\text{Net Income}}$$

The higher the relationship of net nonfund requiring items to net income the greater the funds flow is in relation to reported net income and, thus, the higher the funds flow will be in relation to a given net income figure. An example of the computation of the *net nonfund items* follows:

Depreciation	$3,500,000
Depletion	1,200,000
Patent amortization	400,000
Deferred income taxes	2,800,000
Total nonfund charges	$7,900,000
Less: Unremitted earnings of	
foreign subsidiaries	2,100,000
Net nonfund requiring items	$5,800,000

If net income is $58,000,000, the net nonfund items ratio is as follows:

$$\frac{5,800,000}{58,000,000} = .1 \text{ or } 10 \text{ percent}$$

This means that funds flow will normally be expected to approximate 110 percent of net income.

Cash flow related measures

A ratio, which focuses on cash expenses of the year, and measures how many days of expenses the most liquid current assets could finance, assuming that all other cash inflows were to suddenly dry up, can be computed as follows:

$$\frac{\text{Cash} + \text{Cash Equivalents} + \text{Receivables}}{\text{Year's Cash Expense}}$$

Like the acid test ratio, the sternness of this test is such that its usefulness must be carefully weighed by the analyst.

A variation in the measurement of the relationship of current liabilities to funds which are expected to become available to meet them is to relate them to expected actual cash flows from operations:

$$\frac{\text{Current liabilities}}{\text{Sources of Cash from Operations}}$$

Projecting changes in conditions or policies

It is possible and often very useful to trace through the effects of changes in conditions and/or policies on the funds or cash resources of an enterprise.

ILLUSTRATION 5. Assume that the Foresight Company has the following account balances at December 31, 19X1:

	Debit	Credit
Cash	$ 70,000	
Accounts receivable	150,000	
Inventory	65,000	
Accounts payable		$130,000
Notes payable		35,000
Accrued taxes		18,000
Fixed assets	200,000	
Accumulated depreciation ...		43,000
Capital stock		200,000

The following additional information is available for 19X1:

Sales	$750,000
Cost of sales	520,000
Purchases	350,000
Depreciation	25,000
Net income	20,000

The company anticipates a growth of 10 percent in sales for the coming year. All corresponding revenue and expense items will also increase by 10 percent, except for depreciation which will remain the same. All expenses are paid in cash as they are incurred during the year. 19X2 ending inventory will be $150,000. By the end of 19X2 the company expects to have a notes payable balance of $50,000 and no balance in the accrued taxes account. The company maintains a minimum cash balance of $50,000 as a managerial policy.

I. Assume that the company is considering a change in credit policy so that the ending accounts receivable balance will represent 90 days of sales. What impact will this change have on the company's cash balance. Will it have to borrow?

This can be computed as follows:

Cash 1/1/X2		$ 70,000
Accounts Receivable 1/1/X2	$150,000	
Sales	825,000	
	$975,000	
Less: Accounting Receivable 12/31/X2 (a)	206,250	768,750
Total Cash available		$838,750
Cash Disbursements		
Accounts Payable 1/1/X2	$130,000	
Purchases (b)	657,000	
	787,000	
Accounts Payable 12/31/X2 (c)	244,000	543,000
Notes Payable 1/1/X2	35,000	
Notes Payable 12/31/X2	50,000	(15,000)
Accrued Taxes ...., ...		18,000
Cash Expenses (d)		203,500	749,500
		$ 89,250
Cash Balance Desired		50,000
Cash Excess		$ 39,250

Explanation

(a) $825,000 \times \dfrac{90}{360} = \$206,250$

(b) 19X2 cost of sales: $520,000 \times 1.1 = \$572,000$

Ending inventory	150,000
Goods available for sale	$722,000
Beginning inventory	65,000
Purchases	$657,000

(c) Purchases $\times \dfrac{\text{Old Accounts Payable}}{\text{Old Purchases}} = \$657,000 \times \dfrac{\$130,000}{\$350,000}$

$\qquad\qquad\qquad\qquad\qquad\qquad = \$244,000$

(d)

Gross profit ($825,000 − $572,000)		$253,000
Less: Net income	$24,500*	
Depreciation	25,000	49,500
Other cash expenses		$203,500

  * 110 percent of $20,000 (19X1 N.I.) + 10 percent of $25,000 (19X1 Depreciation).

II. What would the effect be if the change, instead of as in I, is to an *average* accounts receivable turnover of 4?

We compute this as follows:

Excess cash balance as computed above		$39,250
Change from an *ending* to an *average* accounts receivable turnover will increase year-end accounts receivable balance to:		
$\dfrac{825,000}{4} = 206,250 \times 2 =$		
$412,500 - 150,000 =$	$262,500 (e)	
Less: Accounts receivable balance as above (I)	206,250	56,250 (cash decrease)
Cash Required to Borrow		$17,000

(e) $\dfrac{\text{Sales}}{\text{Average A/R Turnover}} = $ Average A/R; Ending A/R = [(Average A/R) $\times$ 2] −

$\qquad\qquad\qquad\qquad\qquad\qquad\qquad\qquad\qquad\qquad\qquad$ Beginning A/R

III. Assuming that, in addition to the conditions prevailing in II above, suppliers require the company to pay within 60 days—What would be the effect on the cash balance?

The computation is as follows:

Cash required to borrow (from II above)		$ 17,000
Ending accounts payable (I above)	$244,000	
Ending accounts payable under 60-day payment =		
Purchases $\times \dfrac{60}{360} = \$657,000 \times \dfrac{60}{360} = $	$109,500	
Additional disbursements required.....................		$134,500
Cash to be borrowed...................................		$151,500

QUESTIONS

1. Why is short-term liquidity so significant? Explain from the viewpoint of various parties concerned.

2. The concept of working capital is simple, that is, the excess of current assets over current liabilities. What are some of the factors that make this simple computation complicated in practice?

3. What are "cash equivalents"? How should an analyst value them in his analysis?

4. Can fixed assets be included in current assets? If so, explain the situation under which the inclusion may be allowed.

5. Some installment receivables are not collectible within one year. Why are they included in current assets?

6. Are all inventories included in current assets? Why or why not?

7. What is the theoretical justification for including prepaid expenses in current assets?

8. The company under analysis has a very small amount of current liabilities but the long-term liabilities section shows a significant balance. In the footnote to the audited statements, it is disclosed that the company has a "revolving loan agreement" with a local bank. Does this disclosure have any significance to you?

9. Some industries are subject to peculiar financing and operating conditions which call for special consideration in drawing the distinction between what is "current" and what is "noncurrent." How should the analyst recognize this in his evaluation of working capital?

10. Your careful computation of the working capitals of Companies A and B reveals that both have the same amount of working capital. Are you ready to conclude that the liquidity position of both is the same?

11. What is the current ratio? What does it measure? What are the reasons for its widespread use?

12. The holding of cash generally does not yield a return. Why does an enterprise hold cash at all?

13. Is there a relationship between the level of inventories and that of sales? Are inventories a function of sales? If there is a functional relationship between the two, is it proportional?

14. What are the major objectives of management in determining the size of inventory and receivables investment?

15. What are the theoretical limitations of the current ratio as a measure of liquidity?

16. If there are significant limitations attached to the current ratio as a measure of liquidity, what is the proper use of this tool?

17. What are cash ratios? What do they measure?

18. How do we measure the "quality" of various current assets?

19. What does the average accounts receivable turnover measure?

20. What is the collection period for accounts receivable? What does it measure?

21. A company's collection period is 60 days this year as compared to 40 days of last year. Give three or more possible reasons for this change.

22. What is an accounts receivable aging schedule? What is its use in the analysis of financial statements?

23. What are the repercussions to an enterprise of (a) overinvestment or (b) underinvestment in inventories?

24. What problems would you expect to encounter in an analysis of a company using the Lifo inventory method in an inflationary economy? What effects do the price changes have (a) on the inventory turnover ratio and (b) on the current ratio?

25. Why does the "nature" of the current liabilities have to be analyzed in assessing the quality of the current ratio?

26. Why is a firm's capacity to borrow significant? What factors does it depend on?

27. An apparently successful company shows a poor current ratio. Explain the possible reasons for this.

28. What is "window dressing"? Is there any way to find out whether the financial statements are "window dressed" or not?

29. What is the "rule of thumb" governing the expected size of the current ratio? What dangers are there in using this rule of thumb mechanically?

30. Describe the importance which the sales level plays in the overall current financial condition and liquidity of the current assets of an enterprise.

31. What is the liquidity index? What significance do the liquidity index numbers have?

32. What do cash flow ratios attempt to measure?

33. What is the importance of projecting the effects of changes in conditions or policies on the cash resources of an enterprise?

3

FUNDS FLOW ANALYSIS AND FINANCIAL FORECASTS

The preceding chapter examined the various measures which are derived from past financial statement data and which are useful in the assessment of short-term liquidity. The chapter which follows will focus on the use of similar data in an evaluation of longer term solvency. The limitations to which these approaches are subject are due mainly to their static nature, that is, to their reliance on status reports, as of a given moment, of claims against an enterprise and the resources available to meet these claims.

An important and, in many cases, superior alternative to such static measures of conditions prevailing at a given point in time is the analysis and projection of more dynamic models of cash and funds flow. Such models use the present only as a starting point, and while building on reliable patterns of past experience, utilize the best available estimates of future plans and conditions in order to forecast the future availability and disposition of cash or working capital.

OVERVIEW OF CASH FLOW AND FUNDS FLOW PATTERNS

Before we examine the methods by means of which funds flow projections are made, it would be useful to get a thorough understanding of the nature of funds flow. Exhibit 3–1 presents a diagram of the flow of funds through an enterprise.

The flow of funds diagram focuses on two concepts of funds: cash and working capital (also known as "funds").

80

EXHIBIT 3-1
Flow of funds through an enterprise

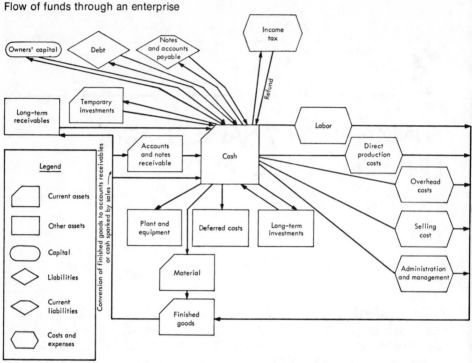

Cash (including cash equivalents) is the ultimate liquid asset. Almost all decisions to invest in assets or to incur costs require the immediate or eventual use of cash. This is why managements focus, from an operational point of view, on *cash* rather than on working capital. The focus on the latter represents mainly the point of view of creditors who consider as part of the liquid assets pool other assets, such as receivables and inventories, which are normally converted into cash within a relatively short time span.

Careful examination of the flows depicted in Exhibit 3–1 should contribute greatly to the reader's understanding of the importance of liquid funds in an enterprise as well as the factors which cause them to be converted into assets and costs. The following factors and relationship are worthy of particular note:

Since the diagram focuses on cash and funds flows only, assets, liabilities, and other items which are not directly involved, such as prepayments and accruals, as well as the income account are not included in it. Some flows are presented in simplified fashion for an easier understanding of relationships. For example, accounts payable are presented as direct sources of cash, whereas in reality they represent a temporary postponement of cash payment for the acquisition of goods and services.

It is recognized that the holding of cash provides no return or a very low return and that in times of rising price levels, cash as a monetary asset is exposed to purchasing power loss. However, these considerations aside, the holding of this most liquid of assets represents, in a business sense, the lowest exposure to risk. Management must make the decision to invest cash in assets or costs, and such a conversion increases risk because the certainty of ultimate reconversion into cash is less than 100 percent. There are, of course, a variety of risks. Thus, the risk involved in a conversion of cash into temporary investments is lower than the risk involved in committing cash to long-term, long-payout assets such as plant, machinery, or research costs. Similarly, the investment of cash in a variety of assets and costs for the creation and marketing of a new product involves serious risk regarding the recovery in cash of amounts so committed. The short-term liquidity as well as the long-term solvency of an enterprise depends on the recovery and realizability of such outlays.

The inflow and outflow of cash (or funds) are highly interrelated. A failure of any part of the system to circulate can affect the entire system. A cessation of sales affects the vital conversion of finished goods into receivables or cash and leads, in turn, to a drop in the cash reservoir. Inability to replenish this reservoir from sources such as owners' capital, debt, or accounts payable (upper left-hand corner of diagram) can lead to a cessation of production activities which will result in a loss of future sales. Conversely, the cutting off of expenses, such as for advertising and marketing, will slow down the conversion of finished goods into receivables and cash. Longer term blockages in the flows may lead to insolvency.

The diagram clarifies the interrelationship between profitability, income, and cash flow. The only real source of funds from operations is sales. When finished goods, which for the sake of simplicity represent the accumulation of *all* costs and expenses in the diagram, are sold, the profit margin will enhance the inflow of liquid funds in the form of receivables and cash. The higher the profit margin the greater the accretion of these funds.

Income, which is the difference between the cash and credit sales and the cost of goods sold, can have a wide variety of effects on cash flow. For example, the costs which flow from the utilization of plant and equipment or from deferred charges generally do not involve the use of current funds. Similarly, as in the case of land sales on long-term installment terms, the creation of long-term receivables through sales reduces the impact of net income on cash flow. It can be readily seen that adding back depreciation to net income creates a very crude measure of cash flow.

The limitation of the cash flow concept can be more clearly seen. As cash flows into its reservoir management has a *degree* of discretion as to where to direct it. This discretion depends on the amount of cash already committed to such outlays as dividends, inventory accumulation, capital expenditures, or debt repayment. The total cash inflow also depends on management's ability to tap sources such as equity capital and debt. With respect to noncommitted cash, management has, at the point of return of the cash to the reservoir, the discretion of directing it to any purpose it deems most important. It is this noncommitted cash flow segment that is of particular interest and importance to financial analysts.

Under present accounting conventions certain cash outlays, such as those for training or sales promotion, are considered as business (period) costs and are not shown as assets. These costs can, nevertheless, be of significant future value in either the increasing of sales or in the reduction of costs.

SHORT-TERM CASH FORECASTS

In the measurement of short-term liquidity the short-term cash forecast is one of the most thorough and reliable tools available to the analyst.

Short-term liquidity analysis is of particular interest to management in the financial operations of an enterprise and to short-term credit grantors who are interested in an enterprise's ability to repay short-term loans. The security analyst will pay particular attention to the short-term cash forecast when an enterprise's ability to meet its current obligations is subject to substantial doubt.

Realistic cash forecasts can be made only for relatively short time spans. This is so because the factors influencing the inflows and outflows of cash are many and complex and cannot be reliably estimated beyond the short term.

Importance of sales estimates

The reliability of any cash forecast depends very importantly on the forecast of sales. In fact, a cash forecast can never reach a higher degree of reliability than the sales forecast on which it is based. Except for transactions involving the raising of money from external sources or the investment of money in long-term assets, almost all cash flows relate to and depend on sales.

The sales forecast involves considerations such as:

1. The past direction and trend of sales volume.
2. Enterprise share of the market.
3. Industry and general economic conditions.
4. Productive and financial capacity.
5. Competitive factors.

These factors must generally be assessed in terms of individual product lines which may be influenced by forces peculiar to their own markets.

Pro forma financial statements as an aid to forecasting

The reasonableness and feasibility of short-term cash forecasts can be checked by means of pro forma financial statements. This is done by utilizing the assumptions underlying the cash forecast and constructing, on this basis, a pro forma statement of income covering the period of the forecast and a pro forma balance sheet as at the end of that period. The ratios and other relationships derived from the pro forma financial statements should then be checked for feasibility against historical relationships which have prevailed in the past. Such relationships must be adjusted for factors which it is estimated will affect them during the period of the cash forecast.

Techniques of short-term cash forecasting

ILLUSTRATION 1. The Prudent Corporation has recently introduced an improved product which has enjoyed excellent market acceptance. As a result, management has budgeted sales for the six months ending June 30, 19X1 as follows:

	Estimated sales
January	$100,000
February	125,000
March	150,000
April	175,000
May	200,000
June	250,000

The cash balance at January 1, 19X1 is $15,000, and the treasurer foresees a need for additional funds necessary to finance the sales expansion. He has obtained a commitment from an insurance company for the sale to them of long-term bonds as follows:

April	$50,000 (less $2,500 debt costs)
May	60,000

He also expects to sell real estate at cost: $8,000 in May and $50,000 in June. In addition, equipment with an original cost of $25,000 and a book value of zero was to be sold for $25,000 cash in June.

The treasurer considers that in the light of the expanded sales volume the following minimum cash balances will be desirable:

January.........................	$20,000
February	25,000
March	27,000
April, May, and June	30,000

He knows that during the next six months he will not be able to meet his cash requirements without resort to short-term financing. Consequently he approaches his bank and finds it ready to consider his company's needs. The loan officer suggests that in order to determine the cash needs and the sources of funds for loan repayment, the treasurer prepare a cash forecast for the six months ending June 30, 19X1 and pro forma financial statements for that period.

The treasurer, recognizing the importance of such a forecast, proceeded to assemble the data necessary to prepare it.

The pattern of receivables collections based on experience was as follows:

Collections	Percent of total receivable
In month of sale	40
In the second month	30
In the third month	20
In the fourth month	5
Write-off of bad debts	5
	100

On the basis of this pattern and the expected sales the treasurer constructed Schedule A shown in Exhibit 3–2.

An analysis of past cost patterns resulted in the estimates of cost and expense relationships for the purpose of the cash forecast (Schedule B) shown in Exhibit 3–3.

It was estimated that all costs in Schedule B (exclusive of the $1,000 monthly depreciation charge) will be paid for in cash in the month incurred, except for material purchases which are to be paid 50 percent in the month of purchase and 50 percent in the following month. Since the product is manufactured to specific order, no finished goods inventories are expected to accumulate.

Schedule C (Exhibit 3–4) shows the pattern of payments of accounts payable (for materials).

EXHIBIT 3-2

SCHEDULE A
Estimates of Cash Collections
For the Months January–June, 19X1

	January	February	March	April	May	June
Sales................	$100,000	$125,000	$150,000	$175,000	$200,000	$250,000
Collections:						
1st month—40%.....	$ 40,000	$ 50,000	$ 60,000	$ 70,000	$ 80,000	$100,000
2nd month—30%....		30,000	37,500	45,000	52,500	60,000
3rd month—20%			20,000	25,000	30,000	35,000
4th month—5%				5,000	6,250	7,500
Total cash collections........	$ 40,000	$ 80,000	$117,500	$145,000	$168,750	$202,500
Write-offs—5%				$5,000	$6,250	$7,500

EXHIBIT 3-3

SCHEDULE B
Cost and Expense Estimates for Six Months
Ending June 30, 19X1

Materials	30% of sales
Labor	25% of sales
Manufacturing overhead:	
Variable	10% of sales
Fixed	$48,000 for six months (including $1,000 of depreciation per month)
Selling expenses	10% of sales
General and administrative expenses:	
Variable	8% of sales
Fixed	$7,000 per month

EXHIBIT 3-4

SCHEDULE C
Pro Forma Schedule of Cash Payments for Materials Purchases
For the Months January–June 19X1

	January	February	March	April	May	June
Materials purchased during month	$40,000	$38,000	$43,000	$56,000	$58,000	$79,000
Payments:						
1st month—50%	$20,000	$19,000	$21,500	$28,000	$29,000	$39,500
2nd month—50%		20,000	19,000	21,500	28,000	29,000
Total payments	$20,000	$39,000	$40,500	$49,500	$57,000	$68,500

EXHIBIT 3–5

THE PRUDENT CORPORATION
Cash Forecast
For the Months January–June 19X1

	January	February	March
Cash balance—beginning	$15,000	$20,000	$ 25,750
Add: Cash receipts:			
Collections of accounts receivable (Schedule A)	40,000	80,000	117,500
Proceeds from sale of real estate			
Proceeds from additional long-term debt			
Proceeds from sale of equipment			
Total cash available	$ 55,000	$100,000	$143,250
Less: Disbursements:			
Payments for:			
Materials purchases (Schedule C)	$20,000	$39,000	$ 40,500
Labor	25,000	31,250	37,500
Fixed factory overhead	7,000	7,000	7,000
Variable factory overhead	10,000	12,500	15,000
Selling expenses	10,000	12,500	15,000
General and administrative	15,000	17,000	19,000
Taxes			
Purchase of fixed assets		1,000	1,000
Total disbursements	87,000	120,250	135,000
Tentative cash balance (negative)	$(32,000)	$ (20,250)	$ 8,250
Minimum cash balance required	20,000	25,000	27,000
Additional borrowing required	$ 52,000	$ 46,000	$ 19,000
Repayment of bank loan			
Interest paid on balance outstanding at rate of ½ per month*			
Ending cash balance	$ 20,000	$ 25,750	$ 27,250
Loan balance	$ 52,000	$ 98,000	$117,000

* Interest is computed at the rate of ½% per month and paid on date of repayment which occurs at month end. Loan is taken out at beginning of month.

Equipment costing $20,000 will be bought in February for notes payable which will be paid off, starting that month, at the rate of $1,000 per month. The new equipment will not be fully installed until sometime in August 19X1.

Exhibit 3–5 presents the cash forecast for the six months ending June 30, 19X1 based on the data given above. Exhibit 3–6 presents the pro forma income statement for the six months ending June 30, 19X1. Exhibit 3–7 presents the actual balance sheet of The Prudent Corporation as at January 1, 19X1 and the pro forma balance sheet as at June 30, 19X1.

The financial analyst should examine the pro forma statements critically and submit to feasibility tests the estimates on which the fore-

April	May	June	Six-month totals
27,250	$ 30,580	$ 30,895	$ 15,000
145,000	168,750	202,500	753,750
	8,000	50,000	58,000
47,500	60,000		107,500
		25,000	25,000
$219,750	$267,330	$308,395	$959,250
$ 49,500	$ 57,000	$ 68,500	$274,500
43,750	50,000	62,500	250,000
7,000	7,000	7,000	42,000
17,500	20,000	25,000	100,000
17,500	20,000	25,000	100,000
21,000	23,000	27,000	122,000
		19,000	19,000
1,000	1,000	1,000	5,000
157,250	178,000	235,000	912,500
$ 62,500	$ 89,330	$ 73,395	$ 46,750,
30,000	30,000	30,000	
—	—	—	$117,000
			(117,000)
$ 30,000	$ 58,000	$ 29,000	
1,920	435	145	2,500
$ 30,580	$ 30,895	$ 44,250	$ 44,250
$ 87,000	$ 29,000	—	—

casts are based. The ratios and relationships revealed by the pro forma financial statements should be analyzed and compared to similar ratios of the past in order to determine whether they are reasonable and feasible of attainment. For example, the current ratio of The Prudent Corporation increased from 2.6 on 1/1/X1 to 3.2 in the pro forma balance sheet as of 6/30/X1. During the six months ended 6/30/X1 a pro forma return on average equity of almost 16 percent was projected. Many other significant measures of turnover, common-size statements, and trends can be computed. The reasonableness of these comparisons and results must be assessed. They can help reveal serious errors and inconsistencies in the assumptions which underly the projections and thus help strengthen confidence in their reliability.

EXHIBIT 3–6

THE PRUDENT CORPORATION
Pro Forma Income Statement
For the Six Months Ending June 30, 19X1

Source of estimate

Sales	$1,000,000	Based on sales budget (page 83)
Cost of sales:		
Materials	$ 300,000	Schedule B
Labor	250,000	Schedule B
Overhead	148,000	Schedule B
	$ 698,000	
Gross profit	$ 302,000	
Selling expense	$ 100,000	Schedule B
Bad debts expense	18,750	Schedule A
General and administrative expense	122,000	Schedule B
Total	$ 240,750	
Operating income	$ 61,250	
Gain on sale of equipment	25,000	
Interest expense	(2,500)	Exhibit 3–5, footnote
Income before taxes	83,750	
Income taxes	38,050	30% of first $25,000; 52% of balance. Pay ½ in June and accrue balance
Net income	$ 45,700	

Differences between short-term and long-term forecasts

The short-term cash forecast is, as we have seen, a very useful and reliable aid in projecting the state of short-term liquidity. Such a detailed approach is, however, only feasible for the short term, that is, up to about 12 months. Beyond this time horizon the uncertainties become so great as to preclude detailed and accurate cash forecasts. Instead of focusing on collections of receivables and on payments for labor and materials, the longer term estimates focus on projections of net income and on other sources and uses of funds. Over the longer term the emphasis on cash becomes less important, and the estimation process centers on funds, that is, working capital. Over the short term the difference between cash and other working capital assets is significant. Over the longer term, however, the distinction between cash, receivables, and inventories becomes less significant because the conversion period of these assets to cash is not significant relative to the period encompassed by the longer term. In other words, if the trade cycle is 90 days long, such a period is not as significant in a 3-year forecast as it is in relation to a 6 or 12 months span. The further we peer

EXHIBIT 3-7

THE PRUDENT CORPORATION
Balance Sheets

	Actual January 1, 19X1		Pro forma June 30, 19X1	
Assets				
Current Assets:				
Cash	$ 15,000		$ 44,250	
Accounts receivable (net)	6,500		234,000	
Inventories–raw materials	57,000		71,000	
Total Current Assets		$ 78,500		$349,250
Real estate	$ 58,000		—	
Fixed assets	206,400		$201,400	
Accumulated depreciation	(36,400)		(17,400)	
Net Fixed Assets		228,000		184,000
Other assets		3,000		3,000
Deferred debt expenses				2,500
Total Assets		$309,500		$538,750
Liabilities and Equity				
Current Liabilities:				
Accounts payable	$ 2,000		$41,500	
Notes payable	28,500		43,500	
Accrued taxes	—		19,050	
Total Current Liabilities.......		$ 30,500		$104,050
Long-term debt	$ 15,000		$125,000	
Common stock.....................	168,000		168,000	
Retained earnings	96,000		141,700	
		279,000		434,700
Total Liabilities and Equity		$309,500		$538,750

into the future, the broader are the financial statement categories which we must estimate and the less detailed can the data behind the estimates be.

The projection of future statements of changes in financial position is best begun with an analysis of prior year funds statements. To this data can then be added all available information and estimates about the future needs for funds and the most likely sources of funds needed to cover such requirements.

ANALYSIS OF STATEMENTS OF CHANGES IN FINANCIAL POSITION

We shall now focus on the analysis of the statement of changes in financial position paying particular attention to the value of such an analysis to a projection of future funds flows.

In any analysis of financial statements the most recent years are the most important because they represent the most recent experience. Since there is an inherent continuity in business events, it is this latest experience that is likely to have the greatest relevance to the projection of future results. So it is with the statement of changes in financial position.

It is important that the analyst obtain statements of changes in financial position for as many years as possible. This is particularly important in the case of an analysis of this statement since the planning and execution of plant expansions, of modernization schemes, of working capital increases as well as the financing of such activities by means of short-term and long-term debt and by means of equity funds is an activity which is likely to encompass many years. Thus, in order for the analyst to be able to assess management's plans and their execution, statements of changes in financial position covering a number of years must be analyzed. In this way a more comprehensive picture of management's financial habits can be obtained and an assessment of them made.

First illustration of statement of changes in financial position analysis

Exhibits 3–8 and 3–9 present the statement of changes in financial position of the Migdal Corporation and the same data expressed in common-size percentages. The common-size statement of changes in financial position is a useful tool of analysis in that it enables the analyst to compare readily the changes which occurred over time in the relative contributions of various categories of sources and uses of funds.

The statements in Exhibit 3–8 and 3–9 reveal that net income has been steadily growing since 19X1 and contributed increasingly, on an absolute basis, to funds from operations. As a percentage of total funds generated, funds from operations fluctuated from a low of 33.5 percent in 19X1 to a high of 97.4 percent in 19X4. This is due to substantial inflows from borrowings in 19X1 and an absence of external financing in 19X4. To finance its significant additions to equipment and to working capital, the company resorted mostly to substantial equity financing in 19X3 and in 19X6. More modest additions to debt occurred in 19X1 to 19X3. The relationship of depreciation to income has exhibited sufficient stability over the years to facilitate the projection of this element.

Deferred taxes have, on the other hand, exhibited a more erratic

EXHIBIT 3-8

MIGDAL CORPORATION
Statement of Changes in Financial Position
For the Years Ended 19X1–19X6

	19X6	19X5	19X4	19X3	19X2	19X1
Funds were provided from:						
Current operations:						
Net income	$1,641,889	$1,385,021	$1,140,113	$ 822,362	$ 532,872	$ 422,065
Depreciation	596,207	436,102	335,019	275,331	193,827	114,096
Amortization of preoperating expenses	152,525	135,156	184,726	73,394	52,885	36,036
Deferred taxes	38,000	(80,000)	43,500	(7,053)	(22,447)	18,881
Funds from operations	$2,428,621	$1,876,279	$1,703,358	$1,164,034	$ 757,137	$ 591,078
Net proceeds from sale of stock	2,526,871			1,340,375		424,982
Exercise of stock options	94,458	7,445	44,663	2,922		
Transfer of deferred taxes to current assets		86,000				
Long-term borrowing				500,000	300,000	750,000
Total	$5,049,950	$1,969,724	$1,748,021	$3,007,331	$1,057,137	$1,766,060
Funds were used for:						
Additions to equipment	$2,256,821	$1,326,761	$ 678,101	$ 535,708	$1,000,593	$ 610,406
Additions to other assets	331,397	188,205	170,063	147,291	127,250	89,017
Reduction in long-term debt	175,000	175,000	100,000	25,000	69,174	32,863
Other		18,975	3,721			30,349
Total	$2,763,218	$1,708,941	$ 951,885	$ 707,999	$1,197,017	$ 762,635
Increase (decrease) in working capital	$2,286,732	$ 260,783	$ 796,136	$2,299,332	$ (139,880)	$1,003,425
Increases (decreases) to working capital:						
Cash and U.S. Treasuries	$ 103,288	$ (60,252)	$ 340,304	$2,124,704	$ (97,370)	$ 263,161
Receivables	279,010	(72,138)	122,950	(79,788)	77,086	30,741
Inventories	2,244,180	1,848,771	737,350	1,184,078	1,416,723	645,078
Prepaid expenses	253,689	149,772	28,075	(4,739)	98,623	62,461
Current portion of long-term debt		(75,000)	(75,000)	500,000	(453,642)	164,515
Accounts payable	(458,504)	(1,394,811)	(87,807)	(809,927)	(897,663)	(681)
Income taxes payable	302,593	217,493	(143,122)	(389,473)	(128,063)	(41,195)
Other payables	(437,524)	(353,052)	(126,614)	(225,523)	(155,574)	(120,655)
Total	$2,286,732	$ 260,783	$ 796,136	$2,299,332	$ (139,880)	$1,003,425

EXHIBIT 3-9

MIGDAL CORPORATION
Statement of Changes in Financial Position
Common Size
For the Years Ended 19X1–19X6

	19X6	19X5	19X4	19X3	19X2	19X1
Funds were provided from:						
Current operations:						
Net income	32.5%	70.3%	65.2%	27.3%	50.4%	23.9%
Depreciation	11.8	22.1	19.1	9.2	18.3	6.5
Amortization of preoperating expenses	3.0	6.9	10.6	2.4	5.0	2.0
Deferred taxes	0.8	(4.1)	2.5	(0.2)	(2.1)	1.1
Funds from operations	48.1%	95.2%	97.4%	38.7%	71.6%	33.5%
Net proceeds from sale of stock	50.0			44.6		24.0
Exercise of stock options	1.9	0.4	2.6	0.1		
Transfer of deferred taxes to current assets		4.4				
Long-term borrowing				16.6	28.4	42.5
Total	100.0%	100.0%	100.0%	100.0%	100.0%	100.0%
Funds were used for:						
Additions to equipment	44.7%	67.4%	38.8%	17.8%	94.7%	34.6%
Additions to other assets	6.6	9.5	9.7	4.9	12.0	5.0
Reduction in long-term debt	3.5	8.9	5.7	0.8	6.5	1.9
Other		1.0	0.2			1.7
Total	54.8%	86.8%	54.4%	23.5%	113.2%	43.2%
Increase (decrease) in working capital	45.2%	13.2%	45.6%	76.5%	(13.2%)	56.8%
Increases (decreases) in working capital:						
Cash and U.S. Treasuries	4.5%	(23.1)%	42.7%	92.4%	(69.6)%	26.2%
Receivables	12.2	(27.7)	15.4	(3.5)	55.1	3.1
Inventories	98.1	708.9	92.6	51.5	1012.8	64.3
Prepaid expenses	11.1	57.4	3.5	(0.2)	70.5	6.2
Current portion of long-term debt		(28.7)	(9.4)	21.7	(324.3)	16.4
Accounts payable	(20.1)	(534.8)	(11.0)	(35.2)	(641.7)	(0.1)
Income taxes payable	13.2	83.4	(18.0)	(16.9)	(91.6)	(4.1)
Other payables	(19.1)	(135.4)	(15.8)	(9.8)	(111.2)	(12.0)
Total	100.0%	100.0%	100.0%	100.0%	(100.0%)	100.0%

pattern. The constantly increasing additions to equipment have not resulted in commensurate increases in the provision for deferred taxes indicating that the company has, in general, probably not elected faster depreciation methods for tax purposes relative to the amounts booked. However, the swing in the provision from 19X5 to 19X6 may indicate some new book–tax differentials.

During the entire period under review, fixed asset additions have significantly exceeded the provision for depreciation. Thus, even allowing for the effects of inflation on replacement costs it is clear that Migdal is going through a period of significant capital investment. The constantly increasing net income is testimony to the productivity of these investments. In all years, except 19X2, funds provided by operations have exceeded additions to equipment. Net borrowing during the period was only about $1 million. New capital from the sale of stock was more significant approaching $4 million. In all years but one working capital increased, probably as a result of increasing sales, and the total increase was substantial. Particularly heavy were investments in inventory, again to support higher sales. The rate of increase in accounts payable, while substantial, did not equal the growth in the investment in receivables further explaining the substantial working capital expansion.

A forecast of future statements of changes in financial position would have to take into consideration all above discussed trends which the enterprise has exhibited, such as those relating to income, the elements that convert it to sources of funds from operations, fixed assets additions, the relationship of sales to growth in working capital and possibly to sources of funds provided by operations as well. The size of nonfund adjustments, such as depreciation, depends on future depreciation policies and equipment acquisitions. The latter as well as write-off methods to be used for tax purposes will in turn determine the size of the deferred tax adjustments. The more we know about factors such as these the more reliable the forecast will be.

Second illustration of statement of changes in financial position analysis

The Exeter Chemical Company presents the five-year statement of changes in financial position shown in Exhibit 3–10. This statement has a column for totals encompassing the period covered by the statement. This is a useful feature since it affords a view of the cumulative totals of sources and uses of funds over the longer term. Since cash and cash equivalents are the most liquid portions of the current assets group, the changes in working capital are separated to indicate

EXHIBIT 3-10

EXETER CHEMICAL COMPANY
Statement of Changes in Financial Position
(in thousands)

	Total	19X4	19X3	19X2	19X1	19X0
Source of funds:						
Net income:	$ 412,712	$114,891	$ 82,990	$ 78,368	$ 68,656	$ 67,807
Provision for:						
Depreciation, depletion, etc.	498,427	120,268	114,606	97,639	86,876	79,038
Deferred income taxes	35,804	11,980	12,373	11,451		
Insurance reserve	2,000	2,000				
Outside financing:						
5¾% promissory notes	99,593			99,593		
Other	4,945	3,276	1,669			
Common shares issued under options	40,245	12,108	14,532	2,639	9,926	1,040
Other–net	(13,622)	(429)	(5,368)	2,366	(7,918)	(2,273)
	$1,080,104	$264,094	$220,802	$292,056	$157,540	$145,612
Disposition of funds:						
Dividends on common shares	$ 155,029	$ 37,606	$ 34,978	$ 29,470	$ 27,316	$ 25,659
Plant additions and replacements	776,511	218,105	114,502	168,833	153,818	121,253
Investment in affiliated companies	60,913	13,340	18,443	9,597	9,810	9,723
Retirement of debt	73,590	10,418	13,452	17,877	21,928	9,915
Increase in working capital*	95,001	29,845	18,042	14,614	5,021	27,479
Increase–(decrease) in cash and securities	(80,940)	(45,220)	21,385	51,665	(60,353)	(48,417)
	$1,080,104	$264,094	$220,802	$292,056	$157,540	$145,612

* Exclusive of cash and securities.

changes in working capital exclusive of these liquid items and changes in the cash items.

An analysis of the statement in Exhibit 3–10 reveals that the sources of funds from operations over the five-year period were as follows:

		Millions
Net income		$413
Nonfund requiring charges:		
Depreciation, depletion, etc.	$498	
Deferred income taxes	36	
Insurance reserves	2	536
Total		$949

From funds provided by operations of $949 million we must deduct essential capital equipment replacement requirements before we can arrive at the balance of discretionary funds available to management for dividend payments (here $155 million), plant expansion and so forth. Here we know only that both replacement and possibly expansion of plant added up to $776 million, an amount which is exceeded by sources of funds from operations less dividends. Thus, investments in affiliated companies, the retirement of debt, and the increase in net working capital over the period were financed by means of promissory notes and the issuance of common stock under options. It is also interesting to note that while working capital increased by $95 million over the five years ending 19X4, cash and marketable securities decreased by almost $81 million. Undoubtedly the substantial increase in activity, as evidenced by a near doubling of net income over the five-year period, necessitated an expansion of funds invested in receivables and inventories.

EVALUATION OF THE STATEMENT OF CHANGES IN FINANCIAL POSITION

The foregoing examples of analyses of the statement of changes in financial position illustrate the variety of information and insights which can be derived from them. Of course, the analysis of statements of changes in financial position is to be performed within the framework of an analysis of all the financial statements, and thus the conclusion reached from an analysis of one statement may be strengthened and corroborated by an analysis of the other financial statements.

There are some useful generalizations that can be made regarding the value of the analysis of the statement of changes in financial position to the financial analyst.

This statement enables the analyst to appraise the quality of management decisions over time, as well as their impact on the results of operations and financial condition of the enterprise. When the analysis encompasses a longer period of time, the analyst can evaluate management's response to the changing economic conditions as well as to the opportunities and the adversities which invariably present themselves.

Evaluation of the statement of changes in financial position analysis will indicate the purposes to which management chose to commit funds, where it reduced investment, the source from which it derived additional funds, and to what extent it reduced claims against the enterprise. Such an analysis will also show the disposition of earnings over the years, as well as how management has reinvested the internal fund inflow over which it had discretion. The analysis will also reveal the size and composition of sources of funds from operations, as well as their pattern and degree of stability.

As depicted in Exhibit 3–1 earlier in this chapter, the circulation of funds in an enterprise involves a constant flow of funds and their periodic reinvestment. Thus, funds are invested in labor, material, and overhead costs as well as in long-term assets, such as inventories and plant and equipment, which join the product-cost stream at a slower rate. Eventually, by the process of sales, these costs are converted back into accounts receivable and into cash. If operations are profitable the funds recovered will exceed the amounts invested, thus augmenting the funds inflow or cash flow. Losses have, of course, the opposite effect.

What constitutes funds inflow, or cash flow, as it is often more crudely referred to, is the subject of considerable confusion. Generally the funds provided by operations, that is, net income adjusted for nonfund requiring or supplying items, is an index of management's ability to redirect funds away from areas of unfavorable profit opportunity into areas of greater profit potential. However, not all the funds provided by operations may be so available because of existing commitments for debt retirement, stock redemption, equipment replacement, and dividend payments. Nor are funds provided by operations the only potential cash inflows, since management can avail itself of external sources of capital in order to bolster its funds inflow. The components of the "sources of funds from operations" figure hold important clues to the stability of that source of funds. Thus, for example, depreciation is a more stable element in the total than net income itself in that it represents a recovery by the enterprise of the investment in fixed assets out of selling prices even before a profit is earned.

In evaluating the statement of changes in financial position, the analyst will judge a company's quality of earnings by the impact which changes in economic and industry conditions have on its flow of funds. The statement will also reveal nonfunds generating income which may have a bearing on the evaluation of earnings quality.

If in his estimates of future earnings potential the analyst foresees a need for additional capital, his analysis of the funds statement will be directed towards a projection of the source from which these funds will be obtained, and what dilution of earnings per share, if any, this will involve.

The analysis and evaluation of the statement of changes in financial position is, as the foregoing discussion suggests, an important early step in the projection of future statements of changes in financial position.

PROJECTION OF STATEMENTS OF CHANGES IN FINANCIAL POSITION

No thorough model of an enterprise's future results is complete without a concurrent forecast of the size of funds needed for the realization of the projections in the model as well as an assessment of the possible sources from which such funds can be derived.

If a future expansion of sales and profits is forecast, the analyst must know whether the enterprise has the "financial horsepower" to see such an expansion through by means of internally generated funds and, if not, where the required future funds are going to come from.

The projection of the statement of changes in financial position will start with a careful estimate of the expected changes in each individual category of assets and the funds which will be derived from or required by such changes. Some of the more important factors to be taken into consideration follow:

1. The net income expected to be generated by future results will be adjusted for nonfund items, such as depreciation, depletion, deferred income taxes, and nonremitted earnings of subsidiaries and investees, in order to arrive at estimates of funds provided by operations.
2. Sources of funds from disposals of assets, sale of investments, and the sale of stocks and bonds will be estimated.
3. The needs for working capital will be arrived at by estimating the required level of the individual working capital items such as cash, receivables, and inventories and reducing this by the expected levels of payables. There is usually a relationship between incremental sales and the corresponding increment in required working capital amounts.
4. Expected capital expenditures will be based on the present level of operations as compared with productive capacity, as well as on

an estimate of the future level of activity implied by the profit projections.

5. Mandatory debt retirement and desirable minimum levels of dividend payments will also be estimated.

The impact of adversity

The projected statement of changes in financial position is useful not only in estimating the funds implications of future expansion and opportunity but also in assessing the impact on the enterprise of sudden adversity.

A sudden adversity, from the point of view of its impact on the flow of funds, will usually manifest itself in a serious interruption in the inflow of funds. This can be brought about by such events as recessions, strikes, or the loss of a major customer or market. In this context a projection of the statement of changes in financial position would be a first step in the assessment of the defensive posture of an enterprise. The basic question to which such an analysis is directed is this: what can the enterprise do; and what resources, both internal and external, can it marshal to cope with a sudden and serious reduction in the inflow of funds?

The strategies and alternatives available to an enterprise faced with such adversities are ably examined and discussed in a work by Professor Donaldson. Dr. Donaldson defines financial mobility as the capacity to redirect the use of financial resources in response to new information about the company and its environment.[1]

The projected "sources and uses of funds" statement is an important tool in the assessment of the resources available to meet such "new information" as well as in planning the changes in financial strategy which this may require.

To the prospective credit grantor such an approach represents an excellent tool in the assessment of risk. In estimating the effects of, for example, a recession, on the future flow of funds he can trace through not only the potential shrinkage in cash inflows from operations but also the effects of such shrinkage on the uses of funds and on the sources from which they can be derived.

The funds flow adequacy ratio

The purpose of this ratio is to determine the degree to which an enterprise generated sufficient funds from operations to cover capital

---

[1] Gordon Donaldson, *Strategy for Financial Mobility* (Boston: Graduate School of Business Administration, Harvard University, 1969).

expenditures, net investment in inventories, and cash dividends. To remove cyclical and other erratic influences a five-year total is used in the computation of the ratio, thus:

$$\frac{\text{Five year sum of sources of funds from operations}}{\text{Five year sum of capital expénditures, inventory additions, and cash dividends}}$$

The investment in the other important working capital item, receivables, is omitted on the theory that it can be financed primarily by short term credit, i.e., growth in payables, and so forth.

A ratio of 1 indicates that an enterprise has covered its needs based on attained levels of growth without the need for external financing. To the degree that the ratio falls below 1 internally generated funds may be inadequate to maintain dividends and current operating growth levels. This ratio may also reflect the effect of inflation on the fund requirements of an enterprise. The reading of this, like any other ratio, can provide no definitive answers and is only a pointer to further analysis and investigation. The ratio for Migdal Corporation (see Exhibit 3–8 above) for the five years ending 19X6 is

$$\frac{7,929}{13,230} = .60.$$

Funds reinvestment ratio

This ratio is useful in measuring the percentage of the investment in assets, which is being retained and reinvested in the enterprise for the replacement of assets and for growth in operations. The formula is:

$$\frac{\text{Funds provided by operations} - \text{Dividends}}{\text{Gross plant} + \text{Investment} + \text{Other assets} + \text{Working capital}}$$

A reinvestment rate of 8 to 10 percent is considered generally to be at a satisfactory level. The ratio for Beta Company (Appendix B in Chapter 1) for 19X6 is

$$\frac{509.4 - 91.4}{4,750.5} \text{ or } 8.8\%.$$

CONCLUSION

In the assessment of future liquidity, the use of cash forecasts for the short term and of projected statements of changes in financial position for the longer term represent some of the most useful tools available to the financial analyst. In contrast to ratio measures of liquidity, these tools involve a detailed examination of sources and uses of cash or funds. Such examination and estimation processes can be subjected to feasibility tests by means of pro forma statements and to the discipline inherent in the double-entry accounting system.

QUESTIONS

1. What is the primary difference between funds flow analysis and ratio analysis? Which is superior and why?
2. "From an operational point of view, management focuses on cash rather than working capital." Do you agree with the statement? Why or why not?
3. What is the relationship between inflows and outflows of cash?
4. Why is the short-term cash forecast important to the financial analyst?
5. What is the first step to be taken in preparing a cash forecast, and what considerations are required in such a step?
6. What are pro forma financial statements? How are they utilized in conjunction with funds flow projections?
7. What are the limitations of short-term cash forecasts?
8. If the usefulness of a short-term cash forecast is limited, what analytical approach is available to the financial analyst who wants to analyze future flows of working capital?
9. What useful information do you, as a financial analyst, expect to get from the analysis of past statements of changes in financial position (funds statement)?
10. What would a forecast of future statements of changes in financial position have to take into consideration?
11. What are the differences between short-term and long-term financial forecasts?
12. What analytical function does the common-size statement of changes in financial position serve?
13. Why is a projected statement of changes in financial position necessary when you have historical data which are based on actual performance?
14. If actual operations are seriously affected by unforeseen adversities, would a projected statement of changes in financial position still be useful?
15. "Cash flow per share" is sometimes used in common stock analysis in the same fashion as *earnings per share*. In financial analysis, shouldn't the former be used more often than the latter? Explain. (C.F.A.)

4

ANALYSIS OF CAPITAL STRUCTURE AND LONG-TERM SOLVENCY

The financial strength and stability of a business entity, the probability surrounding its ability to weather random shocks, and to maintain its solvency in the face of adversity are important measures of risk associated with it. This evaluation of risk is critical because the equity investor as well as the lender require returns which are commensurate with the levels of risk which they assume. This and the preceding two chapters deal with the evaluation of the financial strength and viability of enterprises within different time frames.

KEY ELEMENTS IN THE EVALUATION OF LONG-TERM SOLVENCY

The process of evaluation of long-term solvency of an enterprise differs markedly from that of the assessment of short-term liquidity. In the latter the time horizon is short and it is often possible to make a reasonable projection of funds flows. It is not possible to do this for the longer term, and thus the measures used in the evaluation of longer term solvency are less specific but more all-encompassing.

There are a number of key elements involved in the evaluation of the long-term solvency of an enterprise. The analysis of capital structure is concerned with the types of capital funds used to finance the enterprise, ranging from "patient" and permanent equity capital to short-term funds which are a temporary, and consequently, a much more risky source. There are different degrees of risk associated with the holding of different types of assets. Moreover, assets represent secondary[1] sources of security for lenders ranging from loans secured by specific assets to assets available as general security to unsecured creditors.

On a long-term basis earnings and earning power (which implies the recurring ability to generate cash in the future) are some of the most important and reliable indications of financial strength available. Earnings are the most desirable and reliable sources of funds for the longer term payment of interest and repayment of principal. As a surrogate for funds generated by operations, earnings are the yardstick against which the coverage of interest and other fixed charges is measured. Moreover, a reliable and stable trend of earnings is one of the best assurances of an enterprise's ability to borrow in times of funds shortage and its consequent ability to extricate itself from the very conditions which lead to insolvency.

In addition to general measures of financial strength and long-term solvency lenders rely on the protection afforded by loan covenants or the pledges of specific assets as security. Some loan covenants define default and the legal remedies available when it occurs. Others are designed to insure against deterioration in such key measures of financial health as the current ratio and the debt equity ratio, against the issuance of further debt, or against the disbursement of resources through the payments of dividends above specified levels or through acquisitions. Of course, there can be no prohibition against operating losses, a core problem attending most cases of deterioration in financial condition. Thus, the existence of protective provisions cannot substitute for alertness and a continuous monitoring of the financial condition of an enterprise in which long-term funds are at risk.[2]

The vast amount of public and private debt outstanding has led to standardized approaches to its analysis and evaluation. By far the most important is the rating of debt securities by rating agencies which is discussed in Appendix A to this chapter. Appendix B examines the use of ratios as predictors of failure.

In this chapter we shall examine in further detail the tools and the measures available for the analysis of long-term solvency.

---

[1] When lending to going concerns lenders should regard the liquidation of assets for the purpose of recovery of principal and interest as a measure of last resort and as an undesirable source of funds to rely on at the time credit is granted.

[2] Lenders have learned that senior positions in the debt hierarchy do not afford in practice the security they seem to afford in theory. Thus, subordinated debt is not akin to capital stock because subordinated creditors have a voice in determining whether a debtor should be rescued or be thrown into bankruptcy. This interdependence between junior and senior lenders has led some to the belief that one might as well buy the highest yielding obligation of an enterprise since any situation serious enough to affect the value of the junior security is likely to affect the senior security as well.

IMPORTANCE OF CAPITAL STRUCTURE

The capital structure of an enterprise consists basically of equity funds and debt. It is measured in terms of the relative magnitude of the various sources of funds of the enterprise. The inherent financial stability of an enterprise and the risk of insolvency to which it is exposed are importantly dependent on the sources of its funds as well as on the type of assets it holds and the relative magnitude of such asset categories. Exhibit 4–1 presents an example of the distribution of assets of an enterprise and the sources of funds used to finance their acquisition. It is evident from the diagram in Exhibit 4–1 that within the framework of equality prevailing between assets and liabilities plus capital, a large variety of combinations of assets and sources of funds used to finance them is possible.

ACCOUNTING PRINCIPLES

The amounts at which liabilities and equity accounts are shown on the financial statements are governed by the application of generally

EXHIBIT 4–1
Asset distribution and capital structure of an enterprise

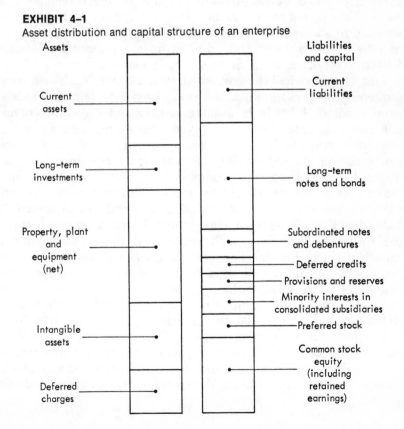

accepted accounting principles. The analyst must keep these principles in mind when analyzing the capital structure and its effect on long-term solvency. While it can be stated, as a broad generalization, that the accounting principles governing the measurement of liabilities and equities do not affect the analysis of financial statements as importantly as do those governing the measurement of assets, a study of the above-mentioned chapters will reveal aspects of real importance to the analyst.

There are liabilities which are not fully reflected in the balance sheet and there are accounts whose accounting classification as debt or equity should not be automatically accepted by the analyst. The proper decision of how to classify or deal with these depends on a thorough understanding of their nature and/or the particular conditions of issue to which they are subject.

Deferred credits

Most deferred credits, such as premiums on bonds, represent allocation accounts designed primarily to aid in the measurements of income. They do not present an important problem of analysis because they are relatively insignificant in size. Deferred income items, such as subscription income received in advance, represent an obligation for future service and are, as such, clearly liabilities.

One type of deferred credit which is much more sizable, and consequently much more important, is *deferred income taxes*. This account is not a liability in the usual sense because the government does not have a definite short-term or even longer term claim against the enterprise. Nevertheless, this account does represent the aggregate exhaustion in tax deductibility of assets and other items, over and above that recorded for book purposes, and this means that at some time in the future the deferred tax account will be used to reduce the higher income tax expense which corresponds to *increased* tax liabilities. Even if the likelihood of the deferred tax account "reversing" in the foreseeable future is quite good, there still remains the question of whether the time-adjusted present value of such future "reversals" should not be used instead of the nominal face value amount of the deferred credit.

To the analyst the important question here is whether to treat the deferred tax account as a liability, as an equity item, or as part debt and part equity. The decision depends on the nature of the deferral, the past experience with the account (e.g., has it been constantly growing?), and the likelihood of future "reversal." To the extent that such future "reversal" is only a remote possibility, the deferred credit can be viewed as a source of funds of such long-term nature as to be classifiable as equity. On the other hand, if the possibility of a "drawing down" of the deferred tax account in the foreseeable future is quite strong, then the account is more in the nature of a long-term liability.[3] In classifying the deferred tax account as between debt and equity, the analyst must be guided by considerations such as the ones discussed above.

Long-term leases

SFAS 13 has, beginning in 1977, restricted further the capital (financing) leases which companies can avoid showing as recorded liabilities. However, until 1980 older financing leases which are exempt from the SEC's immediate disclosure requirements may still not be reflected on balance sheets and the analyst will have to make adjustments on the basis of supplementary data which must be provided in footnotes.

Liabilities for pensions

The excess of vested benefits of employees over pension fund assets represents one kind of unrecorded liability under presently accepted accounting practices. Contingent liabilities which may exist on the liquidation of an enterprise or the termination of a pension plan are other factors which must be taken into consideration by analysts assessing the total obligations to which an enterprise may be subject. Unrecorded pension obligations are particularly substantial in some industries, such as tire and steel.

Unconsolidated subsidiaries

Information on unconsolidated subsidiaries is important because bondholders of such subsidiaries may look only to the latter's assets as security for their bonds. Moreover, bondholders of the parent company (particularly holding companies) may derive a significant portion of their fixed charge coverage from the dividends of the unconsolidated subsidiaries. Yet, in the event of the subsidiary's bankruptcy the parent bondholders may be in a junior position to the bondholders of the subsidiary.

---

[3] H. C. Herring and F. A. Jacobs in "The Expected Behavior of Deferred Tax Credits," *Journal of Accountancy*, August 1976, argue that statistically the probability of the deferred tax accounting reversing is quite good.

Provisions, reserves and contingent liabilities

Provisions such as for guarantees and warranties represent obligations to offer future service and should be classified as such. Generally speaking, reserves created by charges to income may also be considered as liabilities. However, general contingency reserves or reserves for very indeterminate purposes (most of which are now prohibited by SFAS 5) should not be considered as genuine liabilities.

The analyst must make a judgment regarding the probability of commitments or contingencies becoming actual liabilities and should then treat these items accordingly.

Minority interests

Minority interests in consolidated financial statements represent an obligation of the consolidated group to minority shareholders of the subsidiaries included therein. The analyst should recognize, however, that these are not liabilities similar in nature to debt because they have neither mandatory dividend payment nor principal repayment requirements. Capital structure measurements concentrate on the mandatory payments aspects of liabilities. From this point of view, minority interests are more in the nature of outsider's claim to a portion of the equity or an offset representing their proportionate ownership of assets.

Convertible debt

Convertible debt is generally classified among liabilities. However, if the conversion terms are such that the only reasonable assumption that can be made is that the debt will be converted into common stock, then it may be classified as equity for purposes of capital structure analysis.

Preferred stock

Most preferred stock entails no absolute obligation for payment of dividends or repayment of principal, possessing thus the characteristics of true equity. However, preferred stock with a fixed maturity or subject to sinking fund requirements should, from an analytical point of view, be considered as debt.

Effect of intangible assets

Intangible assets and deferred items of dubious value which are included on the asset side of the balance sheet have an effect on the computation of the total equity of an enterprise. To the extent that the analyst cannot evaluate or form an opinion on the present value or future utility of such assets, he may exclude them from consideration and thus reduce the amount of equity capital by the amounts at which such assets are carried. However, the arbitrary exclusion of all intangible assets from the capital base is an unjustified exercise in overconservatism.

The foregoing discussion related to the classification of balance sheet items as between debt and equity. Let us now turn to an examination of the significance of capital structure in financial analysis.

The significance of capital structure

The significance of capital structure is derived, first and foremost, from the essential difference between debt and equity.

The equity is the basic risk capital of an enterprise. Every enterprise must have some equity capital which bears the risk to which it is inevitably exposed. The outstanding characteristic of equity capital is that it has no guaranteed or mandatory return which must be paid out in any event and no definite timetable for repayment of the capital investment. Thus, capital which can be withdrawn at the contributor's option is not really equity capital and has, instead, the characteristics of debt.[4] From the point of view of an enterprise's stability and exposure to the risk of insolvency, the outstanding characteristic of equity capital is that it is permanent, can be counted on to remain invested in times of adversity, and has no mandatory requirement for dividends. It is such funds that an enterprise can most confidently invest in long-term assets and expose to the greatest risks. Their loss, for whatever reason, will not necessarily jeopardize the firm's ability to pay the fixed claims against it.

Both short-term and long-term debt, in contrast to equity capital, must be repaid. The longer the term of the debt and the less onerous its repayment provisions, the easier it will be for the enterprise to service it. Nevertheless, it must be repaid at certain specified times regardless of the enterprise's financial condition; and so must interest be paid in the case of most debt instruments. Generally, the failure to pay principal or interest will result in proceedings under which the common stockholders may lose control of the enterprise as well as part or all of their investment. Should the entire equity capital of the enterprise be wiped out by losses, the creditors may also stand to lose part or all of their principal and interest due.

---

[4] For example, during the financial crisis which befell many brokerage houses in the late 1960s it was discovered that much "equity" capital which was thought to lend strength to the enterprise and additional security to customers and creditors was in effect subject to withdrawal by owners. At the sign of real trouble these owners withdrew their capital thus compounding the financial problems even more.

It can be readily appreciated that the larger the proportion of debt in the total capital structure of an enterprise, the higher the resulting fixed charges and repayment commitments and the greater the probability of a chain of events leading to an inability to pay interest and principal when due.

To the investor in the common stock of an enterprise, the existence of debt represents a risk of loss of his investment, and this is balanced by the potential of high profits arising from financial leverage. Excessive debt may also mean that management's initiative and flexibility for profitable action will be stifled and inhibited.

The creditor prefers as large a capital base as possible as a cushion which will shield him against losses which can result from adversity. The smaller the relative capital base, or conversely, the larger the proportionate contribution of funds by creditors, the smaller is the creditors' cushion against loss and consequently the greater their risk of loss.

While there has been a considerable debate, particularly in academic circles, over whether the *cost of capital* of an enterprise varies with different capital structures, that is, with various mixes of debt and equity, the issue seems significantly clearer from the point of view of outsiders to the enterprise, such as creditors or investors, who must make decisions on the basis of conditions as they are. In the case of otherwise identical entities the creditor exposes himself to greater risk if he lends to the company with 60 percent of its funds provided by debt (and 40 percent by equity capital) than if he lends to a similar company which derives, say, only 20 percent of its funds from debt.

Under the Modigliani-Miller thesis the cost of capital of an enterprise in a perfect market is, except for the tax deductibility of interest, not affected by the debt-equity relationship.[5] This is so, they assert, because each individual stockholder can inject, by use of personally created leverage, his own blend of risk into the total investment position. Thus, under this theory, the advantage of debt will be offset by a markdown in a company's price-earnings ratio.

The degree of risk in an enterprise, as judged by the outside prospective investor is, however, a given; and our point of view, as well as our task here, is to measure the degree of risk residing in the capital structure of an enterprise.

REASONS FOR EMPLOYMENT OF DEBT

In addition to serving as an inflation hedge, a primary reason for the employment of debt by an enterprise is that up to a certain point,

---

[5] F. Modigliani and M. Miller, "The Cost of Capital, Corporation Finance and the Theory of Investment," *American Economic Review*, June 1958, pp. 261–97.

debt is, from the point of view of the ownership, a less expensive source of funds than equity capital. This is so for two main reasons:

1. The interest cost of debt is fixed, and thus, as long as it is lower than the return which can be earned on the funds supplied by creditors, this excess return accrues to the benefit of the equity.
2. Unlike dividends, which are considered a distribution of profits, interest is considered an expense and is, consequently, tax deductible.

A further discussion of these two main reasons follows.

The concept of financial leverage

Financial leverage means the use in the capital structure of an enterprise of debt which pays a fixed return. Since no creditor or lender would be willing to put up loan funds without the cushion and safety provided by the owners' equity capital, this borrowing process is also referred to as "trading on the equity," that is, utilizing the existence of a given amount of equity capital as a borrowing base.

In Exhibit 4–2, a comparison is made of the returns achieved by two companies having identical assets and earnings before interest expense. Company X derives 40 percent of its funds from debt while Company Y has no debt. In Year 1, when the average return on total assets is 7.5 percent, the return on the stockholders' equity of Company X is 10.3 percent. This higher return is due to the fact that the stockholders benefited from the excess return on total assets over the cost of debt. For Company Y the return on equity always equals the return on total assets. In Year 2 the return on total assets of Company X was equal to the interest cost of debt and, consequently, the effects of leverage were neutralized. The results of Year 3 show that leverage is a double-edged sword. Thus, when the return on total assets falls below the cost of debt, Company X's return on the equity is lower than that of debt-free Company Y.

The effect of tax deductibility of interest

The second reason given for the advantageous position of debt is the tax deductibility of interest as opposed to the distribution of dividends. This can be illustrated as follows:

Assume the facts given in Exhibit 4–2 for Year 2, and that the operating earnings of Co. X and Co. Y, $60,000 for each, are both of equal quality.[6] The results of the two companies can be summarized as follows:

---

[6] The concept of the quality of earnings is discussed in Chapter 8.

EXHIBIT 4–2

Trading on the equity—results under different earning assumptions (in thousands of dollars)

	Assets	Debt payable	Stock-holders' equity	Income before interest and taxes	6% debt interest	Taxes (1)	Net income	Net income + (Interest) (1 – tax rate)	Return on Total assets (2)	Return on Stock-holders' equity (3)
Year 1										
Co. X	$1,000,000	$400,000	$ 600,000	$150,000	$24,000	$63,000	$63,000	$75,000	7.5%	10.3%
Co. Y	1,000,000	—	1,000,000	150,000	—	75,000	75,000	75,000	7.5	7.5
Year 2										
Co. X	1,000,000	400,000	600,000	60,000	24,000	18,000	18,000	30,000	3.0	3.0
Co. Y	1,000,000	—	1,000,000	60,000	—	30,000	30,000	30,000	3.0	3.0
Year 3										
Co. X	1,000,000	400,000	600,000	25,000	24,000	500	500	12,500	1.25	.08
Co. Y	1,000,000	—	1,000,000	25,000	—	12,500	12,500	12,500	1.25	1.25

(1) Assuming a 50% effective tax rate.

(2) $\dfrac{\text{Net Income} + \text{Interest} (1 - .50)}{\text{Total Assets}}$

(3) $\dfrac{\text{Net Income}}{\text{Stockholders' Equity}}$

	Company X	Company Y
Operating earnings	$60,000	$60,000
Interest (6% of $400,000)	24,000	
Income before taxes	$36,000	$60,000
Taxes	18,000	30,000
Net income	$18,000	$30,000
Add back interest paid to bondholder	24,000	
Total return to security holders	$42,000	$30,000

Disregarding leverage effects which are neutral in the above example, even if the return on assets is equal to the interest rate, the total amount available for distribution to the bondholders and stockholders of Company X is $12,000 higher than the amount available for the stockholders of Company Y. This is due to the lower total tax liability to which the security holders of Company X are subject.

It should be borne in mind that the value of the tax deductibility of interest is dependent on the existence of sufficient earnings. However, unrecovered interest charges can be carried back and carried forward as part of tax loss carry-overs permitted by law.

Other advantages of leverage

In addition to the advantages accruing to equity stockholders from the successful employment of financial leverage and the tax deductibility of interest expenses, a sound longer term debt position can result in other advantages to the equity owner. A rapidly growing company can avoid earnings dilution through the issuance of debt. Moreover, if interest rates are headed higher, all other things being equal, a leveraged company will be more profitable than its nonleveraged competitor. Finally, there is a financial benefit from advantageously placed debt because debt capital is not always available to an enterprise and the capacity to borrow may disappear should adverse operating results occur.

Measuring the effect of financial leverage

The effect of leverage on operating results is positive when the return on the equity capital exceeds the return on total assets. This difference in return isolates the effect which the return on borrowed money has on the return on the owner's capital. As was seen in the example in Exhibit 4–2, leverage is positive when the return on assets is higher than the cost of debt. It is negative when the opposite conditions prevail. The terms "positive" and "negative" are not used here in the strict algebraic sense.

The effect of financial leverage can be measured by the following formula:

$$\text{Financial Leverage Index} = \frac{\text{Return on Equity Capital}^7}{\text{Return on Total Assets}}$$

Using the data in Exhibit 4–2 we compute the financial leverage indices of Company X for Years 1, 2, and 3 as follows:

Financial leverage index

$$\text{Year 1:} \quad \frac{10.3}{7.5} = 1.4$$

$$\text{Year 2:} \quad \frac{3.0}{3.0} = 1$$

$$\text{Year 3:} \quad \frac{.08}{1.25} = .07$$

In Year 1 when the return on equity exceeded that on total assets, the index at 1.4 was positive. In Year 2 when the return on equity equaled that on total assets, the index stood at 1 reflecting a neutralization of financial leverage. In Year 3 the index, at .07, was way below 1.0, thus indicating the very negative effect of financial leverage in that year. The subject of return on investment is discussed in Chapter 5.

Measuring the effect of capital structure on long-term solvency

From the foregoing discussion it is clear that the basic risk involved in a leveraged capital structure is the risk of running out of cash under conditions of adversity.

Debt involves a commitment to pay fixed charges in the form of interest and principal repayments. While certain fixed charges can be postponed in times of cash shortage, those associated with debt cannot be postponed without adverse repercussion to the ownership and also to the creditor groups.

Another important repercussion of excessive debt is a loss of financing flexibility i.e., the ability to raise funds particularly in adverse capital markets.

Long-term projections—usefulness and limitations

If a shortage of cash required to service the debt is the most adverse possibility envisaged, then the most direct and most relevant measure

---

[7] This can include or exclude preferred stock depending on how the effect of leverage is to be measured.

of risk inherent in the leveraged capital structure of an enterprise would be a projection of future cash resources and flows which would be available to meet these cash requirements. These projections must assume the worst set of economic conditions which are likely to occur, since this is the most realistic and useful test of safety from the creditor's point of view. If only prosperous and normal times are to be assumed, then the creditor would not need his preferred position and would be better off with an equity position where the potential rewards are higher.

In Chapter 3 we concluded that detailed cash flow projections can be reliably made only for the short term. Consequently they are useful only in the measurement of short-term liquidity.

The statement of changes in financial position can be projected over a relatively longer term because such a projection is far less detailed than a projection of cash flows. However, as we saw in the discussion of such projections in the proceding chapter, this lack of detail as well as the longer time horizon reduces the reliability of such projections.

The short term is understood to encompass, generally, a period of up to one year. The longer term, however, is a much wider ranging period. Thus, it may include a solvency analysis with respect to a three-year term loan, or it may encompass the evaluation of risk associated with a 30-year bond issue. Meaningful projections covering the period over which the interest and principal of the term loan will be paid can still reasonably be made. However, a 30-year projection of funds flow covering the bond issue would be an unrealistic exercise. For this reason longer term debt instruments often contain sinking fund provisions which act to reduce the uncertain time horizon, and stipulations of additional security in the form of specific assets pledged as collateral. Moreover, they contain provisions such as for the maintenance of minimum working capital levels or restrictions on the payment of dividends, all of which are designed to insure against a deterioration in the financial ratios prevailing at the time the bonds are issued.

Desirable as funds flow projections may be, their use for the extended longer term is severely limited. For this reason, a number of measures of long-term solvency have evolved which are more static in nature and are based on asset and earnings coverage tests. These measures will be considered below.

CAPITAL STRUCTURE ANALYSIS—COMMON-SIZE STATEMENTS

A simple measure of financial risk in an enterprise is the composition of its capital structure. This can be done best by constructing a common-size statement of the liabilities and equity section of the balance sheet as shown in Exhibit 4–3.

EXHIBIT 4-3
Liabilities and equity section—with common-size percents

Current liabilities	$ 428,000	19.0%
Long-term debt	$ 500,000	22.2%
Equity capital:		
Preferred stock	$ 400,000	17.8%
Common stock	800,000	35.6
Paid-in capital	20,000	.9
Retained earnings	102,000	4.5
Total Equity	$1,322,000	58.8%
Total Liabilities and Equity	$2,250,000	100.0%

An alternative way of analyzing capital structure with common-size percentages would be to focus only on the longer term capital funds by excluding the current liabilities from total funds.

The advantage of a common-size analysis of capital structure is that it presents clearly the relative magnitude of the sources of funds of the enterprise, a presentation which lends itself readily to a comparison with similar data of other enterprises.

A variation of the approach of analyzing capital structure by means of common-size percentages is to analyze it by means of ratios.

CAPITAL STRUCTURE RATIOS

The basic ratio measurements of capital structure relate the various components of the capital structure to each other or to their total. Some of these ratios in common use are explained below.

Equity capital/total liabilities

This ratio measures the relationship of the equity capital, inclusive of preferred stock, to total liabilities, that is, both current and long-term liabilities. A ratio in excess of 1 to 1 indicates that the owners of the enterprise have a greater financial stake in it than do the creditors. Additionally, assuming that the assets are presented at close to realizable values, a ratio of 1 to 1 would mean that creditors have $2 in assets as security for each $1 of credit they extended to the enterprise. This generalization would have to be modified, of course, if some creditors have a prior claim on specific assets or all assets. To the extent that senior creditors have prior claims, the relative security of junior debt is diminished.

A reciprocal measure is total liabilities as a percentage of stockholder's equity.

Equity capital/long-term debt

This ratio measures the relative contributions of equity capital and of long-term debt to the total capitalization of an enterprise.[8] A ratio in excess of 1:1 indicates a higher equity capital participation as compared to long-term debt. The complement of this ratio is the familiar debt/equity ratio which is computed as follows:

$$\frac{\text{Long-Term Debt}}{\text{Equity Capital}}$$

Ratios measuring the proportion which equity capital represents of the total funds invested in the enterprise are a variation the common-size analysis approach. The following are among the ratios which accomplish this purpose.

$$\frac{\text{Equity Capital}}{\text{Equity Capital plus all Liabilities (total capitalization)}}$$

is a ratio which expresses the relationship between equity capital and the total funds available to the entity.

$$\frac{\text{Long-Term Debt}}{\text{Equity Capital plus all Liabilities (total capitalization)}}$$

measures the relative contribution of long-term debt to the total funds available to the enterprise.

Short-term debt

The ratio of debt which matures over the short term (five years) to total debt is an important indicator of the short-run fund and financing needs of an enterprise. Short-term debt, as opposed to maturing long-term debt or sinking fund requirements, is an indicator of enterprise reliance on bank financing.

Equity capital at market value

Accounting principles in current use place primary emphasis on historical costs rather than on current values. Since the shareholder's capital is the residual of assets minus liabilities, this accounting can result in equity capital book value figures which are far removed from realistic market values.

One method of correcting this flaw in the stated equity capital amounts, particularly when they enter importantly into the computation of many of the ratios which we have considered above, is to restate

[8] The term "long-term debt" usually includes *all* liabilities which are not current.

them by converting the assets from historical cost to current market values.

Although SEC disclosure requirements affecting certain companies will provide analysts with some replacement cost data we are still far from having complete market values available.

One way of overcoming the problem of giving recognition to market values is to compute the equity capital at current (or some kind of average) market value of the stock issues which comprise it. On the assumption that the valuation placed by the market on the equity capital recognizes the current values of assets and their earning power, this amount can then be used in the computation of the various debt-equity ratios.

A serious objection to this method is that stock prices fluctuate widely and may, particularly in times of overspeculation, not be representative of "true" values at a given moment. However, this argument can be countered with considerable evidence that the judgment of the marketplace is most of the time superior to that of other judgmental processes and that use of average market prices would solve the problem of temporary aberrations. Thus, the use of equity capital figures computed at current, or at average, market values has much to commend it. Being more realistic they can improve the ratio measurements in which they are used and can provide a more realistic measure of the asset cushion which bondholders can count on.[9]

One important advantage of earnings-coverage ratios, as will be seen in the subsequent discussion of this subject, is that they are based on the earning power of assets rather than on the amount at which they are carried in the financial statements. Market values do, of course, give recognition to such earning power of an entity's assets. Thus, ratio measures, such as debt-equity ratios, which use equity capital amounts at market value, are more consistent with earnings-coverage ratios than are ratios using historical book values.

Interpretation of capital structure measures

The common-size and ratio analyses of capital structure, which have been examined above, are all measures of risk inherent in the capital structure of an enterprise. The higher the proportion of debt, the larger the fixed charges of interest and debt repayment, and the

[9] B. Graham, D. L. Dodd, and S. Cottle in their *Security Analysis*, 4th ed., (New York: McGraw-Hill Book Co., Inc., 1962), p. 361 suggest that the ratio of

$$\frac{\text{Market Value of Junior Equity}}{\text{Par Value of Bonds}}$$

should not be less than .5 and can be used to corroborate earnings coverage measures. It would not be prudent to have to assume, they maintain, that the junior equity is undervalued by the market.

greater the likelihood of insolvency during protracted periods of earnings decline or other adversities.

One obvious value of these measures is that they serve as screening
devices. Thus, when the ratio of débt to equity capital is relatively
small, say 10 percent or less, there is normally no need to be concerned
with this aspect of an enterprise's financial condition; and the analyst
may well conclude that he can spend his time better by directing his
attention to the more critical areas revealed by his analysis.

Should an examination of the debt-equity ratios reveal that debt is
indeed a significant factor in the total capitalization, then further
analysis is necessary.

Such an analysis will encompass many aspects of an enterprise's
financial condition, results of operations, and future prospects.

An analysis of short-term liquidity is always important because before the analyst starts to assess long-term solvency he has to be satisfied
about the short-term financial survival of the enterprise. Chapter 2
examines the analysis of short-term liquidity, and the analyst will use
the tools discussed there to assess the situation and also to relate the
size of working capital to the size of long-term debt. Loan and bond
indenture covenants requiring the maintenance of minimum working
capital ratios attest to the importance attached to current liquidity in
insuring the long-term solvency of an enterprise.

Additional analytical steps of importance will include an examination of debt maturities (as to size and spacing over time), interest costs,
and other factors which have a bearing on the risk. Among those, the
earnings stability of the enterprise and its industry as well as the kind
of assets its resources are invested in are important factors.

MEASURES OF ASSETS DISTRIBUTION

The type of assets an enterprise employs in its operations should
determine to some extent the sources of funds used to finance them.
Thus, for example, it is customarily held that fixed and other long-term
assets should not be financed by means of short-term loans. In fact, the
most appropriate source of funds for investment in such assets is
equity capital, although debt also has a place in such financing. On the
other hand, working capital, and particularly seasonal working capital
needs, can be appropriately financed by means of short-term credit.
The ratio of working capital to long-term debt should not fall below 1
and in most industries which are affected by the business cycle a ratio
below 1.5 to 2 may indicate weakness and vulnerability.

In judging the risk exposure of a given capital structure, the asset
composition is one of the important factors to consider. This asset composition is best measured by means of common-size statements of the
asset side of the balance sheet. For example, Exhibit 4–4 shows the

common-size asset section of the balance sheet whose liabilities and equity section was presented in Exhibit 4–3.

EXHIBIT 4–4
Assets section—with common-size percents

Current Assets:		
Cash	$ 376,000	16.7%
Accounts receivable (net)	425,000	18.9
Merchandise inventory	574,000	25.5
Total Current Assets	$1,375,000	61,1%
Investments	$ 268,000	11.9%
Land, property, and equipment (net)	368,000	16.4
Intangibles	239,000	10.6
Total Assets	$2,250,000	100.0%

Judging *only* by the distribution of assets and the related capital structure, it would appear that since a relatively high proportion of assets is current (61 percent), a 41 percent debt and current liabilities position (see Exhibit 4–3) is not excessive. Other considerations and measurements may, however, change this conclusion.

Asset coverage is an important element in the evaluation of long-term solvency. Assets of value provide protection to holders of debt obligations both because of their earning power and because of their liquidation value. Additionally, they represent the bases on which an enterprise can obtain the financing which may be required to tie it over a period of financial stringency.

The relationship between asset groups and selected items of capital structure can also be expressed in terms of ratios.

Fixed assets/equity capital is a ratio which measures the relationship between long-term assets and equity capital. A ratio in excess of 1 : 1 means that some of the fixed assets are financed by means of debt.

Net tangible assets as a percentage of long-term debt is a measure of asset coverage of long-term obligations. It excludes assets of doubtful realizability or value and represents a measure of safety of debt based on liquidation of assets.

If the financial structure ratios are such that they require further analysis, one of the best means for further investigation are tests which measure an enterprise's ability to service its debt requirements out of earnings. This is the area we shall turn to next.

MEASURES OF EARNINGS COVERAGE

One conclusion of our discussion of debt-equity ratios was that a major usefulness of these measurements lies in their function as a screening device, that is, a means of deciding whether the apparent risk inherent in the capital structure of an enterprise requires further investigation and analysis. An important limitation of the measurements of debt-equity relationships is that they do not focus on the availability of funds, or cash, flows which are necessary to service the enterprise's debt. In fact, as a debt obligation is repaid the debt-equity ratio tends to improve whereas the yearly amount of cash needed to pay interest and sinking fund requirements may remain the same or may even increase, as for example, in the case of level payment debt or loans with "balloon" repayment provisions.

Earnings-coverage ratios measure directly the relationship between debt related fixed charges and the earnings available to meet these charges.[10] While the concept behind this measurement is simple and straightforward, its practical implementation is complicated by the problem of defining what should be included in "earnings" and in "fixed charges."

EARNINGS AVAILABLE TO MEET FIXED CHARGES

Net income determined under the principles of accrual accounting is not the same thing as sources of funds provided by operations. Specifically, certain items of income, such as undistributed earnings of subsidiaries and controlled companies or sales on extended credit terms, do not create funds, that is, working capital. Similarly, certain expenses such as depreciation, amortization, depletion, and deferred income tax charges do not require the outlay of current funds. On the other hand, it should be borne in mind that a parent company can determine the dividend policy of a controlled subsidiary.

Fixed-debt charges are paid out of current funds rather than out of net income. Thus, the analyst must realize that an unadjusted net income figure may not be a correct measure of funds available to meet fixed charges.

Since fixed charges are paid off with cash, a clarification is needed as to why we accept here working capital as a surrogate for cash. The reason is that over the longer term the conversion period of current assets into cash becomes relatively insignificant. Thus, even if the conversion period of inventories into receivables, and ultimately into cash, is 120 days this period is not significant compared with the longer term period over which the fixed charges of debt must be paid.

The use of net income as an approximation of funds provided by

---

[10] Fixed charge coverage ratios represent important inputs in bond rating decisions. Bond indentures often specify that minimum levels of this ratio must be maintained before additional debt can be issued.

operations may, in some instance, be warranted while in others it may significantly overstate or understate the amount actually available for the servicing of debt. Thus, the soundest approach to this problem lies not in generalizations but rather in a careful analysis of the nonfund generating items included in income as well as the nonfund requiring expenses charged to that income. Thus, for example in considering depreciation as a nonfund requiring expense, the analyst must realize that over the long run an enterprise must replace its plant and equipment.

The problem of determining the amount of income to be included in fixed-charge-coverage ratios requires consideration of a number of additional factors:

1. *The treatment of extraordinary gains and losses.* As pointed out in the more comprehensive discussion of this subject in Chapter 8, extraordinary gains and losses enter into the determination of longer term average earnings power. As such they must be recognized as a factor which may, over the longer term, contribute to or reduce the funds available to pay fixed charges. Any computation of earnings-coverage ratios utilizing average earnings figures must recognize the existence of extraordinary gains and losses over the years. This is particularly true of earnings-coverage ratios where what we measure is the risk of loss of sources of funds for payment of fixed charges.

2. *Preferred dividends* need not be deducted from net income because the payment of such dividends is not mandatory. However, in consolidated financial statements, preferred dividends of a subsidiary whose income is consolidated must be deducted because they represent a charge which has priority over the distribution of earnings to the parent.

3. Earnings which are attributed to *minority interests* are usually deducted from net income available for fixed charges even though minority shareholders can rarely enforce a cash claim under normal operating conditions. An exception arises where preferred stock dividend requirements of a consolidated subsidiary are considered fixed charges and where they also represent a significant portion of the total minority interest. In such instances, the coverage ratio should be computed on the basis of earnings before deducting minority interests.

If a subsidiary with a minority interest has a loss, the credit in the income statement which results from the minority's share in the loss should be excluded from consolidated earnings for purposes of the coverage ratio computation. The parent would, in most cases, meet fixed-charge obligations of its subsidiary to protect its own credit standing, whether or not legally obligated to do so.

4. *The impact of income taxes* on the computation of earnings-coverage ratios should always be carefully assessed. Since interest is a tax-deductible expense, it is met out of pretax income. Thus, the income out of which interest payments are met is pretax income. On the other hand, preferred dividends or sinking fund payments are not tax deductible and must be paid out of after-tax earnings.

5. The *level of income* used in the computation of earnings-coverage ratios deserves serious consideration. The most important consideration here is: what level of income will be most representative of the amount that will actually be available in the *future* for the payment of debt-related fixed charges. An average earnings figure encompassing the entire range of the business cycle, and adjusted for any known factors which may change it in the future, is most likely to be the best approximation of the average source of funds from future operations which can be expected to become available for the payment of fixed charges. Moreover, if the objective of the earnings-coverage ratio is to measure the creditor's maximum exposure to risk, then the proper earnings figure to use is that achieved at the low point of the enterprise's business cycle.

FIXED CHARGES TO BE INCLUDED

Having considered the amount of earnings which should be included in the earnings coverage, we shall now turn to an examination of the types of fixed charges properly includable in the computation of this ratio.

1. Interest on long-term debt

Interest on long-term debt is the most direct and most obvious fixed charge which arises from the incurrence of long-term debt. Interest expense includes the amortization of deferred bond discount and premium. The bond discount and issue expenses represent the amount by which the par value of the bond indebtedness exceeded the proceeds from the bond issue. As such, the discount amortization represents an addition to the stated interest expense. The amortization of bond issue premium represents the reverse situation, and thus results in a reduction of interest expense over the period of amortization.[11]

If low coupon bonds have only a short period to run before maturity and it is likely that they will have to be refinanced with higher coupon bonds, it may be appropriate to incorporate in fixed charges the expected higher interest costs.

---

[11] Bond discount or premium amortization, which are usually relatively insignificant in amount, do not, strictly speaking, require a current outlay of funds. They represent cost or income item allocations over the term of the loan.

Interest on income bonds must, at best, be paid only as earned. Consequently, it is not a fixed charge from the point of view of the holder of fixed interest securities. It must, however, be regarded as a fixed charge from the point of view of the income bond issuer.

In public utilities, interest on funds tied up in construction projects which earn, as yet, no return, are usually excluded from interest costs and capitalized as costs of construction. For purposes of earnings-coverage calculations the exclusion of this interest factor from fixed charges results in a failure to measure the total burden of servicing long-term debt. Consequently, a more realistic measure of coverage can be arrived at by adding the "interest during construction" credit back to interest expense. At the same time the total interest amount, without benefit of a credit for interest charged during construction, is used in the coverage computation.

The SEC has been paying increasing attention to the computation of the ratio of earnings to fixed charges in prospectuses and has clarified the point that the amount of interest added back to income must not necessarily equal the interest amount included in the "fixed charges" part of the ratio computation.

In determining the earnings side of the ratio of earnings to fixed charges, interest is to be added back to pretax net earnings. The amount of interest to be added back should include the amount shown as interest expense plus the amount of interest which has found its way into other captions of the income statement such as, for example, capitalized interest expense now being written off to cost of sales as a part of the cost of land, construction, or other items sold. The add-back should not include the amounts of interest expense capitalized which are still carried in the balance sheet as, for instance, inventory, since such interest charges have already been removed from the income statement. The reason for this is to remove from the amount considered to be earnings of the enterprise, all amounts which have been paid out or accrued as interest and which have not been otherwise excluded from the income statement.

For the purpose of determining fixed charges, however, interest expense should include all interest applicable to the period which has been paid or accrued by the company on its total debt structure which existed during the period, including the amounts capitalized, even though some of the capitalized amount will remain in inventory or other balance sheet accounts.

Exhibit 4–5 presents an example of the computation of the ratio of earnings to fixed charges illustrating the principles discussed above: [12]

[12] The basic objective of pro forma earnings coverage computations is to incorporate in them fixed charges associated with contemplated issuances of debt while recognizing at the same time the income statement benefits to be derived from the proceeds of such debt issues.

EXHIBIT 4–5
Computation of actual and pro forma ratio of earnings to fixed charges

	19X1	19X2
Earnings:		
Income before provision for income taxes	$225,700	$370,200
Interest and debt expense included in cost of sales	279,400	523,100
Interest charged direct to income	1,800	9,600
Interest component of noncapitalized leases	1,700	5,100
Total	$508,600	$908,000
Fixed charges:		
Interest and debt expenses capitalized in real estate	$583,700	$727,300
Interest charged direct to income	1,800	9,600
Interest component of noncapitalized leases	1,700	5,100
Total	$587,200	$742,000
Interest on debentures to be issued at assumed		
rate of 7½%...		187,500
Interest on debt to be retired		(5,400)
Pro forma fixed charges		$924,100
Ratio of earnings to fixed charges:		
Historical	.87	1.22
Pro forma		0.98

2. Interest implicit in lease obligations

SFAS 13 now requires the capitalization of most financing leases. When a lease is capitalized, the interest portion of the lease payment is designated as such on the income statement while most of the balance is usually considered as repayment of the principal obligation. A problem arises, however, when the analyst feels that certain leases which should have been capitalized are not so treated in the financial statements. The issue here actually goes beyond the pure accounting question of whether capitalization is, or is not, appropriate. It stems rather from the fact that a long-term lease represents a fixed obligation which must be given recognition in the computation of the earnings coverage ratio. Thus, even long-term leases which, from an accounting theory point of view, need not be capitalized may be considered as including fixed charges which have to be included in the coverage ratio computation.

The problem of extracting the interest portion of long-term lease payments is not a simple one. The external analysts can possibly obtain the implicit interest rate of financing leasing from an examination of the more extensive disclosure now available on the subject. Otherwise a rough rule of thumb, such as that interest represents one third of rentals, originally suggested by Graham and Dodd, may have to be used.[13] The SEC, which had used this rule, no longer accepts it automatically and insists on a more reliable estimate of the portion of rentals which represent interest.[14] "Delay rentals" in the extractive industries represent payment for the privilege of deferring the development of properties and, being in the nature of not regularly recurring compensation to owners, are not considered as rentals includable in the earnings-coverage ratio.

As with the offsetting of interest income against interest expense, the general rule is that rental income should not be offset against rental expense when determining fixed charges. An exception is made, however, where the rental income represents a direct reduction in rental expense.

3. Capitalized interest

The interest cost reflected in the income statement (wherever found, e.g., as financial cost or as part of cost of sales) is not the only one to be considered in arriving at the amount of interest to be included in fixed charges. Thus, interest that is not currently expensed but which is capitalized during the period (e.g., in inventory) must also be considered as a fixed charge. Capitalization occurs, for example, in the case of real estate development companies where interest costs are added to the cost of land held for sale and expensed as part of the cost of land only when it is sold.

4. Other elements to be included in fixed charges

The foregoing discussions concerned the determination of fixed financing charges, that is, interest and the interest portion of lease rentals. These are the most widely used measures of "fixed charges" included in earnings-coverage ratios. However, if the purpose of this ratio is to measure an enterprise's ability to meet fixed commitments which if unpaid could result in repercussions ranging all the way from financial embarrassment to insolvency, there are other fixed charges to be considered. Thus, when consolidated financial statements are presented, preferred stock dividend requirements of consolidated subsidiaries must be included as part of fixed charges. The most important category to be considered here, however, are principal repayment obligations such as sinking fund requirements, serial repayment provisions, and the principal repayment component of lease rentals.

---

[13] Graham, Dodd, and Cottle. *Security Analysis*, p. 344.
[14] SEC *Accounting Series Release 155.*

5. Principal repayment requirements

Principal repayment obligations are, from a cash-drain point of view, just as onerous as obligations to pay interest. In the case of rentals, the obligations to pay principal and interest must be met simultaneously.

A number of reasons have been advanced to indicate why the requirements for principal repayments are not given recognition in earnings-coverage ratio calculations:

1. It is claimed that sinking fund payment requirements do not have the same degree of urgency as do interest payments and that, consequently, they should be excluded. This is based on the assumption that creditors would be willing to agree to a temporary suspension of such payments even though this generally constitutes an act of bankruptcy. This is an assumption of doubtful validity. Moreover, if the coverage ratio is designed to measure safety, then a situation where an enterprise must renegotiate or forego adhering to debt repayment provisions is in itself symptomatic of a rather unsafe condition.

2. Another objection to the inclusion of sinking fund or other periodic principal repayment provisions in the calculation of the earnings-coverage ratio is that this may result in double counting, that is, the funds recovered by depreciation already provide for debt repayment. Thus, if earnings reflect a deduction for depreciation, then fixed charges should not include provisions for principal repayments.

    There is some merit in this argument if the debt was used to acquire depreciable fixed assets and if there is some correspondence between the pattern of depreciation charges and that of principal repayments. It must, moreover, be borne in mind that depreciation funds are recovered generally only out of profitable, or at least break-even, operations, and consequently this argument is valid only under an assumption of such operations.

    Our discussion of the definition of "earnings" to be included in the coverage-ratio calculations emphasized the importance of funds provided by operations as the measure of resources available to meet fixed charges. The use of this concept would, of course, eliminate the double counting problem since nonfund-requiring charges such as depreciation would be added back to net income for the purpose of the coverage computations.

A more serious problem regarding the inclusion of debt repayment provisions among "fixed charges" arises from the fact that not all debt agreements provide for sinking fund payments or similar repayment obligations. Any arbitrary allocation of indebtedness over time would be an unrealistic theoretical exercise and would ignore the fact that to the extent that such payments are not required in earlier years, the immediate pressure on the cash resources of the enterprise is reduced. In the longer run, however, larger maturities as well as "balloon" payments will have to be met.

The most useful solution to this problem lies in a careful analysis and assessment of the yearly debt repayment requirements which will serve as the basis on which to judge the effect of these obligations on the long-term solvency of the enterprise. The assumption that debt can always be refinanced, rolled over, or otherwise paid off from current operations is not the most useful approach to the problem of risk evaluation. On the contrary, the existence of debt repayment obligations as well as the timing of their maturity must be recognized and included in an overall assessment of the long-term ability of the enterprise to meet its fixed obligations. The inclusion of sinking fund or other early repayment requirements in fixed charges is one way of recognizing the impact of such requirements on fund adequacy. Another method would, as a minimum, call for scheduling total debt repayment requirements over a period of 5–10 years into the future and relating these to after tax funds expected to be available from operations.

6. Other fixed charges

While interest payments and debt repayment requirements are the fixed charges most directly related to the incurrence of debt, there is no logical justification to restrict the evaluation of long-term solvency only to these charges and commitments. Thus, a complete analysis of fixed charges which an enterprise is obliged to meet must include all long-term rental payment obligations[15] (not only the interest portion thereof) and particularly those rentals which must be met under any and all circumstances, under noncancellable leases, otherwise known as "hell-and-high-water" leases.

The reason why short-term leases can be excluded from consideration as fixed charges is that they represent an obligation of limited duration, usually less than three years, and can consequently be discontinued in a period of severe financial stringency. Here, the analyst must, however, evaluate how essential the rented items are to the continuation of the enterprise as a going concern.

---

[15] Capitalized long-term leases affect income by the interest charge implicit in them as well as by the amortization of the property right. Thus, to consider the "principal" component of such leases as fixed charges (after income was reduced by amortization of the property right) would amount to double counting.

Other charges which are not directly related to debt, but which must nevertheless be considered as long-term commitments of a fixed nature, are long-term purchase contracts not subject to cancellation and other similar obligations.

7. Guarantees to pay fixed charges

Guarantees to pay fixed charges of unconsolidated subsidiaries should result in additions to fixed charges if the requirement to honor the guarantee appears imminent.

ILLUSTRATION OF EARNINGS-COVERAGE RATIO CALCULATIONS

Having discussed the various considerations which enter into the decision of what factors to include in the earnings-coverage ratio computation, we will address ourselves now to the simpler question of how the ratio is computed. The computation of the various coverage ratios will be based on the illustration in Exhibit 4–6.

EXHIBIT 4–6

THE LEVERED CORPORATION
Abbreviated Income Statement

Net sales		$13,400,000
Equity in earnings of unconsolidated affiliates		600,000
		$14,000,000
Cost of goods sold	$7,400,000	
Selling, general, and administrative expenses	1,900,000	
Depreciation (excluded from above costs)	800,000	
Interest expense (inclusive of interest portion of rents) (1)	700,000	
Rental expense (3)	800,000	
Share of minority interests in consolidated income	200,000	11,800,000
Income before taxes		$ 2,200,000
Income taxes:		
Current	$ 800,000	
Deferred	300,000	1,100,000
Income before extraordinary items		$ 1,100,000
Gain on sale of investment in land (net of $67,000 tax)		200,000
Net income		$ 1,300,000
Dividends:		
On common stock	$ 400,000	
On preferred stock	200,000	600,000
Earnings retained for the year		$ 700,000

Selected notes to the financial statements

1. The interest expense is composed of the following charges:

a.	Interest on $6 million 6% senior notes due 19X0	$360,000
b.	Interest on $4 million 7% subordinated convertible debentures ...	280,000
c.	Interest portion of $160,000 in rents which have been capitalized .	50,000
d.	Other interest costs	10,000
		$700,000

Sinking fund requirements on the 6 percent senior notes are $500,000 annually.
2. The company has a 10-year noncancellable raw material purchase commitment amounting to $100,000 annually.
3. Interest implicit in noncapitalized leases amounts to $300,000.

TIMES-INTEREST-EARNED RATIO

This is the simplest and one of the most widely used coverage ratios. The ratio is computed as follows:

$$\frac{\text{Income before Taxes + Interest Expense}}{\text{Interest Expense}}$$

Using the data in Exhibit 4–6 the computation of the times-interest-earned ratio is as follows:

$$\frac{2,200,000 + 700,000}{700,000} = 4.1 \text{ times}$$

As was pointed out in our discussion earlier in this chapter, since interest is a tax-deductible expense it is met out of pretax income. Interest is added back to pretax income because it was deducted in arriving at such income.

Ratio of earnings to fixed charges

The simplistic computation of the times-interest-earned ratio often omits the interest portion of long-term uncapitalized lease rentals. Under SFAS 13, there should be significantly fewer of these in the future. The ratio of earnings to fixed charges must, as a minimum, include all interest charges including those implicit in noncaptialized lease rentals.

Coverage ratios of senior bonds

If payment of senior bond interest takes precedence over the subordinated or junior bond interest, the fact remains that default in the payment of any contractual obligation may set in motion a chain of events which could prove detrimental to, and perhaps even result in loss, to senior bondholders.

If we compute the coverage ratio for a senior bond only, we omit from fixed charges the interest due to holders of junior issues but include the interest component of rentals on the assumption that the rentals are essential to the conduct of operations. Based on the data in Exhibit 4–6, we compute the fixed-charge coverage ratio for the 6 percent senior notes as follows:

$$\frac{\text{Income before Taxes} + \text{Interest Expense} + \text{Interest in Rentals}}{\text{Interest on Senior Issue} + \text{Interest in Rentals}}$$

$$\frac{2,200,000 + 700,000 + 300,000}{360,000 + 300,000} = 4.8 \text{ times}$$

The analyst should be careful to avoid the error, now rarely made, of computing the fixed-charge coverage ratio on a junior bond issue by omitting the senior bond interest from it. The junior issue can, of course, not be better covered than the senior one.

Fixed-charges-coverage ratio—the SEC standard

According to the SEC's definition, fixed charges include, in addition to *(A)* interest costs (inclusive of amortization of debt discount, expense and premium), *(B)* the interest portion implicit in rentals. Earnings in our example would exclude undistributed income of unconsolidated[16] persons *(C)*. Again, using data in Exhibit 4–6:

$$\frac{\text{Income before Taxes} - (C) + (A) + (B)}{(A) + (B)}$$

$$= \frac{2,200,000 - 600,000 + 700,000 + 300,000}{700,000 + 300,000} = 2.6 \text{ times}$$

Fixed-charges-coverage ratios—expanded concept of fixed charges

If we adopt the point of view that failure to meet any fixed obligations can lead to trouble or to a chain of events leading to insolvency, then we want to establish how well such fixed obligations are covered by earnings. Thus, in addition to the fixed charges included in the computation in the preceding example, the following must now be considered for inclusion:

Annual sinking fund requirements on 6 percent senior note ($500,000). This represents an obligation which if not met may result

---

[16] It is assumed that the enterprise can direct consolidated subsidiaries to transfer funds in the form of dividends or otherwise.

in financial embarrassment or even insolvency. This fixed charge differs from the others considered so far in that it is not tax deductible. In order to bring it to a basis comparable to that of the tax-deductible fixed charges, we must convert it into the pretax amount which is needed to yield an after-tax outlay equal to the fixed charge. This is done by multiplying the fixed charge by a step-up factor computed as follows:

$$\frac{1}{1 - \text{Tax Rate}}$$

Assuming a tax rate of 50 percent in this case we get:

$$\$500,000 \times \left(\frac{1}{1 - 0.50}\right) = \$1,000,000$$

The converted sinking fund fixed charge of \$1,000,000 will be used in the computation of the coverage ratio.

Long-term rental (\$800,000). The earnings coverage computation, defined by the SEC, included as fixed charges only that portion of uncapitalized rentals which is attributable to the interest factor. This approach views as fixed charges only those fixed obligations which are in the nature of interest. Under the expanded concept of fixed charges, any obligation to pay fixed amounts over the longer term is considered a fixed charge because a failure to make such payments can set in motion a chain of events whose end result may be similar to that flowing out of a failure to pay interest.

The data in Exhibit 4–6 indicate that the uncapitalized leases represent long-term obligations. In the case of these lease rentals the interest portion is, from a contractual point of view, indistinguishable from the principal repayment portion (\$500,000). Consequently, under the expanded concept of fixed charges the entire amount of rentals (\$800,000), rather than only the interest portion, is viewed as a fixed charge whose degree of coverage by earnings it is important to establish.

Noninterest portion of capitalized rents (\$110,000)

The principal or noninterest portion of capitalized rentals represents as urgent a call on the liquid resources of the enterprise as does the interest portion. It should, however, be borne in mind that since income is already charged with depreciation of the property rights stemming from the capitalized leases, inclusion in fixed charges of the noninterest portion of capitalized rentals would amount to a double counting.

Noncancellable raw material purchase commitments

According to Exhibit 4–6 the annual noncancellable long-term purchase commitment amounts to $100,000. The reason why this payment may be considered a fixed charge under the "expanded" concept is that it represents a noncancellable obligation to pay out a fixed annual sum of money over a 10-year period.

From the point of view of the income tax impact, this item is akin to interest or rental payments in that it is a tax-deductible charge because it enters ultimately into the cost of goods sold.

Recognition of benefits stemming from fixed charges

Consideration must be given to the question whether the benefits derived by an enterprise from the incurrence of fixed charges are given recognition in the earnings included in the coverage ratio. In the case of interest the benefits stem from the use of the funds derived from the loan. Similarly, rental payments benefit revenues through the productive use of the items leased. The benefits derived from the raw material commitments are reflected in sales revenues. Since outlays for raw materials represent a variable cost, they would ordinarily not be included in fixed charges because they represent an expense that can be varied in accordance with the volume of business transacted. In our example the fixed nature of the charge for raw materials stems from a noncancellable commitment to buy. This reduces discretion and variability. If, in the judgment of the analyst, such commitments represent rock-bottom requirements which will exist even under the most pessimistic estimates of product demand, then he may decide not to consider the purchase commitment as a fixed charge. This will be the assumption in our computational example.

Computation of coverage ratio—expanded concept of fixed charges

In accordance with the preceding discussion the earnings-coverage ratio would, based on the data in Exhibit 4–6, be computed as follows:

$$\frac{\text{Income before Taxes} + \text{Interest} + \text{Rental Expense}}{\text{Interest} + \text{Rental Expense} + \text{Sinking Fund}\left(\dfrac{1}{1-0.50}\right)}$$

$$= \frac{2,200,000 + 700,000 + 800,000}{700,000 + 800,000 + 1,000,000} = 1.48 \text{ Times}$$

Pro forma computations of coverage ratios

In cases where fixed charges yet to be incurred are to be recognized in the computation of the coverage ratio, for example, interest costs under a prospective incurrence of debt, it is quite proper to estimate the benefits which will ensue from such future inflows of funds and to include these estimated benefits in the pro forma income. Benefits to be derived from a propsective loan can be measured in terms of interest savings obtainable from a planned refunding operation, income from short-term investments[17] in which the proceeds may be invested, or similarly reasonable estimates of future benefits.

The SEC will usually insist on the presentation of pro forma computation of the ratio of earnings to fixed charges which reflects changes to be effected under prospective financing plans. Exhibit 4–5 presented an example of such a computation.

Funds flow coverage of fixed charges

The discussion earlier in this chapter pointed out that net income is generally not a reliable measure of funds provided by operations which are available to meet fixed charges. The reason is, of course, that fixed charges are paid with cash or, from the longer term point of view, with funds (working capital) while net income includes items of revenue which do not generate funds as well as expense items which do not require the current use of funds. Thus, a better measure of fixed charges coverage may be obtained by using as numerator funds obtained by operations rather than net income. This figure can be obtained from the statement of changes in financial condition.

Under this concept the coverage ratio would be computed as follows:

$$\frac{\text{Funds provided by Operations} + \text{Fixed Charges}}{\text{Fixed Charges}}$$

Using the data in Exhibit 4–6 and the broadest definition of "fixed charges," we compute the coverage ratio as follows:

Funds provided by operations (pretax)

Income before extraordinary items*	$1,100,000
Add back—income taxes	1,100,000
Pretax income	$2,200,000
Less: Nonfund generating income:	
Equity in earnings of unconsolidated affiliates	600,000
	$1,600,000

---

[17] *Accounting Series Release 119* of the SEC prohibits such offset of investment income.

Add: Expenses not requiring funds:

Depreciation..	$800,000	
Share of minority interests in consolidated income	200,000	
Deferred income taxes (already added above).........	—	1,000,000
Funds provided by operations (before taxes)		$2,600,000

* Assuming that a one-year calculation can properly omit extraordinary items.

Using the fixed charges we discussed under the "expanded concept" in the previous example, that is,

$$
\begin{array}{lr}
\text{Interest} \dotfill & \$\ 700{,}000 \\
\text{Rental expense} \dotfill & 800{,}000 \\
\text{Sinking fund requirement}\left(\dfrac{1}{1-0.50}\right) \dotfill & 1{,}000{,}000 \\
\text{Total} \dotfill & \$2{,}500{,}000
\end{array}
$$

We compute the times fixed charges covered by funds provided by operations as follows:

$$
\frac{\$2{,}600{,}000 + 700{,}000 + 800{,}000}{2{,}500{,}000} = 1.64 \text{ times}
$$

It is interesting to note that the SEC definition of "income to be included in the coverage calculation" recognizes only one type of non fund generating revenue, that is, undistributed earnings of unconsolidated persons. It seems rather arbitrary to insist on only one type of "nonfund" adjustment to the exclusion of others. Perhaps it is a measure of conservatism that the SEC coverage-ratio formula ignores nonfund-requiring charges such as depreciation while requiring deduction of nonfund generating credits. However, it must be recognized that over the long run, and coverage ratios are concerned with the longer term, asset replacement needs may well equal, if not exceed, the amounts charged as depreciation. Thus, while such needs cannot be exactly anticipated and scheduled by external analysts, they must be taken into account, and one way of doing this is to omit depreciation from consideration as a charge not requiring the outlay of funds.

If depreciation is added back to net income, then there is little justification for not including principal repayment requirements, such as sinking fund requirements, among the fixed charges. In this case, the "double counting" problem discussed earlier is clearly eliminated.

A case, similar to the involved in the consideration of depreciation, can be made, under certain circumstances, against considering deferred income taxes as a non fund requiring charge in the computation of the coverage ratio of a long-term bond. Here we must recognize that over the long term, the higher charges of expenses for tax purposes which may have given rise to the tax deferral will result in lower future expense charges for tax purposes, thus causing the tax deferral to "reverse" and requiring higher taxes in the future. The treatment of deferred taxes in the coverage ratio computation will then depend on the analyst's judgment as to the expected future behavior of the deferred tax account, that is, whether it is likely to grow, stabilize, or decline. Also, the fact that deferred tax computations ignore present value concepts may also have to be considered.

Should the analyst wish to base the computation on "cash flow" or, more accurately, cash provided by operations the "funds from operations" figure must be appropriately adjusted for changes in such current items as accounts receivable, inventories, prepayments, accounts payable and accruals.

Other useful tests of funds flow relationships

Net funds (or cash) flows as a percentage of capital expenditures relates funds provided by operations *after* dividends to needed capital plant and equipment replacements and additions. This is a measure of fund committments to outlays which do not enter the fixed charges total but which may nevertheless be vital or important to the continuing operation of an enterprise.

Cash or funds flow as a percentage of long-term debt is an additional measure of safety which relates fund availability to total long term indebtedness.

Stability of "flow of funds from operations"

Since the relationship between the "flow of funds from operations" to the fixed charges of an enterprise is so important to an evaluation of long-term solvency, it is important to assess the stability of that flow. This is done by a careful evaluation of the elements which comprise the sources of funds from operations. For example, the depreciation add-back to net income is a more stable element than is net income itself because the recovery of the depreciation cost from selling prices precedes the earning of any net income, and has thus a higher degree of probability of happening. Even in very competitive industries selling prices must, in the long run, reflect the cost of plant and equipment used up in production.

EARNINGS COVERAGE OF PREFERRED DIVIDENDS

In the evaluation of preferred stock issues, it is often instructive to calculate the earnings coverage of preferred dividends, much in the same way the interest or fixed charges coverage of debt issues is computed.

In our discussion of coverage ratios for individual bond issues, earlier in this chapter, we pointed out the misleading results which can result from a class by class coverage computation where junior and senior bonds are outstanding. Thus, we concluded that the computation of a coverage ratio on an overall basis is a more meaningful approach. The same principle applies to the computation of the coverage of preferred dividends, that is, the computation must include as charges to be covered by earnings all fixed charges which take precedence over the payment of preferred dividends.[18]

As in the case of the interest or fixed-charge coverage computations, the final ratio depends on a definition of "fixed charges."

Since preferred dividends are not tax deductible, after-tax income must be used to cover them. Consequently the basic formula for computing preferred dividend coverage is:

$$\frac{\text{Income before Tax} + \text{Fixed Charges*}}{\text{Fixed Charges*} + \text{Preferred Dividends} \left(\dfrac{1}{1 - \text{Tax Rate}}\right)}$$

* Which *are* tax deductible.

If, for example, we adopt the SEC definition of fixed charges and assume a tax rate of 50 percent, then, based on the data in Exhibit 4–6, we compute the preferred dividend coverage ratio as follows:

Fixed charges:
Interest costs .... $ 700,000
Interest portion implicit in rentals 300,000
Total $1,000,000

$$\frac{2,200,000 - 600,000 + 1,000,000}{1,000,000 + 200,000 \left(\dfrac{1}{1 - 0.50}\right)} = 1.9 \text{ times}$$

If there are two or more preferred issues outstanding, a by-class coverage computation can be made by omitting from it the dividend requirements of the junior issue but always including all prior fixed charges and preferred dividends.

A refinement of the above computation (now required by the SEC) is achieved by substituting for the assumed tax rate the actual composite average tax rate incurred by the entity for the period. This actual tax rate is computed by relating the actual tax provision for the period

---

[18] This is also the position of the SEC as now formalized in *ASR 155* (1974). Care must be exercised in comparing these coverage ratios because some analysts and financial services include only the preferred dividend requirements in the computation.

to income before such taxes. It can, however, be argued that the tax incidence with respect to any one item is measured by the marginal (incremental) rather than the *average* tax rate.

EVALUATION OF EARNINGS-COVERAGE RATIOS

The earnings-coverage ratio test is a test of the ability of an enterprise to meet its fixed charges out of current earnings.[19] The orientation towards earnings is a logical one because the bondholder or other long-term creditor is not as much interested in asset coverage or what he can salvage in times of trouble, as he is interested in the ability of the enterprise to stay out of trouble by meeting its obligations currently and as a going concern. Given the limited returns obtainable from debt instruments, an increase in the interest rate cannot compensate the creditor for a serious risk of loss of principal. Thus, if the probability of the enterprise meeting its obligations as a going concern is not strong, then a creditor relationship can hardly be advantageous.

The coverage ratio is influenced by the level of earnings and by the level of fixed charges which in turn depends importantly on the debt-equity within the capitalization.

Importance of earnings variability

One very important factor in the evaluation of the coverage ratio is the pattern of behavior of cash flows over time, or the behavior of its surrogate—earnings. The more stable the earnings pattern of an enterprise or industry the lower the relative earnings coverage ratio that will be acceptable. Thus, a utility, which in times of economic downturn is likely to experience only a mild falloff in demand, can justify a lower earnings coverage ratio than can a cyclical company such as a machinery manufacturer which may experience a sharp drop in sales in times of recession. Variability of earnings is, then, an important factor in the determination of the coverage standard. In addition, the durability and the trend of earnings are important factors which must be considered apart from their variability.[20]

---

[19] W. B. Hickman, *Corporate Bond Quality and Investor Experience* (Princeton, N.J.: Princeton University Press, 1958), p. 11, found, for example, that bonds with poor earnings coverage had a probability of default 17 times greater than those with good coverage.

[20] Most factors which will affect an entity's equity securities will also affect its bonds. For example, when Consolidated Edison Co. passed its dividend in 1974 its bonds plunged along with its common stock which was the security directly affected. The market, aside from taking its cue from this action, may also have concluded that the company's ability to sell equity securities as well as its overall financing flexibility have been impaired.

Importance of method of computation and of underlying assumptions

The coverage standard will also depend on the method of computation of the coverage ratio. As we saw above, varying methods of computing the coverage ratio assume different definitions of "income" and of "fixed charges." It is reasonable to expect lower standards of coverage for the ratios which employ the most demanding and stringent definitions of these terms. For example, based on data in Exhibit 4–6, the earnings-coverage ratio of interest was 4.1 times, while the coverage ratio under an expanded concept of fixed charges worked out to only 1.46 times.

The standards will also vary with the kind of earnings which are utilized in the coverage computation, that is, average earnings, the earnings of the poorest year, etc. Moreover, the quality of earnings is an important consideration (see Chapter 8).

It is not advisable to compute earnings-coverage ratios under methods which are not theoretically sound and whose only merit is that they are conservative. Thus, using after-tax income in the computation of the coverage ratio of fixed charges which are properly deductible for tax purposes is not logical and introduces conservatism in the wrong place. Any standard of coverage adequacy must, in the final analysis, be related to the willingness and ability of the lender to incur risk.

Example of minimum standard of coverage

A standard suggested by a well-known work on security analysis[21] lists the following minimum coverage ratios of fixed charges:

1. *By seven to ten year average earnings:*

	Coverage	
	Before taxes	After taxes
Public utilities	4x	2.4x
Railroads	5x	2.9x
Industrials	7x	3.8x

2. *By earnings of the poorest year:*

	Before taxes	After taxes
Public utilities	3x	1.9x
Railroads	4x	2.4x
Industrials	5x	2.9x

Over the years an ever growing debt load, undertaken undoubtedly

---

[21] Graham, Dodd, and Cottle, *Security Analysis* p. 348.

in many cases as protection against the effects of inflation, has resulted in lower coverage ratios for most U.S. companies. This lowering in fixed-charge coverage ratios has been accompanied by an apparent erosion of the coverage standards against which they are judged. More recent standards of coverage will be found in Appendix A.

APPENDIX A

THE RATING OF DEBT OBLIGATIONS

Since the turn of the century, there has become established in the United States a comprehensive and sophisticated system for rating debt securities. Most ratings are performed by two highly regarded investment research firms, Moody's and Standard & Poor's (S&P).

A bond credit rating is a composite expression of judgment about the credit worthiness of the bond issuer as well as the quality of the specific security being rated. A rating measures credit risk, that is the probability of occurence of developments adverse to the interests of the creditor.

This judgment of credit worthiness is expressed in a series of symbols which express degrees of credit risk. Thus, the top four rating grades of Standard & Poor's are:

AAA Bonds rated AAA are highest grade obligations. They possess the ultimate degree of protection as to principal and interest. Marketwise they move with interest rates, and hence provide the maximum safety on all counts.

AA Bonds rated AA also qualify as high grade obligations, and in the majority of instances differ from AAA issues only in small degree. Here, too, prices move with the long-term money market.

A Bonds rated A are regarded as upper medium grade. They have considerable investment strength but are not entirely free from adverse effects of changes in economic and trade conditions. Interest and principal are regarded as safe. They predominantly reflect money rates in their market behavior, but to some extent, also economic conditions.

BBB The BBB, or medium grade category is borderline between definitely sound obligations and those where the speculative element begins to predominate. These bonds have adequate asset coverage and normally are protected by satisfactory earnings. Their susceptibility to changing conditions, particularly to depressions, necessitates constant watching. Marketwise, the bonds are more responsive to business and trade conditions than to interest rates. This group is the lowest which qualifies for commercial bank investment.

The major reason why debt securities are widely rated while equity securities are not lies in the fact that there is a far greater uniformity of approach and homogeneity of analytical measures used in the evaluation of credit worthiness than there can be in the evaluation of the future market performance of equity securities. Thus, the wide agreement on what is being measured in credit risk analysis has resulted in a widespread acceptance of and reliance on published credit ratings.

The criteria which enter into the determination of a rating have never been precisely defined and they involve both quantitative measures (e.g., ratio analysis) as well as qualitative factors such as market position and management quality. The major rating agencies refuse to be pinned down on what precise mix of factors enter into their rating process (which is a committee decision) because it is both art and science and also because to do so would cause endless arguments about the validity of the many judgmental factors which enter into a rating decision.

We can then see that in arriving at ratings these agencies must undertake analyses along the lines discussed throughout this work, the differences being mainly in the vast number of debt issues covered and the standardization of approaches which this entails. The following description of factors entering the rating process is based on published sources as well as on discussions with officials of the rating agencies.

The rating of corporate bonds

In rating an industrial bond issue the rating agency will focus on the issuing company's asset protection, financial resources, earning power, management, and the specific provisions of the debt security.

Also of great importance are size of firm, market share, industry position, susceptibility to cyclical influences[1] and other broad economic factors.

Asset protection is concerned with measuring the degree to which a company's debt is covered by the value of its assets. One measure is net tangible assets to long-term debt. At S&P an industrial needs a ratio of 5 to 1 to get an AAA rating; a ratio of over 4 to 1 to qualify for an AA rating; 3 to 3.5 to 1 for an A; and about 2.5 to 1 for a BBB rating.

Understated assets, such as those of companies in the natural resource or real estate fields, are generally accorded recognition in the rating process.

The long term debt as a percentage of total capitalization calls for a ratio of under 25 percent for an AAA, around 30 percent for a AA, 35 percent for an A and about 40 percent for a BBB rating.

---

[1] There are, for example, no AAA rated companies in the steel or paper industries.

Other factors entering the consideration of asset protection include the determination of book value, the makeup of working capital, the quality and age of property, plant, and equipment as well as questions of off balance sheet financing and unrecorded liabilities.

Financial resources encompass, in particular, such liquid resources as cash and other working capital items. Quality measures here include the collection period of receivables and inventory turnover. These are judged by means of industry standards. The use of debt, both short term and long term as well as the mix between the two is also investigated.

Future earning power and the resulting cash generating ability is a factor of great importance in the rating of debt securities because the level and the quality of future earnings determine importantly an enterprise's ability to meet its obligations. Earning power is generally a more reliable source of security than is asset protection.

A prime measure of the degree of protection afforded by earning power is the fixed-charge coverage ratio. To qualify for consideration for an AAA rating an industrial company's earnings should cover its interest and rental charges after taxes above seven to eight times, for an AA rating above six times, for an A rating over four times and a BBB over three times.

Another measure of debt service paying ability is cash flow (crudely-net income plus depreciation) to total funded debt. It should be 65 percent or more for an AAA; 45 to 60 percent for an AA; 35 to 45 percent for an A; and 25 to 30 percent for a BBB rating.

Management abilities, philosophy, depth, and experience always loom importantly in any final rating judgment. Through interviews, field trips, and other analyses the raters probe into the depth and breadth of management, as well as into its goals, the planning process and strategies in such areas as research and development, product promotion, new product planning, and acquisitions.

The specific provisions of the debt security are usually spelled out in the bond indenture. What is analyzed here are the specific provisions in the indenture which are designed to protect the interests of bondholders under a variety of future conditions. Included in consideration here are, among others, conditions for issuance of future debt issues, specific security provisions such as mortgaging, sinking fund and redemption provisions, and restrictive covenants.

As can be seen, debt rating is a complex process involving quantitative as well as qualitative factors all of which culminate in the issuance of a single quality rating. The weights which may be assigned to each factor will vary among analysts but the final conclusion will generally represent the composite judgment of several experienced raters.

THE RATING OF MUNICIPAL SECURITIES

Buyers of Municipal Bonds depend for their security of principal and interest on factors which are quite different from those which determine the quality of corporate debt. Hence, the processes of analysis differ.

Municipal securities, those issued by state and local governmental authorities, comprise a number of varieties. Many are general obligation bonds backed by the full faith and credit of the governmental unit which issues them. Others are special tax bonds that are limited in security to a particular tax that will be used to service and retire them. Then there are revenue bonds secured only by revenues of municipal enterprises. Other categories comprise housing authority bonds, tax anticipation notes, and so forth. Although the amount of information provided to buyers of municipal bonds is of very uneven quality moves are afoot to correct this, primarily by way of legislation.

Raters require a great variety of information from issuers of municipal debt. In case of general obligation bonds, the basic security rests on the issuer's ability and willingness to repay the debt from general revenues under a variety of economic conditions.[2] The fundamental revenue source is the taxing power of the local municipality. Thus, the information they require includes: current population and the trend and composition of population, the largest ten tax payers, the current market value of taxable properties, the gross indebtedness, and the net indebtedness (i.e., after deducting self-sustaining obligations, sinking fund, etc.) recent annual reports, budgets, and estimates of capital improvement and future borrowing programs, as well as an overall description of the area's economy.

While rating techniques have the same objectives as in the case of corporate bonds the ratios used are adapted to the specific conditions which exist with respect to municipal debt obligations. Thus, debt as a percentage of market value of real estate is an important indicator: 10 percent is considered high while 3–5 percent is on the low side. Annual debt service of 10 percent of total revenue is considered comfortable while percentages in the high teens are considered as presenting a warning sign. Per capita debt of $400 or less is considered low while debt in the $900 to $1,000 area is considered excessive and, hence, a

---

[2] The decision of New York State's highest court to overturn the New York City Moratorium on its notes strengthens the meaning of the concept of "full faith and credit." Said Chief Justice C. J. Breitel: "A pledge of the city's faith and credit is both a commitment to pay and a commitment of the city's revenue generating powers to produce the funds to pay . . . that is the way both words "faith" and "credit" are used and they are not tautological."

negative factor. Tax delinquencies should generally not exceed 3–4 percent.

Other factors of interest include unfunded pension liabilities as well as the trend of indebtedness. A steady increase in indebtedness is usually a danger sign. As in all cases of debt rating, the factor of management, though largely intangible and subject to measurement only through ultimate results, is of critical importance.

LIMITATIONS OF THE RATING PROCESS

As valuable and essential as the rating process is to buyers of the thousands upon thousands of bond issues of every description, the limitations of this standardized procedure must also be understood. As is true in any phase of security analysis the analyst who can, through superior analysis, improve on what is conventionally accepted stands to benefit accordingly. This is even more true in the case of debt securities than in the case of equity securities.

Bond ratings are very wide and they consequently present opportunities for those who can identify these differences within a rating classification. Moreover, rating changes generally lag the market and this presents additional opportunities to the analyst who with superior skill and alertness can identify important changes before they become generally recognized.

References

"The Rating Game," The Twentieth Century Fund, New York, 1974.

"Higher Stakes in the Bond-Rating Game," *Fortune*, April 1976.

H. C. Sherwood, *How Corporate and Municipal Debt is Rated: An Inside Look at Standard & Poor's Rating System.* New York: John Wiley & Sons, Inc., 1976.

APPENDIX B

RATIOS AS PREDICTORS OF BUSINESS FAILURE

The most common use to which financial statement ratios are put is to use them as pointers in the direction of further investigation and analysis. Some investigation and experimentation has been undertaken to determine to what extent ratios can be used as predictors of failure. As such they could provide valuable additional tools in the analysis of long-term solvency.

The basic idea behind bankruptcy prediction models is that through observation of the trend and behavior of certain ratios of various firms before failure, those characteristics in ratios which predominate in failing firms can be identified and used for prediction purposes. The expectation is that signs of deterioration observed in ratio behavior can be detected early enough and clearly enough so that timely action can be taken to avoid substantial risk of default and failure.

Empirical studies

Among the earliest studies to focus on the behavior of ratios prior to the failure of firms were those of Winakor and Smith who studied a sample of 183 firms which experienced financial difficulties for as long as 10 years prior to 1931, the year when they failed.[1] Analyzing the 10-year trend of 21 ratios they concluded that the ratio of net working capital to total assets was among the most accurate and reliable indicator of failure.

Fitzpatrick analyzed the three- to five-year trends of 13 ratios of 20 firms that had failed in the 1920–29 period.[2] By comparing them to the experience of a control group of 19 successful firms, he concluded that all of his ratios predicted failure to some extent. However, the best predictors were found to be the return on net worth and the net worth to total debt ratio.

Merwin studied the experience of a sample of 939 firms during the 1926–36 period.[3] Analyzing an unspecified number of ratios he found that three ratios were most sensitive in predicting "discontinuance" of a firm as early as four to five years before such discontinuance. The three ratios were the current ratio, net working capital to total assets, and net worth to total debt. They all exhibited declining trends before "discontinuance" and were at all times below estimated normal ratios.

Focusing on the experience of companies which experienced defaults on debt and bank credit difficulties, Hickman studied the experience of corporate bond issues during 1900–1943 and reached the conclusion that the times-interest-earned ratio and the net-profit-to-sales ratio were useful predictors of bond issue defaults.[4]

In a study using more powerful statistical techniques than used in its predecessors, Beaver found that financial ratios proved useful in the

---

[1] Arthur Winakor and Raymond F. Smith, *Changes in Financial Structure of Unsuccessful Firms,* Bureau of Business Research (Urbana, Ill.: University of Illinois Press, 1935).

[2] Paul J. Fitzpatrick, *Symptoms of Industrial Failures* (Washington: Catholic University of America Press, 1931); and Paul J. Fitzpatrick, *A Comparison of the Ratios of Successful Industrial Enterprises with Those of Failed Companies* (Washington: The Accountants Publishing Co., 1932).

[3] Charles L. Merwin, *Financing Small Corporations: In Five Manufacturing Industries, 1926–36* (New York: National Bureau of Economic Research, 1942).

[4] W. Braddock Hickman, *Corporate Bond Quality and Investor Experience* (Princeton, N.J.: Princeton University Press, 1958), pp. 395–431.

prediction of bankruptcy and bond default at least five years prior to such failure. He determined that ratios could be used to distinguish correctly between failed and nonfailed firms to a much greater extent than would be possible by random prediction.[5]

Among his conclusions were that both in the short-term and the long-term cash-flow-to-total-debt ratios were the best predictors, capital structure ratios ranked second, liquidity ratios third, while turnover ratios were the worst predictors.

In an investigation of the ability of ratios to predict bond rating changes and bond ratings of new issues, Horrigan found that the rating changes could be correctly predicted to a much greater extent by the use of ratios than would be possible through random prediction.[6]

Altman extended Beaver's univariate analysis to allow for multiple predictors of failure.[7] Altman used multiple discriminant analysis (MDA) which attempts to develop a linear function of a number of explanatory variables to classify or predict the value of a qualitative dependent variable; e.g., bankrupt or nonbankrupt. Twenty-two financial ratios, based on data one period before bankruptcy, were examined and Altman selected five of these to be included in his final discriminant function: Working capital/Total assets (liquidity), Retained earnings/Total assets (age of firm and cumulative profitability), Earnings before interest and taxes/Total assets (profitability), Market value of equity/Book value of debt (financial structure), Sales/Total assets (capital turnover rate).

Altman was not able to use a cash flow variable, which Beaver found to be the most discriminating in his study since apart from other elements, Altman did not have depreciation figures.

Conclusions

The above research efforts, while pointing out the significant potential which ratios have as predictors of failure, nevertheless indicate that these tools and concepts are in an early stage of development.

The studies focused on experience with failed firms *after the fact.* While they presented evidence that firms which did not fail enjoyed stronger ratios than those which ultimately failed, the ability of ratios alone to predict failure has not been conclusively proved. Another important question yet to be resolved is whether the observation of

[5] William H. Beaver, "Financial Ratios as Predictors of Failure," *Empirical Research in Accounting, Selected Studies, 1966,* Supplement to vol. 4, *Journal of Accounting Research,* pp. 71–127.

[6] James O. Horrigan, "The Determination of Long-term Credit Standing with Financial Ratios," *Empirical Research in Accounting, Selected Studies, 1966,* Supplement to Vol. 4, *Journal of Accounting Research,* pp. 44–62.

[7] Edward Altman, "Financial Ratios, Discriminant Analysis, and the Prediction of Corporate Bankruptcy," *Journal of Finance* 22 (September 1968) 589–609.

certain types of behavior by certain ratios can be accepted as a better means of the analysis of long-term solvency than is the integrated use of the various tools described throughout this work. Further research may show that the use of ratios as predictors of failure will best complement and precede, rather than supplement, the rigorous financial analysis approaches suggested in this work. However, as screening, monitoring, and attention-directing devices they hold considerable promise.

QUESTIONS

1. Generally speaking, what are the key elements in the evaluation of long-term solvency?
2. Why is the analysis of capital structure important?
3. How should deferred income taxes be treated in the analysis of capital structure?
4. In the analysis of capital structure how should lease obligations which have not been capitalized be treated? Under what conditions should they be considered the equivalent of debt?
5. What are liabilities for pensions? What factors should analysts assessing total pension obligations of the firm take into consideration?
6. How would you classify (i.e., equity or liability) the following items. State your assumptions and reasons:
   a. Minority interest in consolidated financial statement.
   b. General contingency reserve for indefinite purpose.
   c. Reserve for self-insurance.
   d. Guarantee for product performance on sale.
   e. Convertible debt.
   f. Preferred stock.
7. What is meant by "financial leverage," and in what case(s) is such leverage most advantageous?
8. In the evaluation of long-term solvency why are long-term projections necessary in addition to a short-term analysis? What are some of the limitations of long-term projections?
9. What is the difference between common-size analysis and capital structure ratio analysis? Why is the latter useful?
10. The amount of equity capital shown on the balance sheets, which is based on historical cost, at times differs considerably from realizable market value. How should a financial analyst allow for this in the analysis of capital structure?
11. Why is the analysis of assets distribution necessary?
12. What does the earnings coverage ratio measure and in what respects is it more useful than other tools of analysis?
13. Your analysis of additional information leads you to conclude that the rental payment under a long-term lease should have been capitalized. If

it was not capitalized on the financial statement, what approaches would you take?

14. For the purpose of earnings-coverage ratio computation, what are your criteria for inclusion of an item in "fixed charges"?

15. The company under analysis has a purchase commitment of raw materials under a noncancellable contract which is substantial in amount. Under what conditions would you include the purchase commitment in the computation of fixed charges?

16. Is net income generally a reliable measure of funds available to meet fixed charges? Why or why not?

17. What are some of the useful tests of funds flow relationships?

18. Company B is a wholly owned subsidiary of Company A. The latter is also Company B's principal customer. As potential lender to Company B, what particular facets of this relationship would concern you most? What safeguards, if any, would you require?

19. Comment on the statement: "debt is a supplement to, not a substitute for, equity capital."

20. A company in need of additional equity capital decides to sell convertible debt thus postponing equity dilution and ultimately selling its shares at an effectively higher price. What are the advantages and disadvantages of such a course of action?

21. *a.* What is the basic function of restrictive covenants in long-term debt indentures (agreements)?

    b. What is the function of provisions regarding:

    (1) Maintenance of minimum working capital (or current ratio).

    (2) Maintenance of minimum net worth.

    (3) Restrictions on the payment of dividends.

    (4) Ability of creditors to elect a majority of the board of directors of the debtor company in the event of default under the terms of the loan agreement.

22. What is your opinion on the use of ratios as predictors of failure? Your answer should recognize the empirical research which has been recently done in this area.

23. Dogwood Manufacturing, Inc., a successful and rapidly growing company, has always had a favorable difference between the rate of return on its assets and the interest rate paid on borrowed funds. Explain why the company should *not* increase its debt to the 90% level of total capitalization and thereby minimize any need for equity financing. (C.F.A.)

24. Why are debt securities widely rated while equity securities are not?

25. On what aspects do the rating agencies focus in rating an industrial bond? Elaborate.

26. *a.* Municipal securities compromise a number of varieties. Discuss.

    b. What factors are considered in the rating of municipal securities?

27. Can the analyst improve on a rating judgment? Discuss.

5

ANALYSIS OF RETURN ON INVESTMENT AND OF ASSET UTILIZATION

DIVERSE VIEWS OF PERFORMANCE

In this age of increasing social consciousness there exist many views of what the basic objectives of business enterprises are or should be. There are those who will argue that the main objective of a business enterprise should be to make the maximum contribution to the welfare of society of which it is capable. That includes, aside from the profitable production of goods and services, consideration of such immeasurables as absence of environmental pollution and a contribution to the solution of social problems. Others, who adhere to the more traditional *laissez faire* school, maintain that the major objective of a business enterprise organized for profit is to increase the wealth of its owners and that this is possible only by delivering to society (consumers) that which it wants. Thus, the good of society will be served.

An extended discussion of these differing points of view on performance is beyond the purpose of this text. Since the analysis of financial statements is concerned with the application of analytical tools to that which can be measured, we shall concentrate here on those measures of performance which meet the objectives of financial analysis. In that context performance is the source of the rewards required to compensate investors and lenders for the risks which they are assuming.

CRITERIA OF PERFORMANCE EVALUATION

There are many criteria by which performance can be measured. Changes in sales, in profits, or in various measures of output are among the criteria frequently utilized.

No one of these measurements, standing by itself, is useful as a comprehensive measure of enterprise performance. The reasons for this are easy to grasp. Increases in sales are desirable only if they result in increased profits. The same is true of increases in volume of production. Increases in profits, on the other hand, must be related to the capital that is invested in order to attain these profits.

IMPORTANCE OF RETURN ON INVESTMENT (ROI)

The relationship between net income and the capital invested in the generation of that income is one of the most valid and most widely recognized measures of enterprise performance. In relating income to invested capital the ROI measure allows the analyst to compare it to alternative uses of capital as well as to the return realized by enterprises subject to similar degrees of risk. The investment of capital can always yield some return. If capital is invested in government bonds, the return will be relatively low because of the small risk involved. Riskier investments require higher returns in order to make them worthwhile. The ROI measure relates income (reward) to the size of the capital that was needed to generate it.

MAJOR OBJECTIVES IN THE USE OF ROI

Economic performance is the first and foremost purpose of business enterprise. It is, indeed, the reason for its existence. The effectiveness of operating performance determines the ability of the enterprise to survive financially, to attract suppliers of funds, and to reward them adequately. ROI is the prime measure of economic performance. The analyst uses it as a tool in two areas of great importance:

1. An indicator of managerial effectiveness.
2. A method of projecting earnings.

An indicator of managerial effectiveness

The earning of an adequate or superior return on funds invested in an enterprise depends first and foremost on the resourcefulness, skill, ingenuity, and motivation of management. Thus, the longer term ROI is of great interest and importance to the financial analyst because it offers a prime means of evaluating this indispensible criterion of business success: the quality of management.

A method of projecting earnings

A second important function served by the ROI measure is that of a means of earnings projection. The advantage of this method of earnings projection is that it links the amount of earnings which it is estimated an enterprise will earn to the total invested capital. This adds discipline and realism to the projection process, which applies to the present and expected capital investment the return which is expected to be realized on it. The latter will usually be based on the historical and incremental rates of return actually earned by the enterprise, and adjusted by projected changes, as well as on expected returns on new projects.

The rate of ROI method of earning projection can be used by the analyst as either the primary method of earnings projection or as a supplementary check on estimates derived from other projection methods.

Internal decision and control tool

While our focus here is on the work of the external financial analyst, mention should be made of the very important role which ROI measures play in the individual investment decisions of an enterprise as well as in the planning, budgeting, coordination, evaluation, and control of business operations and results.

It is obvious that the final return achieved in any one period on the total investment of an enterprise is composed of the returns (and losses) realized by the various segments and divisions of which it is composed. In turn, these returns are made up of the results achieved by individual product lines, projects, and so forth.

The well-managed enterprise exercises rigorous control over the returns achieved by each of its "profit centers" and rewards its managers on the basis of such results. Moreover, in evaluating the advisability of new investments of funds in assets or projects, management will compute the estimated returns it expects to achieve from them and use these estimates as a basis for its decision.

BASIC ELEMENTS OF ROI

The basic concept of ROI is relatively simple to understand. However, care must be used in determining the elements entering its computation because there exist a variety of views, which reflect different objectives, of how these elements should be defined.

The basic formula for computing ROI is as follows:

$$\frac{\text{Income}}{\text{Investment}}$$

We shall now examine the various definitions of "investment" and of the related "income."

Defining the investment base

There is no one generally accepted measure of capital investment on which the rate of return is computed. The different concepts of investment reflect different objectives. Since the term "return on investment (ROI)" covers a multitude of concepts of investment base and income, there is need for more specific terms to describe the actual investment base used.

Total assets. Return on total assets is perhaps the best measure of the *operating efficiency* of an enterprise. It measures the return obtained on *all* the assets entrusted to management. By removing from this computation the effect of the method used in financing the assets, the analyst can concentrate on the evaluation or projection of operating performance.

Modified asset bases. For a variety of reasons some ROI computations are based not on total assets but rather on an adjusted amount.

One important category of adjustments relates to "unproductive" assets. In this category assets omitted from the investment base include idle plant, facilities under construction, surplus plant, surplus inventories and surplus cash, intangible assets, and deferred charges. The basic idea behind these exclusions is not to hold management responsible for earning a return on assets which apparently do not earn a return. While this theory may have validity in the use of ROI as an internal management and control tool, it lacks merit when applied as a tool designed to evaluate management effectiveness on an overall basis. Management is entrusted funds by owners and creditors, and it has discretion as to where it wants to invest them. There is no reason for management to hold on to assets which bring no return. If there are reasons for keeping funds invested in such assets, then there is no reason to exclude them from the investment base. If the long-run profitability of an enterprise is benefited by keeping funds invested in assets which have no return or a low return in the interim, then the longer term ROI should reflect such benefits. In conclusion, it can be said that from the point of view of an enterprise evaluation by the external analyst there is rarely any justification to omit assets from the investment base merely because they are not productively employed or do not earn a current return.

The exclusion of intangible assets from the investment base is often due to skepticism regarding their value or their contribution to the earning power of the enterprise. Under generally accepted accounting principles intangibles are carried at cost. However, if the cost exceeds their future utility, they must be written down or else the analyst will at least find an uncertainty exception regarding their carrying value included in the auditor's opinion. The exclusion of intangible assets from the asset (investment) base must be justified on more substantial evidence than a mere lack of understanding of what these assets represent or an unsupported suspicion regarding their value.

Depreciable assets in the investment base. An important difference of opinion prevails with respect to the question of whether depreciable assets should be included in the investment base at original cost or at an amount net of the accumulated allowances for depreciation.

One of the most prominent advocates of the inclusion of fixed assets at gross amount in the investment base, for purposes of computing the return on investment, is the management of E. I. duPont de Nemours and Company which pioneered the use of ROI as an internal management tool.

In a pamphlet describing the company's use of the ROI method in the appraisal of operating performance, this point of view is expressed as follows:

Calculation of return on investment. Return on investment as presented in the chart series is based upon *gross* operating investment and earnings *net* of depreciation.

Gross operating investment represents all the plant, tools, equipment and working capital made available to operating management for its use; no deduction is made for current or other liabilities or for the reserve for depreciation. Since plant facilities are maintained in virtually top productive order during their working life, the depreciation reserve being considered primarily to provide for obsolescence, it would be inappropriate to consider that operating management was responsible for earning a return on only the net operating investment. Furthermore, if depreciable assets were stated at net depreciated values, earnings in each succeeding period would be related to an ever-decreasing investment; even with stable earnings, Return on Investment would continually rise, so that comparative Return on Investment ratios would fail to reveal the extent of trend of management performance. Relating earnings to investment that is stable and uniformly compiled provides a sound basis for comparing the "profitability of assets employed" as between years and between investments.

In the case of any commitment of capital—e.g., an investment in a security—it is the expectation that in addition to producing earnings while committed, the principal will eventually be recovered. Likewise, in the case of funds invested in a project, it is expected that in addition to the return earned while invested, the working capital will be recovered through liquidation at the end of the project's useful life and the plant investment will be recovered through depreciation accruals. Since earnings must allow for this recovery of plant investment, they are stated net of depreciation.[1]

It is not difficult to take issue with the above reasoning. It must, however, be borne in mind that the duPont system is designed for use in the internal control of separate productive units as well as for the control of operating management. Our point of view here is, however, that of evaluating the operating performance of an enterprise taken as a whole. While the recovery of capital out of sales and revenues (via depreciation), by an enterprise operating at a profit, can be disregarded in the evaluation of a *single* division or segment, it cannot be disregarded for an enterprise taken as a whole because such recovery is reinvested somewhere within that enterprise even if it is not reinvested in the particular segment which gave rise to the depreciation and which is evaluated for internal purposes. Thus, for an enterprise taken as a whole, the "net of depreciation" asset base is a more valid measure of investment on which a return is computed. This is so for the reasons given above and also because the income which is usually related to the investment base is net of the depreciation expense.

The tendency of the rate of return to rise as assets are depreciated is offset by the retention of capital recovered by means of depreciation, on which capital a return must also be earned. Moreover, maintenance and repair costs rise as equipment gets older, thus tending to offset the reduction, if any, in the asset base.

Among other reasons advanced in support of the use of fixed assets at their gross amount is the argument that the higher amounts are designed to compensate for the effects of inflation on assets expressed in terms of historical cost. Price level adjustments can validly be made only within the framework of a complete restatement of all elements of the financial statements. Crude "adjustments," such as using the gross asset amount, are apt to be misleading and are generally worse than no adjustments at all.

Long-term liabilities plus equity capital. The use of long-term liabilities plus equity capital as the investment base differs from the "total assets" base only in that current liabilities are excluded as suppliers of funds on which the return is computed. The focus here is on the two major suppliers of longer term funds, that is, long-term creditors and equity shareholders.

---

[1] American Management Association, *Executive Committee Control Charts*, AMA Management Bulletin No. 6, 1960, p. 22.

Shareholders' equity.   The computation of return on shareholders' equity measures the return accruing to the owners' capital. As was seen in the discussion of financial leverage in Chapter 4, this return reflects the effect of the employment of debt capital on the owners' return. Since preferred stock, while in the equity category, is usually nevertheless entitled only to a fixed return, it is also omitted from the calculation of the final return on equity computation.

BOOK VERSUS MARKET VALUES IN THE INVESTMENT BASE

Return on asset calculations are most commonly based on book values appearing in the financial statements rather than on market or fair values which are, in most cases, analytically more significant and relevant. Also, quite often, a return is earned by enterprises on assets which either do not appear in the financial statements or are significantly understated therein. Examples of such assets are intangibles such as patents, trademarks, expensed research and development costs, advertising and training costs, and so forth. Other excluded assets may include leaseholds and the value of natural resources discovered.

There exists a trend toward fair value accounting and information on the replacement cost of assets of large corporations is already available. In the interim one alternative to the use of such sketchy data is to rely on the valuation which the market places the equity securities of the enterprise in order to approximate fair values. Thus we can substitute the market value of equity securities and debt for the book value of total assets in computing a proper investment base.

Difference between investor's cost and enterprise investment base

For purposes of computing the ROI, a distinction must be drawn between the investment base of an enterprise and that of an investor. The investor's investment base is, of course, the price he paid for his equity securities. Except for those cases in which he acquired such securities at book value, his investment base is going to differ from that of the company in which he has invested. In general, the focus in ROI computations is on the return realized by the enterprise rather than the return realized on the investment cost of any one shareholder.

Averaging the investment base

Regardless of the method used in arriving at the investment base, the return achieved over a period of time is always associated with the investment base that was, on average, actually available to the enterprise over that period of time. Thus, unless the investment base did not change significantly during the period, it will be necessary to average it. The most common method of averaging for the external analyst is that of adding the investment base at the beginning of the year to that at the end of the year and dividing their total by two. A more accurate method of averaging, where the data is available, is to average by month-end balances, that is, adding the month-end investment bases and dividing the total by 12.

Relating income to the investment base

In the computation of ROI, the definition of return (income) is dependent on the definition of the investment base.

If the investment base is defined as comprising total assets, then income *before* interest expense is used. The exclusion of interest from income deductions is due to its being regarded as a payment for the use of money to the suppliers of debt capital in the same way that dividends are regarded as a reward to suppliers of equity capital. Income, before deductions for interest or dividends, is used when it is related to total assets or to long-term debt plus equity capital.

When the return on the equity capital is computed, net income after deductions for interest and preferred dividends is used. If the preferred dividends are cumulative, they are deducted in arriving at the balance of earnings accruing to the common stock, whether these dividends were declared or not.

The final ROI must always reflect all applicable costs and expenses and that includes income taxes. Some computations of ROI nevertheless omit deductions of income taxes. One reason for this practice is the desire to isolate the effects of tax management from those of operating performance. Another reason is that changes in tax rates affect comparability over the years. Moreover, companies which have tax loss carry-forwards find that the deduction of taxes from income adds confusion and complications to the ROI computations.

It must, however, be borne in mind that income taxes reduce the final return and that they must be taken into consideration particularly when the return on shareholders' equity is computed.

Illustration of ROI computations

The computation of ROI under the various concepts of "investment base" discussed above will now be illustrated by means of the data contained in Exhibits 5–1 and 5–2. The computations are for the year 19X9 and based on figures rounded to the nearest million dollars.

EXHIBIT 5-1

AMERICAN COMPANY
Statement of Income
For Years Ended December 31, 19X8 and 19X9
(in thousands of dollars)

	19X8	19X9
Net sales	$1,636,298	$1,723,729
Costs and expenses	1,473,293	1,579,401
Operating income	$ 163,005	$ 144,328
Other income net.........................	2,971	1,784
	$ 165,976	$ 146,112
Interest expense*	16,310	20,382
Provision for federal and other taxes		
on income	71,770	61,16⌊
Net income	$ 77,896	$ 64,569
Less dividends:		
Preferred stock	2,908	2,908
Common stock	39,209	38,898
	$ 42,117	$ 41,806
Net income reinvested in the business	$ 35,779	$ 22,763

* All assumed to be on long-term debt.

Return on total assets

$$\frac{\text{Net Income} + \text{Interest}}{\text{Total Assets}}$$

$$\frac{65 + 20}{1,372} = 6.2\%$$

Two refinements are possible in this computation and become necessary if their use would make a significant difference in the result.

One refinement recognizes that the year-end total asset figure may be different from the average amount of assets employed during the year. This calls for adding the total assets at the beginning and end of the year and dividing by two.

The second refinement recognizes that interest is a tax-deductible expense and that if the interest cost is excluded the related tax benefit must also be excluded from income. If we assume the average tax rate[2] to be 50 percent that means that we add back only *half* the interest cost.

Reflecting these two refinements the formula becomes:

$$\frac{\text{Net Income} + \text{Interest Expense} \times (1 - \text{Tax Rate})}{(\text{Beginning Total Assets} + \text{Ending Total Assets}) \div 2}$$

---

[2] As was already argued in Chapter 4, the incremental (marginal) tax rate, rather than the average effective tax rate of the enterprise may be the appropriate rate to use.

EXHIBIT 5–2

AMERICAN COMPANY
Statements of Financial Position
As at December 31, 19X8 and 19X9
(in thousands of dollars)

	19X8	19X9
Assets		
Current Assets:		
Cash	$ 25,425	$ 25,580
Eurodollar time deposits and temporary cash investments	38,008	28,910
Accounts and notes receivable—net	163,870	176,911
Inventories	264,882	277,795
Total Current Assets	$ 492,185	$ 509,196
Investments in and receivables from nonconsolidated subsidiaries	33,728	41,652
Miscellaneous investments and receivables	5,931	6,997
Funds held by trustee for construction	6,110	
Land, buildings, equipment, and timberlands—net	773,361	790,774
Deferred charges to future operations	16,117	16,452
Goodwill and other intangible assets	6,550	6,550
Total Assets	$1,333,982	$1,371,621
Liabilities		
Current Liabilities:		
Notes payable to banks—principally Eurodollar	$ 7,850	$ 13,734
Accounts payable and accrued expenses	128,258	144,999
Dividends payable	10,404	10,483
Federal and other taxes on income	24,370	13,256
Long-term indebtedness payable within one year	9,853	11,606
Total Current Liabilities	$ 180,735	$ 194,078
Long-term indebtedness	350,565	335,945
Deferred taxes on income	86,781	101,143
Total Liabilities	$ 618,081	$ 631,166
Capital		
Preferred, 7% cumulative and noncallable, par value $25 per share; authorized 1,760,000 shares	$ 41,538	$ 41,538
Common, par value $12.50 per share; authorized 30,000,000 shares	222,245	222,796
Capital in excess of par value	19,208	20,448
Earnings reinvested in the business	436,752	459,515
Less: Common treasury stock	(3,842)	(3,842)
Total Capital	$ 715,901	$ 740,455
Total Liabilities and Capital	$1,333,982	$1,371,621

Using the data in Exhibits 5–1 and 5–2,

$$\frac{65 + 20(1 - 0.5)}{(1,334 + 1,372) \div 2} = 5.5\%$$

Since the return on total assets shown by the refined method differs significantly from the uncorrected method, the use of the refined method, which is the theoretically correct one, is indicated.

Return on modified asset bases. Since our discussion earlier in the chapter came to the conclusion that in normal circumstances most of the modifications in the amount of total assets are not logically warranted, no illustrations of such computation will be given.

Return on long-term liabilities plus equity capital

$$\frac{\text{Net Income} + \text{Interest Expense*} \times (1 - \text{Tax Rate})}{\text{Average Long-Term Liabilities plus Equity Capital}}$$

Using the data in Exhibits 5–1 and 5–2:

$$\frac{65 + (20 \times 0.5)}{(437 + 716 + 437 + 740) \div 2} = 6.4\%$$

* On long-term debt.

It should be noted that deferred taxes on income are included among the long-term liabilities. In the computation of return on long-term liabilities and equity capital, the question of how to classify deferred taxes does not really present a problem because after careful consideration of the circumstances giving rise to the deferrals, the analyst will decide whether they are to be considered as either debt or equity. In this computation both debt and equity are aggregated anyway. The problem of classification becomes more real in computing the return on shareholders' equity. In the examples which follow we assume circumstances where deferred taxes are considered to be more in the nature of a long-term liability than of an equity nature.

Return on stockholders' equity. The basic computation of return on the equity excludes from the investment base all but the common stockholders' equity.

$$\frac{\text{Net Income} - \text{Preferred Dividends}}{\text{Average Common Stockholders' Equity}}$$

Using data in Exhibits 5–1 and 5–2:

$$\frac{65 - 3}{(674 + 699) \div 2} = 9 \text{ percent}$$

The higher return on shareholders' equity as compared to the return on total assets reflects the positive workings of financial leverage.

Should it be desired, for whatever reason, to compute the return on total stockholders' equity, the investment base would include the preferred shareholders' equity, while net income would not reflect a deduction for preferred dividends. The formula[3] would then be:

$$\frac{\text{Net Income}}{\text{Average Total Shareholders' Equity (common and preferred)}}$$

Where convertible debt sells at a substantial premium above par and is clearly held by investors for its conversion feature, there is justification for treating it as the equivalent of equity capital. This is particularly true when the company can choose at any time to force conversion of the debt by calling it.

Analysis and interpretation of ROI

Earlier in the chapter we mentioned that ROI analysis is particularly useful to the analyst in the areas of evaluation of managerial effectiveness, enterprise profitability, and as an important tool of earnings projection.

Both the evaluation of management and the projection of earnings by means of ROI analysis are complex processes requiring thorough analysis. The reason for this is that the ROI computation usually includes components of considerable complexity.

Components of the ROI ratio. If we focus first on return on total assets we know that the primary formula for computing this return 's:

$$\frac{\text{Net Income} + \text{Interest } (1 - \text{Tax Rate})}{\text{Average Total Assets}}$$

For purposes of our discussion and analysis let us look at this computation in a simplified form:

$$\frac{\text{Net Income}}{\text{Total Assets}}$$

Since sales are a most important yardstick in relation to which profitability is measured and are, as well, a major index of activity, we can recast the above formula as follows:

$$\frac{\text{Net Income}}{\text{Sales}} \times \frac{\text{Sales}}{\text{Total Assets}}$$

The relationship of net income to sales measures operating performance and profitability. The relationship of sales to total assets is a

---

[3] The return on common stockholders equity may also be computed thus:

$$\frac{\text{Earnings per Share}}{\text{Book Value per Share}}$$

but the results will often not be identical because the earnings per share computation includes adjustments for common stock equivalents, etc.

measure of asset utilization or turnover, a means of determining how effectively (in terms of sales generation) the assets are utilized. It can be readily seen that both factors, profitability as well as asset utilization, determine the return realized on a given investment in assets.

Profitability and asset utilization are, in turn, complex ratios which normally require thorough and detailed analysis before they can be used to reach conclusions regarding the reasons for changes in the return on total assets.

Exhibit 5–3 presents the major factors which influence the final return on total assets. In the next section we shall be concerned with the interaction of profitability (net income/sales) and of asset utilization or turnover (sales/total assets) which, in Exhibit 5–3 is regarded as the first level of analysis of the return on total assets. As can be seen from Exhibit 5–3, the many important and complex factors which, in turn, determine profitability and asset utilization represent a second level of analysis of the return on total assets. Chapters 6 and 7 will take up the analysis of results of operations, and Chapter 8 will deal with the evaluation and projection of earnings. The analysis of asset utilization will be discussed in subsequent sections of this chapter.

EXHIBIT 5–3

Levels of analysis ▷

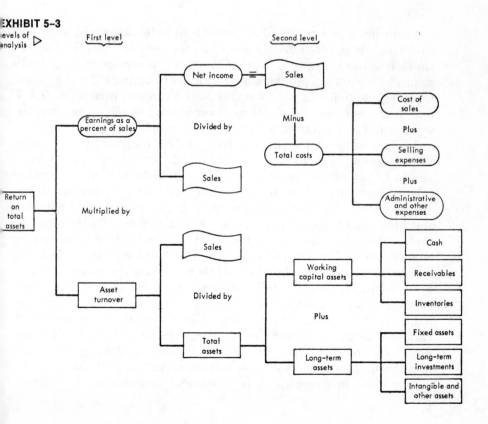

Relationship between profitability and asset turnover. The relationship between return on total assets, profitability, and capital turnover (utilization) is illustrated in Exhibit 5–4, which indicates that when we multiply profitability (expressed as a percentage) by asset utilization (expressed as a turnover) we obtain the return on total assets (expressed as a percentage relationship).

EXHIBIT 5–4
Analysis of return on total assets

	Company X	Company Y	Company Z
1. Sales	$5,000,000	$10,000,000	$10,000,000
2. Net income	500,000	500,000	100,000
3. Total assets	5,000,000	5,000,000	1,000,000
4. Profit as % of sales $\left(\frac{2}{1}\right)$	10%	5%	1%
5. Asset turnover $\left(\frac{1}{3}\right)$	1	2	10
Return on total assets (4 × 5)	10%	10%	10%

Company X realizes its 10 percent return on total assets by means of a relatively high profit margin and a low turnover of assets. The opposite is true of Company Z, while Company Y achieves its 10 percent return by means of a profit margin half that of Company X and an asset turnover rate twice that of Company X. It is obvious from Exhibit 5–4 that there are many combinations of profit margins and turnover rates which can yield a return on assets of 10 percent.

In fact, as can be seen from Exhibit 5–5, there exist an infinite variety of combinations of profit margin and asset turnover rates which yield a 10 percent return on assets. The chart in the exhibit graphically relates asset turnover (vertical axis) to profitability (horizontal axis).

The curve, sloping from the upper left area of low profit margins and high asset turnover rates, traces out the endless combinations of profitability and asset turnover rates which yield a 10 percent return on total assets. The data of Companies X and Y (from Exhibit 5–4) are represented by dots on the graph, while the data of Company Z cannot be fitted on it since the full curve has not been shown. The other lettered dots represent the profit-turnover combination of other companies within a particular industry. This clustering of the results of various companies around the 10 percent return on assets slope is a useful way of comparing the returns of many enterprises within an industry and the major two elements which comprise them.

The chart in Exhibit 5–5 is also useful in assessing the relative

EXHIBIT 5–5

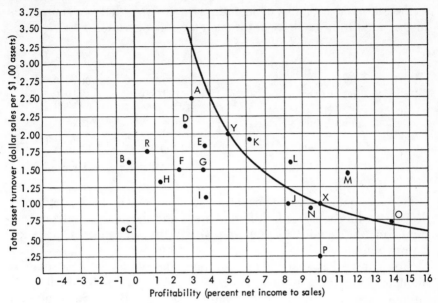

courses of action open to different enterprises which want to improve their respective returns on investments.

Companies B and C must, of course, restore profitability before the turnover rate becomes a factor of importance. Assuming that all the companies represented in Exhibit 5–5 belong to the same industry and that there is an average representative level of profitability and turnover in it, Company P will be best advised to pay first and particular attention to improvement in its turnover ratio, while Company R should pay foremost attention to the improvement of its profit margin. Other companies, such as Company I, would best concentrate on both the turnover and the profit margin aspects of ROI improvement.

While the above analysis treats profitability and turnover as two independent variables, they are, in fact, interdependent. As will be seen from the discussion of break-even analysis in Chapter 7, a higher level of activity (turnover), when fixed expenses are substantial, will tend to increase the profit margin because, within a certain range of activity, costs increase proportionally less than sales. In comparing two companies within an industry the analyst, in evaluating the one having the lower asset turnover, will make allowance for the potential increase in profitability that can be associated with a projected increase in turnover that is based primarily on an expansion of sales.

Analysis of return on total assets can reveal the weaknesses as well as the potential strengths of an enterprise. Assume that two companies in the same industry have returns on total assets as follows:

		Company A	Company B
1.	Sales	$ 1,000,000	$20,000,000
2.	Net income	100,000	100,000
3.	Total assets	10,000,000	10,000,000
4.	Profitability $\left(\frac{2}{1}\right)$	10%	0.5%
5.	Turnover of assets $\left(\frac{1}{3}\right)$	0.1 times	2 timés
	Return on investment (4×5)	1%	1%

Both companies have poor returns on total assets. However, remedial action for them lies in different areas and the analyst will concentrate on the evaluation of the feasibility of success of such improvement.

Company A has a 10 percent profit on sales which, let us assume, is about average for the industry. However, each dollar invested in assets supports only 10 cents in sales whereas Company B gets $2 of sales for each dollar invested in its assets. The analyst's attention will naturally be focused on Company A's investment in assets. Why is its turnover so low? Are there excess assets which yield little or no return or are there idle assets which should be disposed of? Or, as often is the case, are the assets inefficiently or uneconomically utilized? Quite obviously, Company A can achieve more immediate and significant improvements by concentrating on improving turnover (by increasing sales, reducing investment, or both) than by striving to increase the profit margin beyond the industry average.

The opposite situation prevails with respect to Company B where attention should first be focused on the reasons for the low profit margin and to the improvement of it as the most likely avenue of success in increasing ROI. The reasons for low profitability can be many, including inefficient equipment and production methods, unprofitable product lines, excess capacity with attendant high fixed costs, excessive selling or administrative costs, etc.

The company with the low profitability may discover that changes in tastes and in technology have resulted in an increased investment in assets being needed to finance a dollar of sales. This means that in order to maintain its return on assets the company must increase its profit margin or else production of the product is no longer worthwhile.

There is a tendency to regard a high profit margin as a sign of high earnings quality. This view was rebutted by W. M. Bennett who pointed out the importance of return on capital as the ultimate test of profitability.[4] He presented the following table comparing during a given year the similar profit margins of five companies with their respective returns on capital:

	Profit margin as % of sales	Profit as % of capital
Whirlpool	5.3%	17.1%
Com Products	5.9	12.0
Goodyear	5.5	9.6
U.S. Plywood	5.5	8.0
Distillers Seagram	5.0	6.7

It is evident that in the case of these five companies, which have similar profit margins, the rate of capital turnover made the difference in the return on capital performance, and this must be taken into account by the analyst. Thus, a supermarket chain will be content with a net profit margin of 1 percent or less because it has a high rate of turnover due to a relatively low investment in assets and a high proportion of leased assets (such as stores and fixtures). Similarly, a discount store will accept a low profit margin in order to obtain a high rate of asset turnover (primarily of inventories). On the other hand, capital intensive industries such as steels, chemicals, and autos, which have heavy investments in assets and resulting low asset turnover rates, must achieve high net profit margins in order to offer investors a reasonable return on capital.

ANALYSIS OF ASSET UTILIZATION

As is graphically illustrated in Exhibit 5–3, the return on total assets depends on (1) getting the largest profit out of each dollar of sales and (2) obtaining the highest possible amount of sales per dollar of invested capital (net assets).

The intensity with which assets are utilized is measured by means of asset turnover ratios. That utilization has as its ultimate measure the amount of sales generated since sales are in most enterprises the first and essential step to profits. In certain special cases, such as with enterprises in developmental stages, the meaning of turnover may have to be modified in recognition of the fact that most assets are committed to the development of future potential. Similarly, abnormal supply problems and strikes are conditions which will affect the state of capital utilization and, as such, will require separate evaluation and interpretation.

[4] William M. Bennett, "Capital Turnover vs. Profit Margins," *Financial Analysts Journal*, March–April 1966, pp. 88–95.

Evaluation of individual turnover ratios

Changes in the basic turnover ratio which enters the determination of the ROI calculation, that is,

$$\frac{\text{Sales}}{\text{Total Assets}}$$

can be evaluated meaningfully only by an analysis of changes in the turnover rates of individual asset categories and groups which comprise the total assets.

Sales to cash. As was seen in the discussion in Chapter 2, cash and cash equivalents are held primarily for purposes of meeting the needs of day-to-day transactions as well as a liquidity reserve designed to prevent the shortages which may arise from an imbalance in cash inflows and outflows. In any type of business there is a certain logical relationship between sales and the cash level that must be maintained to support it.

Too high a rate of turnover of cash may be due to a cash shortage which can ultimately result in a liquidity crisis if the enterprise has no other ready sources of funds available to it.

Too low a rate of turnover may be due to the holding of idle and unnecessary cash balances. Cash accumulated for specific purposes or known contingencies may result in temporary decreases in the rate of turnover.

The basic trade-off here is between liquidity and the tying up of funds which yield no return or a very modest return.

Sales to receivables. Any organization which sells on credit will find that the level of its receivables is a function of sales. A relatively low rate of turnover here is, among other reasons, likely to be due to an overextension of credit, to an inability of customers to pay, or to a poor collection job.

A relatively high rate of turnover may indicate a strict credit extension policy or a reluctance or inability to extend credit. Determining the rate of turnover here is the trade-off between sales and the tying up of funds in receivables.

Sales to inventories. The maintenance of a given level of sales generally requires a given level of inventories. This relationship will vary from industry to industry depending on the variety of types, models, colors, sizes, and other classes of varieties of items which must be kept in order to attract and keep customers. The length of the production cycle as well as the type of item (e.g., luxury versus necessity;

perishable versus durable) has a bearing on the rate of turnover. A slow rate of turnover indicates 'the existence of problems such as overstocking, slow-moving or obsolete inventories, overestimating of sales or a lack of balance in the inventory. Temporary problems such as strikes at important customers may also be responsible for this.

A higher than normal rate of turnover may mean an underinvestment in inventory which can result in lack of proper customer service and in loss of sales.

In this case the trade-off is between tying up funds in inventory, on one hand, and sacrificing customer service and sales on the other.

Sales to fixed assets. While the relationship between property, plant, and equipment and sales is a logical one on a long-term basis, there are many short-term and temporary factors which may upset this relationship. Among these factors are conditions of excess capacity, inefficient or obsolete equipment, multishift operations, temporary changes in demand, and interruptions in the supply of raw materials and parts.

It must also be remembered that increases in plant capacity are not gradual but occur, instead, in lumps. This too can create temporary and medium-term changes in the turnover rates. Often, leased facilities and equipment, which do not appear on the balance sheet, will distort the relationship between sales and fixed assets.

The trade-off here is between investment in fixed assets with a correspondingly higher break-even point on one hand, and efficiency, productive capacity, and sales potential on the other.

Sales to other assets. In this category we find, among others, such assets as patents and deferred research and development costs. While the direct relationship between these individual categories of assets and current sales levels may not be evident, no assets are held or should be held by an enterprise unless they contribute to sales or to the generation of income. In the case of deferred research and development costs, the investment may represent the potential of future sales. The analyst, must, in his evaluation of rates of asset utilization, allow for such factors.

Sales to short-term liabilities. The relationship between sales and short-term trade liabilities is a predictable one. The amount of short-term credit which an enterprise is able to obtain from suppliers depends on its needs for goods and services, that is, on the level of activity (e.g., sales). Thus, the degree to which it can obtain short-term credit depends also importantly on the level of sales. This short-term credit is relatively cost-free and, in turn, reduces the investment of enterprise funds in working capital.

Use of averages

Whenever the level of a given asset category changes significantly during the period for which the turnover is computed, it is necessary to use averages of asset levels in the computation. The computation then becomes

$$\frac{\text{Sales}}{(\text{Asset at beginning of period} + \text{Asset at end of period}) \div 2}$$

To the extent that data is available and the variation in asset levels during the period warrants it, the average can be computed on a monthly or quarterly basis.

Other factors to be considered in return on asset evaluation

The evaluation of the return on assets involves many factors of great complexity. As will be seen from the discussion in Chapter 8, the inclusion of extraordinary gains and losses in single period and average net income must be evaluated. The effects of price level changes on ROI calculations must also be taken into account by the analyst.

In analyzing the trend of return on assets over the years, the effect of acquisitions accounted for as poolings of interest must be isolated and their chance of recurrence evaluated.

The external analyst will not usually be able to obtain data on ROI by segments, product lines, or divisions of an enterprise. However, where his bargaining power or position allows him to obtain such data, they can make a significant contribution to the accuracy and reliability of his analysis.

A consistently high return on assets is the earmark of an effective management and can distinguish a growth company from one experiencing merely a cyclical or seasonal pickup in business.

An examination of the factors which comprise the return on assets will usually reveal the limitations to which their expansion is subject. Neither the profit margin nor the asset turnover rate can expand indefinitely. Thus, an expanding asset base via external financing and/or internal earnings retention will be necessary for further earnings growth.

Equity growth rate

The equity growth rate by means of earnings retention can be calculated as follows:

$$\frac{\text{Net Income} - \text{Dividend Payout}}{\text{Common Shareholders' Equity}} = \text{Percent Increase in Common Equity}$$

This is the growth rate due to the retention of earnings. It indicates the possibilities of earnings growth without resort to external financing. These increased funds, in turn, will earn the rate of return which the enterprise can obtain on its assets and thus contribute to growth in earnings.

Return on shareholders' equity

Up to now we have examined the factors affecting the return on total assets. However, of great interest to the owner group of an enterprise is the return on the stockholders' equity. The rate of return on total assets and that on the stockholders' equity differs because a portion of the capital with which the assets are financed is usually supplied by creditors who receive a fixed return on their capital or, in some cases, no return at all. Similarly, the preferred stock usually receives a fixed dividend. These fixed returns differ from the rate earned on the assets (funds) which they provide, and this accounts for the difference in returns on assets and those of stockholders' equity. This is the concept of financial leverage which was already discussed at length in Chapter 4.

Equity turnover

The computation of the return on shareholders' equity is composed of the following two major elements:

$$\frac{\text{Net Income}}{\text{Sales}} \times \frac{\text{Sales}}{\text{Average Shareholders' Equity}}$$

The equity turnover (sales/average shareholder's equity) can be further analyzed by breaking it down into two elements:

$$\frac{\text{Sales}}{\text{Net Operating Assets}} \times \frac{\text{Net Operating Assets}}{\text{Average Shareholders' Equity}}$$

The first factor measures asset utilization which we have discussed earlier in the chapter. The second factor is a measure of the use of financial leverage by the enterprise. The more an enterprise uses borrowed funds to finance its assets the higher this ratio will be.

Measuring the financial leverage index

The financial leverage index, as we already saw in Chapter 4, can be measured as follows:

$$\frac{\text{Return on Equity}}{\text{Return on Total Assets}} = \frac{\text{Assets}}{\text{Equity}}$$
$$\times \frac{\text{Net Income}}{\text{Net Income} + \text{Interest}\,(1 - \text{Tax Rate})}$$

The formula for return on total assets

$$\frac{\text{Net Income} + \text{Interest}\,(1 - \text{Tax Rate})}{\text{Total Assets}}$$

can be converted to a return on stockholders' equity formula by multiplying it by the financial leverage index.

$$\frac{\text{Net Income} + \text{Interest}\,(1 - \text{Tax Rate})}{\text{Total Assets}} \times (\text{Financial leverage index})$$

In the discussion that follows, the leverage index for American Company, based on the data of Exhibits 5–1 and 5–2 in this chapter, is as follows:

$$\frac{\text{Return on Stockholders' Equity}}{\text{Return on Total Assets}} = \frac{8.8\%}{5.47\%} = 1.61$$

A financial leverage index greater than 1 is positive, that is, it indicates that the use of borrowed and other noncommon equity funds increases the common stockholders' return. A leverage index below 1 has the opposite effect.

Analysis of financial leverage effects

The effect which each noncommon equity capital source has on the return on the common equity can be analysed in detail. Using the data of American Company which was included in Exhibits 5–1 and 5–2, earlier in this chapter we can undertake such an analysis as follows:

An analysis of the American Company balance sheet as at 12/31/X9 discloses the following major sources of funds (in thousands):

Current liabilities (exclusive of current portion of long-term debt)		$ 182,472
Long-term debt	$335,945	
Current portion	11,606	347,551
Deferred taxes		101,143
Preferred stock		41,538
Common stockholders' equity		698,917
Total Investment or Total Assets		$1,371,621

The income statement for 19X9 includes (in thousands):

Income before taxes	$ 125,730
Income (and other) taxes	61,161*
Net income	$ 64,569
Preferred dividends	2,908
Income accruing to common shareholders	$ 61,661
Total Interest Expense	$ 20,382
Assumed interest on short-term notes (5%)	687
Balance of interest on long-term debt	$ 19,695

* Average tax rate of 49%.

The return on total assets is computed as follows:

$$\frac{\text{Net Income} + \text{Interest } (1 - \text{Tax Rate})}{\text{Total Assets}}$$

$$= \frac{64,569 + 20,382 \ (1 - 0.49)}{1,371,621} = 5.47\%$$

The 5.47 percent return represents the average return on all assets employed by the company. To the extent that suppliers of capital other than the common stockholders get a lower reward than an average of 5.47 percent the common equity benefits by the difference. The opposite is true when the suppliers of capital receive more than a 5.47 percent reward in 19X9.

Exhibit 5–6 presents an analysis showing the relative contribution and reward of each of the major suppliers of funds and their effect on the returns earned by the common stockholders.

EXHIBIT 5–6

Analysis of composition of return on shareholders' equity (slide rule accuracy computations in thousands of dollars)

Category of fund supplier	Fund supplied	Earnings on fund supplied at rate of 5.47%	Payment to suppliers of funds	Accruing to (detracting from) return on common stock
Current liabilities	182,472	9,981	350 (1)	9,631
Long-term debt	347,551	19,011	10,044 (2)	8,967
Deferred taxes	101,143	5,533	None	5,533
Preferred stock	41,538	2,272	2,908 (3)	(636)
Earnings in excess of compensation to suppliers of funds				23,495
Add: Common stockholder's equity	698,917	38,231	—	38,231
Totals	1,371,621	75,028 (4)	13,302	
Total income (return) on stockholders' equity				61,726 (4)

(1) Interest cost of $687 less 49% tax.
(2) Interest cost of $19,695 less 49% tax.
(3) Preferred dividends—not tax deductible.
(4) Slight differences with statement figures are due to rounding.

As can be seen from Exhibit 5–6 the $9,631,000 accruing to the common equity from use of current liabilities is largely due to its being free of interest costs. The advantage of $8,967,000 accruing from the use of long-term debt is substantially due to the tax deductability of interest. Since the preferred dividends are not tax deductible, the unimpressive return on total assets of 5.45 percent resulted in a disadvantage to the common equity of $636,000. The value of tax deferrals can be clearly seen in this case where the use of cost-free funds amounted to an annual advantage of $5,533,000.

We can now carry this analysis further (all dollar amounts in thousands):

The return on the common stockholder equity is as follows:

$$\frac{\text{Net Income less Preferred Dividends}}{\text{Common Stockholders' Equity}} = \frac{61,661^5}{698,917} = 8.8\%$$

The net advantage which the common equity reaped from the working of financial leverage (Exhibit 5–6) is $23,495.

As a percentage of the common stockholders' equity, this advantage is computed as follows:

$$\frac{\begin{array}{c}\text{Earnings in excess of compensation}\\ \text{to outside suppliers of funds}\end{array}}{\text{Common Stockholders' Equity}} = \frac{\$23,495}{\$698,917} = 3.36\%$$

The return on common stockholders' equity can now be viewed as being composed as follows:

Return on assets	5.47%
Leverage advantage accruing to common equity	3.36
Return on common equity	8.8%

QUESTIONS

1. Why is "return on investment (ROI)" one of the most valid measures of enterprise performance? How is this measure used by the financial analyst?
2. How is ROI used as an internal management tool?
3. Discuss the validity of excluding "nonproductive" assets from the asset base used in the computation of ROI. Under what circumstances is the exclusion of intangible assets from the asset base warranted?
4. Why is interest added back to net income when the ROI is computed on total assets?
5. Under what circumstances may it be proper to consider convertible debt as equity capital in the computation of ROI?

[5] Ties in (except for rounding difference) with total income accruing to common stockholders in Exhibit 5–6.

6. Why must the net income figure used in the computation of ROI be adjusted to reflect the asset base (denominator) used in the computation?

7. What is the relationship between ROI and sales?

8. Company A acquired Company B because the latter had a record of profitability (net income to sales ratio) exceeding that of its industry. After the acquisition took place a major stockholder complained that the acquisition resulted in a low return on investment. Discuss the possible reasons for his complaint.

9. Company X's profitability is 2 percent of sales. Company Y has a turnover of assets of 12. Both companies have ROIs of 6 percent which is considered unsatisfactory by industry standards. What is the asset turnover of Company X and what is the profitability ratio of Company Y? What action would you advise to the managements of the respective companies?

10. What is the purpose of measuring the asset utilization of different asset categories?

11. What factors enter into the evaluation of the ROI measures?

12. How is the equity growth rate computed? What does it signify?

13. How is the "financial leverage index" computed? What is the significance of a financial leverage index reading of 1?

14. a. What is "equity turnover" and how is it related to the rate of return on equity?

   b. "Growth in per share earnings generated from an increase in equity turnover probably cannot be expected to continue indefinitely." Do you agree or disagree? Explain briefly, bringing out in your answer the alternative causes of an increase in equity turnover. (C.F.A.)

6

ANALYSIS OF RESULTS OF OPERATIONS—I

THE SIGNIFICANCE OF INCOME STATEMENT ANALYSIS

The income statement presents in summarized fashion the results of operations of an enterprise. These results, in turn, represent the major reason for the existence of a profit-seeking entity, and they are important determinants of its value and solvency.

Some of the most important decisions in security analysis and credit evaluation are based on an evaluation of the income statements. To the security analyst income is often the single most important determinant of security values, and hence the measurement and the projection of income are among his most important analytical objectives. Similarly, to the credit grantor income and funds or cash provided by operations are the most natural as well as the most desirable source of interest and principal repayment. In almost all other aspects of financial analysis the evaluation and projection of operating results assume great importance.

THE MAJOR OBJECTIVES OF INCOME ANALYSIS

In the evaluation of the income of an enterprise the analyst is particularly interested in an answer to the following questions:

1. What is the relevant net income of the enterprise and what is its quality?
2. What elements in the income statement can be used and relied upon for purposes of earnings forecasting?

3. How stable are the major elements of income and expense and what is their trend?
4. What is the "earning power" of the enterprise?

What is the relevant net income of the enterprise?

Based on the simple proposition that net income is the excess of revenues over costs and expenses during an accounting period, many people, including astute professional analysts, are exasperated at the difficulties they encounter in their search for the "true earnings" or the "real earnings" of an enterprise.

Why, they ask, should it be possible for so many different "acceptable" figures of "net income" to flow out of one set of circumstances? Given the economic events which the enterprise experienced during a given period, is there not only *one* "true" result, and is it not the function of accountancy to identify and measure such result?

The answer to the last question must be "no". In this chapter, dealing with the analysis of income, it is appropriate to summarize *why* this is so.

"Net income" is not a specific quantity. Net income is not a specific flow awaiting the perfection of a flawless meter with which it can be precisely measured. There are a number of reasons for this:

1. The determination of income is dependent on estimates regarding the outcome of future events. This peering into the future is basically a matter of judgment involving the assessment of probabilities based on facts and estimates.

While the judgment of skilled and experienced professionals, working on the basis of identical data and information, can be expected to fall within a narrow range, it will nevertheless *vary* within such a range. The estimates involve the allocation of revenues and costs as between the present and the future. Put another way, they involve the determination of the future utility and usefulness of many categories of unexpired costs and of assets as well as the estimation of future liabilities and obligations.

2. The accounting principles governing the determination and measurement of income at any given time are the result of the cumulative experience of the accounting profession, of regulatory agencies, of businessmen, and others. They reflect a momentary equilibrium which is based partly on knowledge and experience and partly on the compromise of widely differing views on methods of measurement. While the accounting profession has moved to narrow the range of acceptable alternative measurement principles, alternatives nevertheless remain; and their complete elimination in the near future is unlikely.

3.   Beyond the problem of honest differences in estimation and other judgments, as well as of the variety of alternative acceptable principles, is also the problem arising from the diverse ways in which the judgments and principles are applied.

Theoretically, the independent professional accountant should be concerned first and foremost with the fair presentation of the financial statements. He should make accounting a "neutral" science which gives expression and effect to economic events but does not itself affect the results presented. To this end he should choose from among alternative principles those most applicable to the circumstances and should disclose all facts, favorable and adverse, which may affect the user's decision.

In fact, the accounting profession as a whole has not yet reached such a level of independence and detachment of judgment. It is subject to the powerful pressures on the part of managements who have, or at least feel that they have, a vital interest in the way in which results of operations are presented. The auditors are most vulnerable to pressures in those areas of accounting where widely differing alternatives are equally acceptable and where accounting theory is still unsettled. Thus, they may choose the lowest level of acceptable practice rather than that which is most appropriate and fair in the circumstances. Although relatively less frequent, cases of malpractice and collusion in outright deception by independent accountants nevertheless still surface from time to time.

The analyst cannot ignore these possibilities, must be aware of them and be ever alert to them. It calls for constant vigilance in the analysis of audited data, particularly when there is reason to suspect a lack of independence and objectivity in the application of accounting principles.

In addition to the above reasons which are inherent in the accounting process, there exists another reason why there cannot be such a thing as an absolute measure of "real earnings." It is that financial statements are general-purpose presentations designed to serve the diverse needs of many users. Consequently, a single figure of "net income" cannot be relevant to all users, and that means that the analyst must use this figure and the additional information disclosed in the financial statements and elsewhere as a starting point and adjust it so as to arrive at a "net income" figure which meets his particular interests and objectives.

ILLUSTRATION 1.   To the buyer of an income-producing property, the depreciation expense figure which is based on the seller's cost is not relevant. In order to estimate the net income he can derive from such property, depreciation based on the expected purchase price of the property must be substituted.

ILLUSTRATION 2.   To the analyst who exercises independent judgment and uses knowledge of the company he is analyzing and the industry of which it is a part, the reported "net income" marks the start of his analysis. He adjusts the "net income" figure for changes in income and expense items which he judges to be warranted. These may include, for example, estimates of bad debts, of depreciation, and of research costs as well as the treatment of gains and losses which are labeled "extraordinary." Comparisons with other companies may call for similar adjustments so that the data can be rendered comparable.

From the above discussion it should be clear that the determination of *a* figure of "net income" is from the point of view of the analyst secondary to the objective of being able to find in the income statement all the disclosures needed in order to arrive at an income figure which is relevant for the purpose at hand.

The questions regarding the quality of earnings, of what elements in the income statement can be relied on for forecasting purposes, of what the stability and the trend of the earning elements are, and finally, of what the "earning power" of the enterprise is, will all be considered in Chapter 8.

We shall now proceed to examine the specific tools which are useful in the analysis of the various components of the income statement.

ANALYSIS OF COMPONENTS OF THE INCOME STATEMENT

The analysis of the income statements of an enterprise can be conceived as being undertaken at two levels: (1) obtaining an understanding of the accounting principles used and of their implication and (2) using the appropriate tools of income statement analysis.

Accounting principles used and their implication

The analyst must have a thorough understanding of the principles of income, cost, and expense accounting and measurement employed by the enterprise. Moreover, since most assets, with the exception of cash and receivables actually collectible, represent costs deferred to the future, the analyst must have a good understanding of the principles of asset and liability measurements employed by the enterprise so that he can relate them to the income accounting of the enterprise as a means of checking the validity of that accounting. Finally, he must understand and assess the implications which the use of one accounting principle, as opposed to another, has on the measurement of the income of an enterprise and its comparison to that of other enterprises.

Tools of income statement analysis

The second level of analysis consists of applying the appropriate tools of analysis to the components of the income statement and the interpretation of the results shown by these analytical measures. The application of these tools is aimed at achieving the objectives of the analysis of results of operations mentioned earlier, such as the projection of income, the assessment of its stability and quality, and the estimation of earning power.

The remainder of this chapter will be devoted to an examination of these tools and to the interpretation of the results achieved through their use.

THE ANALYSIS OF SALES AND REVENUES

The analysis of sales and revenues is centered on answers to these basic questions:

1. What are the major sources of revenue?
2. How stable are these sources and what is their trend?
3. How is the earning of revenue determined and how is it measured?

Major sources of revenue

Knowledge of major sources of revenues (sales) is important in the analysis of the income statement particularly if the analysis is that of a

EXHIBIT 6–1
Analysis of sales by product line over time

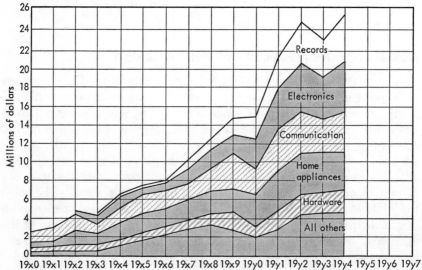

EXHIBIT 6-2

	Year ended				
	Sept. 25, 19X0	Sept. 24, 19X1	Sept. 29, 19X2	Sept. 28, 19X3	Sept. 27, 19X4
Net sales	(dollar amounts in thousands)				
Mining systems equipment	$133,927	$149,673	$157,096	$145,889	$191,345
Industrial and general products	76,971	72,699	67,964	84,806	97,634
Air pollution control equipment	28,391	40,610	62,679	58,702	55,811
Ore processing and petroleum equipment	34,113	37,868	36,062	38,784	51,652
Total	$273,402	$300,850	$323,801	$328,181	$396,442
Income before income taxes and extraordinary items*					
Mining systems equipment	$ 15,869	$ 20,434	$ 19,622	$ 13,301	$ 20,038
Industrial and general products	5,524	2,647	2,304	8,216	9,120
Air pollution control equipment	2,560	3,636	(1,852)	(2,747)	663
Ore processing and petroleum equipment	3,907	4,507	3,610	2,839	5,823
Total	$ 27,860	$ 31,224	$ 23,684	$ 21,609	$ 35,644

* Generally, corporate costs and expenses have been allocated to each of the lines of business on the basis of sales or investment employed depending on the nature of the item.

multimarket enterprise. Each major market or product line may have its own separate and distinct growth pattern, profitability, and future potential.

The best way to analyze the composition of revenues is by means of a common-size statement which shows the percentage of each major class of revenue to the total. This information can also be portrayed graphically on an absolute dollar basis as shown in Exhibit 6–1. With inclusion of an increasing amount of product line information in published financial statements the external analyst will be able to obtain more readily the data necessary for this analysis. Exhibit 6–2 presents an example of disclosure in a prospectus.

FINANCIAL REPORTING BY DIVERSIFIED ENTERPRISES

The user of the financial statements of diversified enterprises faces, in addition to the usual problems and pitfalls of financial analysis, the problem of sorting out and understanding the impact which the different individual segments of the business have on the sum total of reported results of operations and financial condition. The author of an important study in the reporting by diversified companies has defined a conglomerate company as follows:

. . . one which is so managerially decentralized, so lacks operational integration, or has such diversified markets that it may experience rates of profitability, degrees of risk, and opportunities for growth which vary within the company to such an extent that an investor requires information about these variations in order to make informed decisions.[1]

Reasons for the need for data by significant enterprise segments

The above definition suggests some of the most significant reasons why financial analysts require as much information and detailed data as possible about the various segments of an enterprise. The analysis, evaluation, projection, and valuation of earnings requires that these be broken down into categories which share similar characteristics of variability, growth potential, and risk. Similarly, the asset structure and the financing requirements of various segments of an enterprise can vary significantly and thus require separate analysis and evaluation. Thus, the credit grantor may be interested in knowing which segments of an enterprise provide funds and which are net users of funds.

TABLE 6–1
Earnings contribution and growth rates by industry segments

Industry	Earnings contributions (in $000)	Growth rate of earnings contribution over the past 3 years (in %)
Leisure time:		
1. Camp equipment	100	11
2. Fishing equipment	50	2
3. Boats	72	15
4. Sporting goods	12	3
	234	
Agribusiness:		
1. Milk processing	85	2
2. Canning	72	8
3. Chicken farming	12	15
	169	
Education:		
1. Text publishing	40	3
2. Papers and supplies	17	6
	57	
Total	460	

---

[1] R. K. Mautz, "Identification of the Conglomerate Company," *Financial Executive*, July 1967, p. 26.

TABLE 6-2
Segmented earnings contribution matrix

	Growth rate (in %)			
Industry	0–5	5–10	10–15	Total
Leisure time	$ 62	$ 0	$172	$234
Agribusiness	85	72	12	169
Education	40	17	0	57
Total	$187	$89	$184	$460

The composition of an enterprise, the relative size and profitability of its various segments, the ability of management to make profitable acquisitions, and the overall performance of management represents additional important information which the analyst seeks from its segmented data.[2] As will be seen from the discussion in Chapter 8, among the best ways to construct an earnings forecast is to build the projections, to the extent possible, segment by segment.

The evaluation of the growth potential of earnings requires that as much information as possible be obtained about the different product lines or segments which make up the aggregate earnings. Rappaport and Lerner have illustrated the use of a segmented earnings contribution matrix which may prove useful in an assessment of earnings quality and growth potential, as well as in the valuation of aggregate earnings.[3] These are shown in Tables 6–1 and 6–2.

Disclosure of "line of business" data

The degree of informative disclosure about the results of operations and the asset base of segments of a business can vary widely. Full disclosure would call for providing detailed income statements, statements of financial position, and statements of changes in financial position for each significant segment. This is rarely found in practice because of the difficulty of obtaining such breakdowns internally, and also because of management's reluctance to divulge information which could harm the enterprise's competitive position. Short of the disclosure of complete financial statements by business segment, a great variety of partial detail has been suggested.

[2] D. W. Collins in a study of 150 multisegment firms found that "SEC product-line revenue and profit disclosures together with industry sales projections published in various government sources provide significantly more accurate estimates of future total-entity sales and earnings than do those procedures that rely totally on consolidated data." *Journal of Accounting Research*, Spring 1976, pp. 163–77.

[3] A. Rappaport and E. M. Lerner, *A Framework for Financial Reporting by Diversified Companies* (New York: National Association of Accountants, 1969), pp. 18–19.

Income statement data

Revenues only. In most enterprises this should not present great difficulties.

Gross profit. This involves complex problems of interdivisional transfer pricing as well as allocation of indirect overhead costs.

Contribution margin. Contribution margin reporting (see also Chapter 7) is based on assigning to each segment the revenues, costs, and expenses for which that segment is solely responsible. It is a very useful concept in management accounting, but for purposes of public reporting of segment data it presents problems because there are no generally accepted methods of cost allocation and, consequently, they can vary significantly from company to company and even within one enterprise. Disclosure of allocation methods, while helpful, will not remove all the problems facing the user of such data.

Net income (after full cost allocation). The further down the income statement we report by segment, the more pervasive and the more complex the allocation procedures become. Reporting segment net income would require allocating all joint expenses to each specific business activity on some rational basis, even though they may not be directly related to any particular one.

Balance sheet data

A breakdown by segments of assets employed would be needed in an assessment of the efficiency of operations by segment, in the evaluation of segmental management, as well as in the computation of divisional return on investment.

In most companies only certain assets, such as, for example, plant and equipment, inventories, and certain intangibles, are identified directly with a specific segment. An allocation of all assets would have to be arbitrary since in many enterprises cash, temporary investments, and even receivables are centralized at the group or corporate headquarters level.

Research studies

Interest in the subject of reporting by diversified companies has sparked research efforts into the types of disclosures which are necessary and feasible and the problems related thereto.[4] The most exten-

[4] See Morton Backer and Walter B. McFarland, *External Reporting for Segments of a Business* (New York: National Association of Accountants, 1968). Also see Robert T. Sprouse, "Diversified Views about Diversified Companies," *Journal of Accounting Research*, Vol. 7, No. 1 (Spring 1969), pp. 137–59; and A. Rappaport and E. H. Lerner, *A Framework for Financial Reporting by Diversified Companies* (New York: National Association of Accountants, 1969).

sive research effort was that undertaken by Professor R. K. Mautz[5] and in 1974 the FASB published an extensive Discussion Memorandum on the subject.

Statement of Financial Accounting Standards 14

In late 1976, the FASB issued *Statement of Financial Accounting Standards No. 14,* "Financial Reporting for Segments of a Business Enterprise." This *Statement,* which is effective for fiscal years beginning on or after 12/16/76, establishes requirements for disclosures to be made in company financial statements concerning information about operations in different industries, foreign operations, export sales, and major customers.

The *Statement* recognizes that evaluation of risk and return is the central element of investment and lending decisions. Since an enterprise operating in various industry segments or geographic areas may have different rates of profitability, degrees and types of risk and opportunities for growth, disaggregated information will assist analysts in analyzing the uncertainties surrounding the timing and amount of expected cash flows—and hence the risks—related to an investment in or a loan to an enterprise that operates in different industries or areas of the world.

The *Statement* requires companies to report in their financial statements the revenues, operating profit (revenue less operating expenses), and identifiable assets of each significant industry segment of their operations. Certain other related disclosures are required. The *Statement* does not prescribe methods of accounting for transfer pricing or cost allocation. However, it does require that the methods in use be disclosed.

A segment is regarded as significant, therefore reportable, under the *Statement* if its sales, operating profit, or identifiable assets are 10 percent or more of the related combined amounts for all of a company's industry segments.[6] To ensure that the industry segments for which a company reports information represent a substantial portion of the company's overall operations, the *Statement* requires that the

---

[5] R. K. Mautz, *Financial Reporting by Diversified Companies* (New York: Financial Executives Research Foundation, 1968).

[6] Specifically, an industry segment is significant if in the latest period for which statements are presented:

1. Its revenue is 10 percent or more of the *combined* revenue of all industry segments; or
2. Its operating profit (loss) is 10 percent or more of the greater of: (a) the combined operating profit of all segments that did not incur a loss, or (b) the combined operating loss of all segments that did incur a loss; or
3. Its identifiable assets are 10 percent or more of the combined identifiable assets of all industry segments.

combined sales of all segments for which information is reported shall be at least 75 percent of the company's total sales. The Statement also suggests ten as a practical limit to the number of industry segments for which a company reports information. If that limit is exceeded, it may be appropriate to combine certain segments into broader ones to meet the 75 percent test with a practical number of segments.

Under SFAS *14*, if a company derives 10 percent or more of its revenue from sales to any single customer, that fact and the amount of revenue from each such customer also must be disclosed.

The *Statement* provides guidelines for determining a company's foreign operations and export sales and for grouping operations by geographic areas. Information similar to that required for industry segments also is required for a company's operations in different geographic areas of the world.

SEC reporting requirements

In 1969 the SEC amended its registration forms S-1 and S-7 under the 1933 Act, and Form 10 under the 1934 Act. The effect of the amendment was to include a requirement for comprehensive lines of business information to be disclosed by registrants who, with their subsidiaries, are engaged in more than one line of business.

In 1970 the Commission revised its annual report form (Form 10-K) to include a requirement of annual reporting of line of business information identical with the requirements referred to above.

These provisions are intended to elicit information with respect to those lines of business that contributed, during either of the last two fiscal years, a certain proportion of (1) the total of sales and revenues, or (2) income before income taxes and extraordinary items and without deduction of loss resulting from operations of any line of business. For companies with total sales and revenues of more than $50 million, the proportion is 10 percent; for smaller companies, 15 percent. Similar disclosure is also required with respect to any line of business which resulted in a loss of 10 percent or more (15 percent or more for smaller companies) of income before income taxes, extraordinary items, and loss operations. The period to be covered by the information is each of a maximum of the last five fiscal years.

In 1974 these reporting requirements were extended to annual reports to security holders of companies filing with the SEC. It is likely that, following issuance of SFAS *14*, the SEC will conform its requirements to those of that statement.

Implications for analysis

The increasing complexity of diversified business entities and the loss of identity which acquired companies suffer in the published financial statements of conglomerates have created serious problems for the financial analyst.

The disclosure requirements of SFAS *14* and those of the SEC which preceded them will increase the amount of segmental information available for analysis. However the analyst will have to be very careful in his assessment of the reliability of the data on which he bases his conclusions.

The more specific and detailed the information provided is the more likely it is to be based on extensive allocations of costs and expenses. Allocation of common costs, as practiced for internal accounting purposes, are often based on such concepts as "equity," "reasonableness," and "acceptability to managers." These concepts have often little relevance to the objective of financial analysis.

Bases of allocating joint expenses are largely arbitrary and subject to differences of opinions as to their validity and precision. Some specific types of joint expenses which fall into this category are general and administrative expenses of central headquarters, research and development costs, certain selling costs, advertising, interest, pension costs, and federal and state income taxes.

There are, at present, no generally accepted principles of cost and expense allocation or any general agreement on the methods by which the costs of one segment should be transferred to another segment in the same enterprise. Moreover, the process of formulating such principles or of reaching such agreement has barely begun. The analyst who uses segmented data must bear these limitations firmly in mind.

In SFAS *14* the board has, in effect, recognized the above described limitations and realities. Consequently the disclosure of profit contribution (revenue less only those operating expenses that are directly traceable to a segment), which was proposed in the exposure draft issued for public comment was not required in the final Statement. Similarly, the board concluded that revenue from intersegment sales or transfers shall be accounted for on whatever basis is used by the enterprise to price intersegment sales or transfers. No single basis was prescribed or proscribed.

Moreover, the board concluded that certain items of revenue and expense either do not relate to segments or cannot always be allocated to segments on the basis of objective evidence and consequently there is no requirement in SFAS *14* that net income be disclosed for reportable segments. The board also noted in the *Statement* that "determination of an enterprise's industry segments must depend to a considerable extent on the judgment of the management of the enterprise."

The implication for analysts of this lack of firmer guidelines and definitions is that segmental disclosures are and must be treated as "soft" information which is subject to manipulation and pre-interpretation by managements. Consequently, such data must be treated with a healthy degree of skepticism and conclusions can be derived from them only through the exercise of great care as well as analytical skill.

Stability and trend of revenues

The relative trend of sales of various product lines or revenues from services can best be measured by means of trend percentages as illustrated in Table 6–3.

TABLE 6–3
Trend percentage of sales by product line (19X1 = 100)

	19X1	19X2	19X3	19X4	19X5
Product A	100	110	114	107	121
Product B	100	120	135	160	174
Product C	100	98	94	86	74
Service A	100	101	92	98	105

Sales indices of various products lines can be correlated and compared to composite industry figures or to product sales trends of specific competitors.

Important considerations bearing on the quality and stability of the sales and revenues trend include:

1. The sensitivity of demand for the various products to general business conditions.
2. The ability of the enterprise to anticipate trends in demand by the introduction of new products and services as a means of furthering sales growth and as replacement of products for which demand is falling.
3. Degree of customer concentration (now required to be disclosed by SFAS 14), dependence on major customers, as well as demand stability of major customer groups.[7]
4. Degree of product concentration and dependence on a single industry.
5. Degree of dependence on relatively few star salesmen.
6. Degree of geographical diversification of markets.

---

[7] Statement on Auditing Standards 6 (AICPA) requires disclosure of the economic dependency of a company on one or more parties with which it transacts a significant volume of business, such as a sole or major customer, supplier, franchisor, franchisee, distributor, borrower or lender.

MANAGEMENT'S DISCUSSION AND ANALYSIS OF THE SUMMARY OF EARNINGS

A significant new concept of disclosure from the analyst's point of view was instituted in 1974 with the promulgation by the SEC of *ASR 159*.

The release is concerned with additional disclosures of an interpretative or explanatory nature which are necessary to enable investors to understand and evaluate significant period-to-period changes in the various items included in the summary of earnings (or summary of operations). A separate section to be captioned "Management's Discussion and Analysis of the Summary of Earnings" must contain an explanation of such changes as well as changes in accounting principles or practices or in the method of their application that have a material effect on reported net income. An explanation is also required when due to the presence of "material facts" historical operations or earnings as reported are not indicative of future operations or earnings.

To help determine whether a change should be discussed or elaborated upon, the release offers the following guide as to materiality:

A change in an item of revenue or expense is generally required to be discussed when it increased or decreased by more than 10 percent compared to its level in a prior period presented *and* it also increased or decreased by more than 2 percent of the average net income or loss for the most recent three years presented. In the calculation of the three year average, loss years are excluded; if losses were incurred in each of the most recent years, the average net loss shall be used for purposes of this test of materiality.

If a change is immaterial under the foregoing test, it should still be discussed or explained if that is necessary for a full understanding of the earnings summary. Conversely, if management finds that a change exceeds the percentage criteria but need not be explained, it must furnish to the SEC a written *supplemental* statement explaining why, in its opinion, such explanation is not necessary.

While it is recognized that the release cannot cover all situations which may arise it cites the following as examples of the types of subjects which should be covered:

1. Material changes in product mix or in the relative profitability of lines of business.
2. Material changes in advertising, research, development, product introduction or other discretionary costs.
3. The acquisition or disposition of a material asset other than in the ordinary course of business.
4. Material and unusual charges or gains, including credits or charges associated with discontinuation of operations.

5. Material changes in assumptions underlying deferred costs and the plan for amortization of such costs.
6. Material changes in assumed investment return and in actuarial assumptions used to calculate contributions to pension funds.
7. The closing of a material facility or material interruption of business or completion of a material contract.

Disclosure of the dollar amount of each item or change covered and its effect on reported results as well as a discussion of causes of material changes in each item are also required.

The discussion of "material facts" is not intended to be retrospective only. Such discussion must also cover material factors known to management which are likely to influence, favorably or unfavorably, *future* trends and results. However, a discussion of such factors may be in broad terms only; no specific quantitative estimates or projections are required.

Implications for analysis

In the explanatory portion of the release the commission staff sets forth the following objectives of the required narrative disclosure:

a. They should enable investors to appraise the "quality of earnings".
b. They should facilitate an understanding of the extent to which changes in accounting as well as changes in business activity affect the comparability of year-to-year data.
c. They should facilitate an assessment of the source as well as the probability of recurrence of net income (or loss).

While *ASR 159* leaves to the discretion of management the determination of how to communicate most effectively to the reader the significant elements which are necessary for a clear understanding of the company's financial results, it is emphasized that a mechanistic approach which uses "boiler plate or compliance jargon" should be avoided. Thus, the aim is meaningful disclosure in narrative form by those in charge of operations who are really in a position to know and who can supply significant additional details not usually found in the financial statements.

Since the issuance of *ASR 159*, experience has shown that the quality and the depth of the disclosures is uneven. The analyst, without having to take them at face value, can nevertheless use them as valuable analytical supplements for both the information that they provide and the insights into the thinking and the attitude of managements which they afford.

Methods of revenue recognition and measurement

A variety of methods of revenue recognition and measurement coexist in various industries. Some of these methods are more conservative than others. The analyst must understand the income recognition methods used by the enterprise and their implications as well as the methods used by companies with which the results of the enterprise under analysis are being compared. A foremost consideration is whether the revenue recognition method in use accurately reflects an entity's economic performance and earnings activities.

QUESTIONS

1. What are the major objectives of income analysis?
2. Why can "net income" not be a single specific quantity?
3. Two levels can be identified in the analysis of the income statement. Name them.
4. Why is knowledge of major sources of revenue (sales) of an enterprise important in the analysis of the income statement?
5. Why are information and detailed data about the segments of diversified enterprises important to financial analysts?
6. What are the major provisions of SFAS 14?
7. Disclosure of various types of information by "line of business" has been proposed. Comment on the value of such information and the feasibility of providing it in published financial statements.
8. To what limitations of public segmental data must the analyst be alert?
9. Which important considerations have a bearing on the quality and the stability of a sales and revenue trend?
10. *a.* What is the test, offered by ASR 159, of the materiality of a change that should be discussed by management in its discussion and analysis of the summary of earnings?
    b. If a change is immaterial under the above test, should it still be discussed?
11. Cite some of the examples of the types of subjects which should be covered in the management's discussion and analysis of the summary of earnings.
12. What are the objectives of discussions required by ASR 159?

7

ANALYSIS OF RESULTS OF OPERATIONS—II

This chapter continues and concludes the discussion of the analysis of results of operations begun in the preceding chapter.

ANALYSIS OF COST OF SALES

In most enterprises[1] the cost of goods or services sold is, as a percentage of sales, the single most significant cost category. The methods of determining cost of sales encompass a wide variety of alternatives. Moreover, there is, particularly in unregulated industries, no agreed-to uniform cost classification method which would result in a clear and generally accepted distinction among such basic cost and expense categories as cost of sales, administrative, general, sales, and financial expenses. This is particularly true in the classification of general and administrative expenses. Thus, in undertaking cost comparisons the analyst must be ever alert to methods of classification and the effect they can have on the validity of comparisons within an enterprise or among enterprises.

GROSS PROFIT

The excess of sales over the cost of sales is the gross profit or gross margin. It is commonly expressed as a percentage:

---

[1] Exceptions can be found, for example, in some land sales companies where selling and other costs may actually exceed the cost of land sold.

Sales	$10,000,000	100%
Cost of sales	7,200,000	72
Gross profit	$ 2,800,000	28%

The gross profit percentage is a very important operating ratio. In the above example the gross profit is $2,800,000 or 28 percent of sales. From this amount all other costs and expenses must be recovered and any net income that is earned is the balance remaining after all expenses. Unless an enterprise has an adequate gross profit, it can be neither profitable nor does it have an adequate margin with which to finance such essential future-directed discretionary expenditures as research and development and advertising. Gross profit margins vary from industry to industry depending on such factors as competition, capital investment, the level of costs other than direct costs of sales which must be covered by the gross profit, and so forth.

Factors in the analysis of gross profit

In the analysis of gross profit the analyst will pay particular attention to—

1. The factors which account for the variation in sales and costs of sales.
2. The relationship between sales and costs of sales and management's ability to control this relationship.

ANALYSIS OF CHANGES IN GROSS MARGIN[2]

A detailed analysis of changes in gross margin can usually be performed only by an internal analyst because it requires access to data such as the number of physical units sold, unit sales prices, as well as unit costs. Such data are usually not provided in published financial statements. Moreover, unless the enterprise sells a single product, this analysis requires detailed data by product line. The external analyst, unless he has special influence on the company analyzed, will usually not have access to the data required for the analysis of gross margin.

Despite the above limitations to which gross margin analysis is subject, it is instructive to examine its process so that the elements accounting for variations in gross margin can be more fully understood.

---

[2] In this discussion the terms "gross profit" and "gross margin" are used interchangeably. Some writers reserve the term "gross margin" for situations where the cost of goods sold excludes overhead costs, that is, direct costing. This is not the intention here.

EXAMPLE OF ANALYSIS OF CHANGE IN GROSS MARGIN

Company A shows the following data for two years:

	Unit of measure	Year ended December 31, 19X1	Year ended December 31, 19X2	In-crease	De-crease
1. Net sales	Thousands of dollars	657.6	687.5	29.9	
2. Cost of sales	Thousands of dollars	237.3	245.3	8.0	
3. Gross margin	Thousands of dollars	420.3	442.2	21.9	
4. Units of product sold	Thousands	215.6	231.5	15.9	
5. Selling price per unit (1 ÷ 4)	Dollars	3.05	2.97		.08
6. Cost per unit (2 ÷ 4)	Dollars	1.10	1.06		.04

Based on the above data, Exhibit 7–1 presents an analysis of the change in gross margin of $21,900 from 19X1 to 19X2. This analysis is

EXHIBIT 7–1

COMPANY A
Statement Accounting for Variation in Gross Margin
Between Years 19X1 and 19X2

Thousands of dollars

I. Analysis of variation in sales
   (1) Variation due to change in volume of products sold
      Change in volume (15.9) × 19X1 unit selling price (3.05) $48.5
   (2) Variation due to change in selling price
      Change in selling price (−$0.08) × 19X1 sales
       volume (215.6) ....   −17.2
                                  $31.3
   (3) Variation due to combined change in sales volume
      (15.9) and unit sales price (−$0.08) ....   − 1.3
   Increase in net sales $30.0*

II. *Analysis of variation in cost of sales*
   (1) Variation due to change in volume of products sold:
      Change in volume (15.9) × 19X1 cost per unit ($1.10) $17.5
   (2) Variation due to change in cost per unit sold: change in
      cost per unit (−$0.04) × 19X1 sales volume (215.6) ....   − 8.6
                                  $ 8.9
   (3) Variation due to combined change in volume (15.9)
      and cost per unit (−$0.04) ....   − .6
   Increase in cost of sales .... $ 8.3*
        Net variation in gross margin $21.7*

* Differences are due to rounding.

based on the principle of focusing on one element of change at a time. Thus, in Exhibit 7–1 the analysis of variation in sales involves the following steps:

Step 1: We focus on the year-to-year change in volume while *assuming* that the unit selling price remained unchanged at the former, 19X1, level. Since both the volume change (15.9) and the unit selling price ($3.05) are positive, the resulting product ($48.5) is positive.

Step 2: We focus now on the change in selling price which represents a year-to-year decrease (−$0.08) and *assume* the volume (215.6) to be unchanged from the prior year level so as to single out the change due to price change. Algebraically here the multiplication of a negative (price change) by a positive (volume) results in a negative product (−$17.2).

Step 3: We must now recognize that the *assumptions* used in steps 1 and 2 above, that is, that the volume remained unchanged while the unit price changed and vice versa, are temporary expedients used to single out major causes for change. To complete the computation we must recognize that by making these assumptions we left out the *combined* change in volume and unit price. The change in volume of 15.9 represents an *increase* and, consequently, is *positive*. The unit selling price change represents a *decrease* (−$0.08) and hence is *negative*. As a result the product is negative (−$1.3).

Step 4: Adding up the—

Variation due to volume change	$48.5
Variation due to price change	−17.2
Combined change of volume and unit price	− 1.3
We account for the causes behind the sales increase	$30.0

The analysis of variation in the cost of sales follows the same principles.

Interpretation of changes in gross margin

The analysis of variation in gross margin is useful in identifying major causes of change in the gross margin. These changes can consist of one or a combination of the following factors:

1. Increase in sales volume.
2. Decrease in sales volume.
3. Increase in unit sales price.
4. Decrease in unit sales price.
5. Increase in cost per unit.
6. Decrease in cost per unit.

192

The presence of the "combined change of volume and unit sales price" and the "combined volume and unit cost" in the analysis presents no problem in interpretation since their amount is always minor in relation to the main causative factors of change.

The interpretation of the results of the analysis of gross margin involves the identification of the major factors responsible for change in the gross margin and an evaluation of the reasons for change in the factors. Such an analysis can also focus on the most feasible areas of improvement (i.e., volume, price, or cost) and the likelihood of realizing such improvements. For example, if it is determined that the major reason for a decline in gross margin is a decline in unit sales prices and that it reflects a situation of overcapacity in the enterprise's industry with attendant price cutting, then the situation is a serious one because of the limited control management has on such a development. If, on the other hand, the deterioration in the gross margin is found to be due to increases in unit costs, then this may be a situation over which management can exercise a larger measure of control and, given its ability to do so, an improvement is a more likely possibility.

BREAK-EVEN ANALYSIS

The second level of cost analysis is importantly concerned with the relationship between sales and the cost of sales but goes beyond that segment of the income statement. This level encompasses break-even analysis and is concerned with the relationship of sales to most costs, including, but not limited to, the cost of sales.

Concepts underlying break-even analysis

The basic principle underlying break-even analysis is the behavior of costs. Some costs vary directly with sales while others remain essentially constant over a considerable range of sales. The first category of costs is classified as *variable* while the latter are known as *fixed* costs.

The distinction among costs according to their behavior can be best understood within the framework of an example. In order to focus first on the basic data involved and on the technique of break-even analysis, we shall examine it by means of a simple illustration:

An enterprising graduate student saw an opportunity to sell pocket calculators at a financial analysts convention due to take place in his hometown. Upon inquiry he learned that he would have to get a vendor's license from the convention organizing committee at a cost of $10 and that the rental of a room in which to sell would amount to $140. The cost of calculators was to be $3 each with the right to return any that were not sold. The student decided that $8 was the proper sales price per calculator and wondered whether the undertaking will be worthwhile. As a first step he decided to compute the number of calculators he will have to sell in order to break even.

Equation approach

We start from the elementary proposition that

Sales = Variable Cost + Fixed Costs + Profit (or − Loss)

Since at break even there is neither gain nor loss the equation is

Sales = Variable Cost + Fixed Costs

If we designate the number of calculators which must be sold to break even as X, we have

$$8X = 3X + 150$$

where

Sales = Unit sales Price (8) × X
Variable Costs = Variable cost per unit (3) × X
Fixed Costs = License fee ($10) + Rental ($140)

These costs are fixed because they will be incurred regardless of the number of calculators sold.
Solving the equation we get

$$5X = 150$$
$$X = 30 \quad \text{units or calculators}$$
$$\text{to be sold to break even}$$

In this example the number of calculators to be sold is important information because the student needs to assess the likelihood of obtaining the size of demand which will make his venture profitable. This approach is, however, limited to a single product enterprise.

If, as is common in business, an enterprise sells a mix of goods, the unit sales break-even computation becomes impracticable and the focus is on dollar sales. This would be the situation if our student sold stationery and books in addition to calculators.

This more prevalent break-even computation can be illustrated with the data already given.

If we designate the dollar sales at break even as Y, we get:

$$Y = \text{Variable cost percentage } Y + \text{Fixed costs}$$
$$= 0.375Y + 150$$
$$0.625Y = 150$$
$$Y = \$240 \text{ (sales at break even)}$$

In this computation the variable cost percentage is the ratio of variable costs ($3) to sales price ($8). This means that each dollar of sales entails an incurrence of $.375 for variable costs or 37.5 percent of the sales price.

Graphic presentation

Exhibit 7–2 portrays the results attained above in graphic form. A graph drawn to scale will yield a solution approximating in accuracy that obtained by the formula method. Moreover it portrays under one set of assumptions not only the break-even point but also a whole range of profitable operations above that point as well as the losses below it.

EXHIBIT 7–2
Calculator illustration—break-even chart

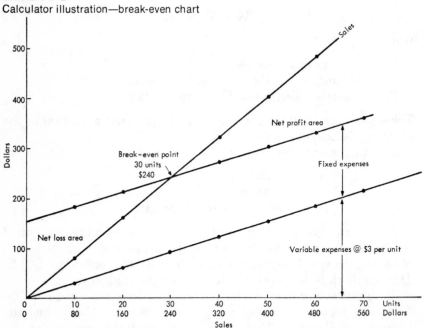

Contribution margin approach

Another technique of break-even analysis which can produce additional insights into the relationship of sales, costs, and profits is the contribution margin approach. It will be illustrated here by means of the foregoing pocket calculator example.

The contribution margin is what is left of the net sales price after deduction of the variable costs. It is from this margin that fixed costs must first be met and after that a profit earned.

Sales price per calculator	$8.00
Variable costs per calculator	3.00
Unit contribution margin	$5.00

Since each unit (calculator) sold contributes $5 to overhead and for profit, the break-even point in units is

$$\frac{\text{Fixed Costs}}{\text{Unit Contribution Margin}} = \frac{\$150}{\$5} = 30 \text{ units}$$

Thus, after 30 units are sold the fixed costs are covered and each additional unit sale yields a profit equal to the unit contribution margin, that is, $5.

If, as is more usual, the break-even point is to be expressed in dollars of sales, the formula involves use of the contribution margin ratio rather than the unit contribution margin. The contribution margin ratio is a percentage relationship computed as follows:

$$\frac{\text{Unit Contribution Margin}}{\text{Unit Sales Price}} = \frac{5}{8} = 0.625 \text{ or } 62.5 \text{ percent}$$

The calculator problem dollar break-even point can now be calculated as follows:

$$\frac{\text{Fixed Costs}}{\text{Contribution Margin Ratio}} = \frac{150}{0.625} = \$240$$

The contribution margin is an important tool in break-even analysis, and its significance will be the subject of further discussion later in this section.

Pocket calculator problem—additional considerations

The break-even technique illustrated above lends itself to a variety of assumptions and requirements. The following are additional illustrations, all using the original data of our example, unless changed assumptions are introduced:

ILLUSTRATION 1: Assume that our student decided that in order to make the venture worthwhile he requires a net profit of $400. How many calculators must be sold to achieve this objective?

$$\text{Sales} = (\text{Variable cost \%})(\text{sales}) + \text{Fixed costs} + \text{Profit}$$
$$S = 0.375S + \$150 + \$400$$
$$0.625S = 550$$
$$S = \$880$$
$$\frac{880}{8} = 110 \text{ units}$$

ILLUSTRATION 2: Assume that the financial analysts convention committee offered to provide the student with a room free of charge if he agreed to imprint on the calculators the Financial Analysts Society's seal. However, this would increase the cost of calculators from $3 to $4 per unit. Under the original assumptions the break-even point was 30 calculators. What should it be if the student accepts the committee's proposal?

Here we have a reduction of fixed costs by $140 and an increase in variable costs of $1 per unit.

If X be the number of calculators sold at break-even point, then:

$$\text{Sales} = \text{Variable costs} + \text{Fixed costs}$$
$$8X = 4X + \$10$$
$$4X = 10$$
$$X = 2.5 \text{ calculators (rounded to 3)}$$

This proposal obviously involves a much lower break-even point and hence reduced risk. However, the lower contribution margin will at higher sales levels reduce total profitability. We can determine at what level of unit sales the original assumption of a $3 per unit variable cost and $150 fixed cost will equal the results of the $4 per unit variable cost and $10 fixed costs.

Let X be the number of units (calculators) sold, then:

$$4X + \$10 = 3X + \$150$$
$$1X = 140$$
$$X = 140 \text{ calculators}$$

Thus, if more than 140 calculators are sold, the alternative which includes the $3 variable cost will be more profitable.

Having examined the break-even analysis technique and some types of decisions for which it is useful, we will now turn to a discussion of the practical difficulties and the theoretical limitations to which this approach is subject.

Break-even technique—problem areas and limitations

The intelligent use of the break-even technique and the drawing of reasonably valid conclusions therefrom depends on a resolution of practical difficulties and on an understanding of the limitations to which the techniques are subject.

Fixed, variable, and semivariable costs. In the foregoing simple examples of break-even analysis, costs were clearly either fixed or variable. In the more complex reality found in practice, many costs are not so clearly separable into fixed and variable categories. That is, they do not either stay constant over a considerable change in sales volume or respond in exact proportion to changes in sales.

We can illustrate this problem by reference to the costs of a food supermarket. As was discussed above, some costs will remain fixed within a certain range of sales. Rent, depreciation, certain forms of maintenance, utilities, and supervisory labor are examples of such fixed costs. The level of fixed costs can, of course, be increased by simple management decision unrelated to the level of sales, for example, the plant superintendent's salary may be increased.

Other costs, such as the cost of merchandise, trading stamps, supplies, and certain labor will vary closely with sales. These costs are truly variable. Certain other costs may, however, contain both fixed and variable elements in them. Examples of such "semivariable" costs are repairs, some materials, indirect labor, fuel, utilities, payroll taxes, and rents which contain a minimum payment provision and are also related to the level of sales. Break-even analysis requires that the variable component of such expenses be separated from the fixed component. This is often a difficult task for the management accountant and an almost impossible task for the outside analyst to perform without the availability of considerable internal data.

Simplifying assumptions in break-even analysis. The estimation of a variety of possible results by means of break-even calculations or charts requires the use of simplifying assumptions. In most cases these simplifying assumptions do not destroy the validity of the conclusions reached. Nevertheless, in reaching such conclusions the analyst must be fully aware of these assumptions and of their possible effect.

The following are some of the more important assumptions implicit in break-even computations:

1. The factors comprising the model, implicit in any given break-even situation, actually behave as assumed, that is,
    a. That the costs have been reasonably subdivided into their fixed and variable components;
    b. That variable costs fluctuate proportionally with volume;
    c That fixed costs remain fixed over the range relevant to the situation examined; and
    d. That unit selling prices will remain unchanged over the range encompassed by the analysis.
2. In addition, there are certain operating and environmental assumptions which emphasize the static nature of any one break-even computation. It is assumed:
    a. That the mix of sales will remain unchanged,
    b. That efficiency of operations will remain constant,
    c. That prices of costs factors will not change,
    d. That the only factor affecting costs is volume,
    e. That beginning and end of period inventory levels will remain substantially unchanged, and
    f. That there is no substantial change in the general price level during the period.

The formidable array of assumptions enumerated above points out the susceptibility of break-even computations to significant error. Not all the assumptions are, however, equally important, or, if not justified, will have an equal impact on the validity of conclusions. For example, the assumption that the selling price will not change with volume is contrary to economic theory and often is contrary to reality. Thus, the sales line is a curved rather than a linear function. However, the degree of error will depend on the actual degree of deviation from a strict linear relationship. Another basic assumption is that volume is *the* major, if not the only, factor affecting costs. We know, however, that strikes, political developments, legislation, and competition, to name a few other important factors, have a decided influence on costs. The analyst must, consequently, keep these simplifying assumptions firmly in mind and be aware of the dynamic factors which may require modifications in his conclusions.

Break-even analysis—uses and their implications

The break-even approach can be a useful tool of analysis if its limitations are recognized and its applications are kept in proper perspective.

The emphasis on the break-even, that is, zero profit, point is an unfortunate distortion of the objective of this type of analysis. Instead, the break-even situation represents but one point in a flexible set of projections of revenues and of the costs which will be associated with them under a given set of future conditions.

The managerial applications of break-even analysis are many. It is useful, among others, in price determination, expense control, and in the projection of profits. Along with standard cost systems it gives management a basis for pricing decisions under differing levels of activity. In conjunction with flexible budgets it represents a powerful tool of expense control. The break-even chart is also a useful device with which to measure the impact of specific managerial decisions, such as plant expansion and new product introduction or of external influences, on the profitability of operations over various levels of activity.

To financial analysts the function of profit projections is one of vital importance. Moreover, the ability to estimate the impact of profitability of various economic conditions or managerial courses of action is also an extremely important one. Both of these are importantly aided by break-even analysis. The intelligent use of this technique and a thorough understanding of its operation are the factors which account for its importance to the external financial analyst.

Illustration of break-even technique application. Exhibit 7–3 presents the break-even chart of the Multi-Products Company at a

EXHIBIT 7–3
Multi-Products Company
Break-even chart—all operations

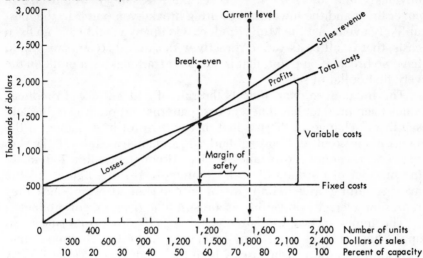

given point in time. It is subject to the various assumptions which were discussed above including that relating to the ability to separate costs into their fixed and variable components.

At break even a very condensed income statement of Multi-Products Company will be as follows:

Sales		$1,387,000
Costs:		
Variable	$887,000	
Fixed	500,000	1,387,000
Net income		0

The variable cost percentage is 887/1387 or about 64 percent. The contribution margin ratio is 36 percent (100 − Variable cost percentage of 64). The variable cost percentage means that on average, out of every dollar of sales 64 cents go to meet variable costs, that is, costs which would not be incurred if the sale did not occur. The contribution margin ratio is basically the complement of the variable cost percentage.

Break-even point:	
Sales	$1,387,000
Units	1,156,000
Average selling price per unit	$1.20

It indicates that each dollar of sales generates a contribution of 36 cents towards meeting fixed expenses and the earning of a profit beyond the break-even point. The contribution margin earned on sales of $1,387,000 is just sufficient to cover the $500,000 in fixed costs. Quite obviously, the lower the fixed costs, the less sales it would take to cover them and the lower the resulting break-even point. In the most unlikely event that the Multi-Products Company would have no fixed costs, that is, all costs varied directly with sales, the company would have no break-even point, that is, it would start making a profit on the very first dollar of sales.

The break-even chart reflects the sale of a given mix of products. Since each product has different cost patterns and profit margins, any significant change in the product mix will result in a change in the break-even point and consequently in a change in the relationship between revenues, costs, and results. Although Exhibit 7–3 shows the number of units on the sales (volume) axis, this figure and the average selling price per unit are of limited significance because they represent averages prevailing as a result of a given mix of products.

The importance of a relatively stable sales mix to the successful application of break-even analysis suggests that this technique cannot be usefully employed in cases where the product mix varies greatly over the short term. Nor, for that matter, can break-even analysis be usefully applied in cases where there are sharp and frequent fluctuations in sales prices or in costs of production, such as raw materials.

Exhibit 7–3 indicates that given the existing mix of products, the present level of fixed costs of $500,000 can be expected to prevail up to a sales level of approximately $2,400,000. This is the point at which 100 percent of theoretical capacity will be reached. The break-even point is at 60 percent of capacity while the current level of sales is at about 75 percent of capacity. This means that when the 100 percent capacity level is reached, the fixed costs may have to undergo an upward revision. If Multi-Products is reluctant to expand its capacity and thus increase its fixed costs and break-even point, assuming that variable costs do not decrease, it may have to consider other alternatives such as:

1. Forgoing an increase in sales.
2. Increasing the number of shifts, which could increase variable costs significantly.
3. Subcontracting some of its work to outsiders, thus forgoing some of the profit of increased activity.

Exhibit 7–3 also presents to the analyst at a glance the company's present position relative to the break-even point. The current level of sales of $1,800,000 is about $413,000 above the break-even point. This is also known as the "safety margin," that is, the margin that separates the company from a no-profit condition. This concept can be expanded to indicate on the chart at what point the company will earn a desired return on investment, at what point the common dividend may be in jeopardy, and at what point the preferred dividend may no longer be covered by current earnings.

It is obvious that the data revealed by a reliably constructed break-even chart or by the application of break-even computations is valuable in profit projection, in the assessment of operating risk, as well as in an evaluation of profit levels under various assumptions regarding future conditions and managerial policies.

Analytical implications of break-even analysis

From the above discussion of a specific situation, such as that illustrated in Exhibit 7–3, we will now turn to a more general review of conclusions which can be derived from break-even analysis.

The concept of operating leverage.   Leverage and fixed costs go together. As we have seen in Chapter 4, financial leverage is based on fixed costs of funds for a portion of the resources used by the enterprise. Thus, earnings above that fixed cost magnify the return on the residual funds and vice versa.

The fixed costs of a business enterprise, in the sense in which we have discussed them so far in this chapter, form the basis of the concept of operating leverage. Until an enterprise develops a volume of sales which is sufficient to cover its fixed costs, it will incur a loss. Once it has covered the fixed costs, further increments in volume will result in more than proportionate increases in profitability. The following will illustrate the nature of operating leverage:

Illustration of the working of operating leverage.   In a given enterprise the cost structure is as follows:

$$\text{Fixed costs} = \$100,000$$
$$\text{Variable cost percentage} = 60 \text{ percent}$$

The following tabulation presents the profit or loss at successively higher levels of sales and a comparison of relative percentage changes in sales volume and in profitability:

Sales	Variable costs	Fixed costs	Profit (loss)	Percentage increase over preceding step Sales	Profit
$100,000	$ 60,000	$100,000	$(60,000)	—	—
200,000	120,000	100,000	(20,000)	100%	—
250,000	150,000	100,000	—	25	—
300,000	180,000	100,000	20,000	20	Infinite
360,000	216,000	100,000	44,000	20	120%
432,000	259,200	100,000	72,800	20	65%

The working of operating leverage is evident in the above tabulation. Starting at break even, the first 20 percent sales increase resulted in an infinite increase in profits because they started from a zero base. The next 20 percent increase in sales resulted in a 120 percent profit increase over the preceding level while the sales increase that followed resulted in a 65 percent profit increase over the preceding level. The effects of leverage diminish as the sales increase above the break-even level because the bases to which increases in profits are compared get progressively larger.

Leverage, of course, works both ways. It will be noted that a drop in sales from $200,000 to $100,000, representing 50 percent decrease, resulted in a tripling of the loss.

One important conclusion from this to the analyst is that enterprises operating near their break-even point will have relatively larger percentage changes of profits or losses for a given change in volume. On the upside the volatility will, of course, be desirable. On the downside, however, it can result in adverse results which are significantly worse than those indicated by changes in sales volume alone.

Another aspect is operating *potential,* sometimes erroneously referred to as leverage, which derives from a high level of sales accompanied by very low profit margins. The potential here, of course, is the room for improvements in profit margins. Even relatively slight improvements in profit margins, applied on a large sales level, can result in dramatic changes in profits. Thus, the popular reference to a semblance of leverage for what is really a potential for improvement.

Another aspect of the same *potential* occurs when the sales volume *per share* is large. Obviously an improvement in profitability will be translated into larger earnings per share improvements.

The significance of the variable cost percentage

The volatility of profits is also dependent on the variable cost percentage. The low variable cost enterprise will achieve higher profits for a given increment in volume once break-even operations are reached than will the high variable-cost enterprise.

ILLUSTRATION 3. Company A has fixed costs of $700,000 and a variable cost equal to 30 percent of sales. Company B has fixed costs of $300,000 and variable costs equal to 70 percent of the sales. Assume that both companies have now reached sales of $1,000,000 and are, consequently, at break even. A $100,000 increment in sales will result in a profit of $70,000 for Company A and only in a profit of $30,000 for Company B. Company A has not only greater operating leverage but can, as a result, afford to incur greater risks in going after the extra $100,000 in sales than can Company B.

From the above example it is evident that the *level* of the break-even point is not the only criterion of risk assessment but that the analyst must also pay attention to the variable cost ratio.

The significance of the fixed-cost level

Given a certain variable cost percentage, the higher the fixed costs, the higher the break-even point of an enterprise. In the absence of change in other factors, a given percentage change in fixed costs will result in an equal percentage change in the break-even point. This can be illustrated as follows:

First break-even situation

Sales.....................		$100,000
Variable expenses	$60,000	
Fixed costs	40,000	100,000
Profit		–0–

Second break-even situation—20% increase in fixed costs

Sales (increase of 20%)		$120,000
Variable expenses (60%)	$72,000	
Fixed cost (40,000 + 20%)	48,000	120,000
		–0–

Thus a fixed cost increase of 20 percent, with the variable cost ratio remaining unchanged, resulted in a 20 percent increase in the break-even point.

An increase in the break-even point of an enterprise generally increases operational risk. It means that the enterprise is dependent on a higher volume of sales in order to break even. Looked at another way, it means that the enterprise is more vulnerable to economic downturns as compared to its situation with a lower break-even point. The substantial acquisition of the large capacity Boeing 747 aircraft by the airlines provides an example of the effects of high break-even points. While these large aircraft lowered the variable cost per passenger, they relied also on a projected increase in the number of passengers. When this failed to materialize, the airlines' profit margins deteriorated swiftly with many of them going into the red. There are other repercussions to high levels of fixed costs. Thus, for example, a higher break-even point may mean that the enterprise has less freedom of action in fields such as labor relations. A high level of fixed costs makes strikes more expensive and subjects the enterprise to added pressure to submit to higher wage demands.

Often, added fixed costs in the form of automatic machinery are incurred in order to save variable costs, such as labor, and to improve efficiency. That can be very profitable in times of reasonably good demand. In times of low demand, however, the higher level of fixed costs sets in motion the process of reverse operational leverage discussed above, with attendant rapidly shrinking profits or even growing losses. High fixed costs reduce an enterprise's ability to protect its profits in the face of shrinking sales volume.

Investments in fixed assets, particularly in sophisticated machinery, can bring about increases in fixed costs far beyond the cost of maintaining and replacing the equipment. The skills required to operate such equipment are quite specialized and require skilled personnel which the enterprise may be reluctant to dismiss for fear of not being able to replace them when business turns up again. This converts what should be variable costs into de facto fixed costs.

While fixed costs are incurred in order to increase capacity or to decrease variable costs, it is often advisable to cut fixed costs in order to reduce the risks associated with a high break-even point. Thus, a company may reduce fixed costs by switching from a salaried sales force to one compensated by commissions based on sales. It can avoid added fixed costs by adding work shifts, buying ready-made parts, subcontracting work, or discontinuing the least profitable product lines.

In evaluating profit performance, past and future, of an enterprise, the analyst must always keep in mind the effect that the level of fixed costs can have on operating results under a variety of business conditions. Moreover, in projecting future results the analyst must bear in mind that any given level of fixed costs is valid only up to the limits of practical capacity within a range of product mixes. Beyond such a point a profit projection must take into consideration not only the increased levels of fixed costs required but also the financial resources which an expansion will require as well as the cost and sources of the funds which will be needed.

The importance of the contribution margin

The analyst must be alert to the absolute size of an enterprise's contribution margin because operating leverage is importantly dependent on it. He must, moreover, be aware of the factors which can change this margin, that is, changes in variable costs as well as changes in selling prices.

While we have focused on the individual factors which affect costs, revenues, and profitability, in practice changes result from a combination of factors. Projected increases in sales volume will increase profits only if costs, both fixed and variable, are controlled and kept within projected limits. Break-even analysis assumes that efficiency remains constant. However, experience teaches us that cost controls are more lax in times of prosperity than they are in times of recession. Thus, the analyst cannot assume constant efficiency any more than he can assume a constant product mix. The latter is also an important variable which must be watched by the analyst. Questions of why an enterprise realized lower profits on a higher volume of sales can often be explained, at least in part, by reference to changes in sales mix.

In spite of its important limitations, the break-even approach is an important tool of analysis to the financial analyst.

Its ability to aid the external analyst in performance evaluation and in profit projection makes its use worthwhile to him in spite of the laborious work which it often entails and the fragmentary and scarce amounts of information on which, of necessity, it must be based.

ADDITIONAL CONSIDERATIONS IN THE ANALYSIS OF COST OF SALES

Gross margin analysis focuses on changes in costs, prices, and volume. Break-even analysis, in turn, focuses on the behavior of costs in relation to sales volume and on management's ability to control costs in the face of rising and falling revenues. The effectiveness of these and other methods of cost analysis depends on the degree of data availability as well as on an understanding of the accounting principles which have been applied.

The ability of the analyst to make the rough approximations which are necessary to separate costs into fixed and variable components depends on the amount of detail available. Disclosure of major cost components such as materials, labor, and various overhead cost categories can be helpful. The more detailed the breakdowns of expense categories the more likely is the analyst to be able to construct meaningful break-even estimates.

In the evaluation of the cost of sales and the gross margin, and particularly in its comparison with those of other enterprises, the analyst must pay close attention to distortions which may arise from the utilization of a variety of accounting principles. While this is true of all items of cost, attention must be directed particularly to inventories and to depreciation accounting. These two areas merit special attention not only because they represent costs which are usually substantial in amount but also because of the proliferation of alternative principles which may be employed in accounting for them.

DEPRECIATION

Depreciation is an important cost element particularly in manufacturing and service enterprises. It is mostly fixed in nature because it is computed on the basis of elapsed time. However, if its computation is based on production activity the result is a variable cost.

Because depreciation is computed in most cases on the basis of time elapsed, the ratio of depreciation expense to income is not a particularly meaningful or instructive relationship. In the evaluation of depreciation expense the ratio of depreciation to gross plant and equipment is more meaningful. The ratio is computed as follows:

$$\frac{\text{Depreciation Expense}}{\text{Assets subject to Depreciation}}$$

This ratio can, of course, be computed by major categories of assets. The basic purpose is to enable the analyst to detect changes in the composite rate of depreciation used by an enterprise as a means of evaluating its adequacy and' of detecting attempts at income smoothing.

AMORTIZATION OF SPECIAL TOOLS AND SIMILAR COSTS

The importance of the cost of special tools, dies, jigs, patterns, and molds costs varies from industry to industry. It is of considerable importance, for example, in the auto industry where special tool costs are associated with frequent style and design changes. The rate of amortization of such costs can have an important effect on reported income and is important to the analyst in an assessment of that income as well as in its comparison with that of other entities within an industry. The ratios that can be used to analyze changes in the deferral and amortization policies of such costs are varied and focus on their relationship to sales and other classes of assets.

The yearly expenditure for special tools can be related to and expressed as a percentage of (1) sales and (2) net property and equipment.

The yearly amortization of special tools can be related to (1) sales, (2) unamortized special tools, and (3) net property and equipment.

A comparison of the yearly trend in these relationships can be very helpful in an analysis of the consistency of income reporting of a single enterprise. The comparison can be extended further to an evaluation of the earnings of two or more enterprises within the same industry. This approach is indicative of the type of analysis which various elements of costs lend themselves to.

MAINTENANCE AND REPAIRS COSTS

Maintenance and repairs costs vary in significance with the amount invested in plant and equipment as well as with the level of productive activity. They have an effect on the cost of goods sold as well as on other elements of cost. Since maintenance and repairs contain elements of both fixed and variable costs, they cannot vary directly with sales. Thus, the ratio of repairs and maintenance costs to sales, while instructive to compare from year to year or among enterprises, must be interpreted with care. To the extent that the analyst can determine the fixed and the variable portions of maintenance and repairs costs, his interpretation of their relationship to periodic sales will be more valid.

Repairs and maintenance are, to a significant extent, discretionary costs. That is, the level of expense can, within limits, be regulated by management for a variety of reasons including those aimed at the improvement of reported income or at the preservation of liquid resources. Certain types of repairs cannot, of course, be postponed without resulting breakdowns in productive equipment. But many types of preventive repairs and particularly maintenance can be postponed or skimped on with results whose effects lie mainly in the future. Thus, the level of repair and maintenance costs both in relation to sales and to plant and equipment is of interest to the analyst. It has, of course, a bearing on the quality of income, a subject which we shall consider in the next chapter.

The level of repair and maintenance costs is also important in the evaluation of depreciation expense. Useful lives of assets are estimated by the use of many assumptions including those relating to the upkeep and maintenance of the assets. If, for instance, there is a deterioration in the usual or assumed level of repairs and maintenance, the useful life of the asset will, in all probability, be shortened. That may, in turn, require an upward revision in the depreciation expense or else income will be overstated.

OTHER COSTS AND EXPENSES—GENERAL

Most, although not all, cost and expense items found in the income statement have some identifiable or measurable relationship to sales. This is so because sales are the major measure of activity in an enterprise except in instances when production and sales are significantly out of phase.

Two analytical tools whose usefulness is based, in part, on the relationship that exists between sales and most costs and expenses should be noted here:

1. The *common-size income statement* expresses each cost and expense item in terms of its percentage relationship to net sales. This relationship of costs and expenses to sales can then be traced over a number of periods or compared with the experience of other enterprises in the same industry. Appendix B of Chapter 1 contains an illustration of a common-size income statement covering a number of years.

2. The *index number analysis of the income statement* expresses each item in the income statement in terms of an index number related to a base year. In this manner relative changes of income statement items over time can be traced and their significance assessed. Expense item changes can thus be compared to changes in sales and to changes in related expense items. Moreover, by use of common-size balance sheets, percentage changes in income statement items can be related to changes in assets and liabilities. For example, a given change in sales would normally justify a commensurate change in inventories and in accounts receivable. Appendix B of Chapter 1 contains an illustration of an index number analysis.

Selling expenses

The analysis of selling costs has two main objectives:

1. The evaluation over time of the relationship between sales and the costs needed to bring them about.
2. An evaluation of the trend and the productivity of future-directed selling costs.

The importance of selling costs in relation to sales varies from industry to industry and from enterprise to enterprise. In some enterprises selling costs take the form of commissions and are, consequently, highly variable in nature, while in others they contain important elements of fixed costs.

After allowing for the fixed and variable components of the selling expenses, the best way to analyze them is to relate them to sales. The more detailed the breakdown of the selling expense components is—the more meaningful and penetrating can such analysis be. Exhibit 7–4 presents an example of such an analysis.

Analysis of Exhibit 7–4 indicates that for the entire period selling costs have been rising faster than sales and that in 19X3 they took 5.6 percent more of the sales dollar than they did in 19X0. In this period salesmen's salaries increased by 1.0 percent of sales, advertising by 3.6 percent of sales, and branch expenses by 2.2 percent of sales. The drop in delivery expense may possibly be accounted for by the offsetting increase in freight costs.

EXHIBIT 7–4

TRYON CORPORATION
Comparative Statement of Selling Expenses
(dollar amounts in thousands)

	19X3		19X2		19X1		19X0	
	$	%	$	%	$	%	$	%
Sales	1,269		935		833		791	
Trend percentage		160		118		105		100
Selling expenses (% are of sales):								
Advertising	84	6.6	34	3.6	28	3.4	24	3.0
District branch expenses*	80	6.3	41	4.4	38	4.6	32	4.1
Delivery expense (own trucks)	20	1.6	15	1.6	19	2.3	22	2.8
Freight-out	21	1.7	9	1.0	11	1.3	8	1.0
Salesmen's salary expense	111	8.7	76	8.1	68	8.1	61	7.7
Salesmen's travel expense	35	2.8	20	2.1	18	2.2	26	3.3
Miscellaneous selling expense	9	.7	9	1.0	8	.9	7	.9
Total	360	28.4	204	21.8	190	22.8	180	22.8

* Includes rent, regional advertising, etc.

A careful analysis should be made of advertising costs in order to determine to what extent the increase is due to the promotion of new products or the development of new territories which will benefit the future.

When selling expenses as a percentage of sales show an increase, it is instructive to focus on the selling expense increase which accompanies a given increase in sales. It can be expected that beyond a certain level greater sales resistance is encountered in effecting additional sales. That sales resistance or the development of more remote territories may involve additional cost. Thus, it is important to know what the percentage of selling expense to sales is or to new sales as opposed to old ones. This may have, of course, implications on the projection of future profitability. If an enterprise can make additional sales only by spending increasing amounts of selling expenses, its profitability may suffer. Offsetting factors, such as those related to break-even operations or to economies of scale must also be considered.

Future directed marketing costs

Certain categories of sales promotion costs, particularly advertising, result in benefits which extend beyond the period in which they were incurred. The measurement of such benefits is difficult if not impossible, but it is a reasonable assumption that there is a relationship between the level of expenditures for advertising and promotion and the sales level, present and future.

Since expenditures for advertising and other forms of promotion are discretionary in nature, the analyst must carefully follow the year to year trend in these expenditures. Not only does the level of such expenditures have a bearing on future sales estimates, but it also indicates whether management is attempting to "manage" reported earnings. The effect of discretionary costs on the "quality" of earnings reported will be the subject of further discussion in the chapter that follows.

GENERAL, ADMINISTRATION, FINANCIAL, AND OTHER EXPENSES

Most costs in this category tend to be fixed in nature. This is largely true of administrative costs because such costs include significant amounts of salaries and occupancy expenditures. However, there may be some "creep" or tendency for increases in this category, and this is particularly true in prosperous times. Thus, in analyzing this category of expense the analyst should pay attention to both the trend of administrative costs as well as to the percentage of total sales which they consume.

Financial costs

Financial costs are, except for interest on short-term indebtedness, fixed in nature. Moreover, unless replaced by equity capital, most borrowed funds are usually refinanced. This is because of the long-term nature of most interest-bearing obligations. Included in these costs are the amortization of bond premium and discount as well as of debt issue expenses. A good check on an enterprise's cost of borrowed money as well as credit standing is the calculation of the average effective interest rate paid. This rate is computed as follows:

$$\frac{\text{Total Interest Cost}}{\text{Total Indebtedness subject to Interest}}$$

The average effective interest rate paid can be compared over the years or compared to that of other enterprises. It is also significant in that it sheds light on the credit standing of the enterprise.

A measure of sensitivity to interest changes is obtained by determining the portion of debt which is tied to the prime rate. In periods of rising interest rates a significant amount of debt tied to the prime rate exposes an enterprise to sharply escalating interest costs. Conversely, falling interest rates are a beneficial factor to such an enterprise.

"Other" expenses

"Other" expenses are, of course, a nondescript category. The total amount in this category should normally be rather immaterial in relation to other costs. Otherwise, it can obscure substantial costs which, if revealed, may provide significant information about the enterprise's current and future operations. Nonrecurring elements may also be included in the "other expense" category, and this may add to the significance of this category to the analyst.

The analyst must also be alert to the tendency to offset "other" expenses against "other" income. Here too the major problem is one of concealment of important information and data. Here it is important that details of the major items comprising the offset amount be given.

OTHER INCOME

Miscellaneous income items which are small in amount are usually of no significance to the analyst. However, since "other income" may include returns from various investments, it may contain information about new ventures and data regarding investments which is not available elsewhere. Such investments may, of course, have future implications, positive or negative, which exceed in significance the amounts of current income which are involved.

INCOME TAXES

Income taxes represent basically a sharing of profits between an enterprise and the governmental authority by which they are imposed. Since most enterprises with which this text is concerned are organized in corporate form, we shall focus primarily on corporate income taxes.

Income taxes are almost always significant in amount and normally can take about half of a corporation's income before taxes. For this reason the analyst must pay careful attention to the impact which income taxes have on net income.

Except for a lower rate on a first modest amount of income, corporate income is normally taxed at the rate of about 50 percent. Differences in the timing of recognition of income or expense items as between taxable income and book income should not influence the effective tax rate because of the practice of interperiod income tax allocation which aims to match the tax expense with the book income regardless of when the tax is paid.

The relationship between the tax accrual and the pretax income, otherwise known as the effective tax rate or tax ratio, will, however, be influenced by permanent tax differences. These are differences which arise from provisions in the tax law which:

1. Do not tax certain revenues (e.g., interest on municipal obligations and proceeds from life insurance).
2. Do not allow certain expenses as deductions in arriving at taxable income (e.g., goodwill amortization, fines, premiums on officers' life insurance).
3. Tax certain income at reduced rates (e.g., dividend income, capital gains).
4. Allow certain costs beyond the amount taken for book purposes (e.g., excess of statutory depletion over book depletion).

The effective tax rate or tax ratio is computed as follows:

$$\frac{\text{Income Tax Expense for Period}}{\text{Income before Income Taxes}}$$

This ratio may also deviate from the normal or expected rate because, among others, of the following additional reasons:

1. The basis of carrying property for accounting purposes may differ from that for tax purposes as a result of reorganizations, business combinations, etc.
2. Nonqualified as well as qualified stock-option plans may result in book-tax differences.
3. Certain industries, such as savings and loan associations, shipping lines, and insurance companies enjoy special tax privileges.
4. Credits, such as the Investment Tax Credit.

The important thing is that both for income evaluation as well as for net income projection the analyst must know the reasons why the tax ratio deviates from the normal or the expected. Income taxes are such an important element of cost that even relatively small changes in the effective tax rate can explain important changes in net income. Moreover, without an understanding of the factors which cause changes in the effective tax rate of a company, the analyst is missing an important ingredient necessary in the forecasting of future net income.

In *ASR 149* (1973) the SEC issued rules which expanded significantly the analytical disclosures concerning regular and deferred income taxes.

While the focus on net income and on earnings per share requires a thorough analysis of changes in the effective tax rate, it must be borne in mind that many analysts attach relatively greater importance to pretax earnings. This is due to the greater importance which is assigned to pretax operating results, which require management skills of a high order, as compared with changes due to variations in the effective tax rate over which, it is assumed, management has comparatively more limited control.

THE OPERATING RATIO

The operating ratio is yet another intermediate measure in the analysis of the income statement. It measures the relationship between all operating costs and net sales and is computed as follows:

$$\frac{\text{Cost of Goods Sold} + \text{Other Operating Expenses}}{\text{Net Sales}}$$

The ratio is designed to enable a comparison within an enterprise or with enterprises of the proportion of the sales dollar absorbed by all operating costs. Only other income and expense items as well as income taxes are excluded from the computation of this ratio.

In effect this ratio represents but an intermediate step in the commonsize analysis of the income statement. It is, in and of itself, not of great analytical significance because it is a composite of many factors which require separate analysis. These factors comprise the analysis of gross margin and of other major expense categories discussed earlier. Thus, the operating ratio cannot be properly interpreted without a thorough analysis of the reasons accounting for variations in gross margin and for changes in selling, general, administrative, and other costs.

NET INCOME RATIO

The net income ratio is the relationship between net income and total revenues and is computed as follows:

$$\frac{\text{Net Income}}{\text{Total Revenues}}$$

It represents the percentage of total revenue brought down to net income. In addition to its usefulness as an index of profitability, the net profit ratio represents, as was seen in Chapter 5, a main component of the computation of the return on investment.

Statement accounting for variation in net income

In the analysis of year-to-year changes in net income it is useful to separate the elements which contributed to an increase in net income from those which contributed to a decrease. A statement which does that and which also indicates the percentage increase or decrease in these factors is the "statement accounting for the variations in net income."

Exhibit 7–5 presents comparative statements of income of the Alliance Company. Based on the data in these income statements, Exhibit 7–6 presents a "statement accounting for variations in net income." This statement is simple to prepare and allows the analyst to single out for further analysis those elements of income and expense which had the greatest impact on the change in net income from one period to another.

EXHIBIT 7–5

ALLIANCE COMPANY
Income Statements
For Years Ended March 31, 19X1, 19X2
(amounts in thousands)

	19X1	19X2	Dollar increase (decrease) 19X2	Percentage increase (decrease) 19X2
Net sales	$94,313	$102,888	$8,575	9%
Cost of sales	71,516	77,922	6,406	9
Gross profit	$22,797	$ 24,966	$2,169	10
Selling, general, and administrative and other expenses:				
Selling expenses	$ 3,300	$ 4,298	$ 998	30
General and administrative expenses	2,610	3,191	581	22
Financing expenses	4,627	4,916	289	6
Total Operating Expenses	$10,537	$ 12,405	$1,868	18
Operating profit	$12,260	$ 12,561	$ 301	2
Other income and expenses (Net)	1,447	1,752	305	21
Profit before taxes on income	$13,707	$ 14,313	$ 606	4
Taxes on income	4,500	4,604	104	2
Net income	$ 9,207	$ 9,709	$ 502	5

EXHIBIT 7-6

ALLIANCE COMPANY
Statement Accounting for Variation in Net Income
For the Year Ended December 31, 19X2
(amounts in thousands)

			Percentage increase
Items tending to increase net income:			
Increase in gross margin on sales:			
Increase in net sales:			
Net sales, 19X2	$102,888		
Net sales, 19X1	94,313	$8,575	9
Deduct: Increase in cost of goods sold:			
Cost of goods sold, 19X2	77,922		
Cost of goods sold, 19X1	71,516	6,406	9
Net increase in gross margin:			
Gross margin, 19X2	24,966		
Gross margin, 19X1	22,797	2,169	10
Increase in other revenue and expense (net)			
Net 19X2	1,752		
Net 19X1	1,447	305	21
Total of items tending to increase net income		$2,474	
Items tending to decrease in income:			
Increase in selling expenses:			
Selling expenses, 19X2	4,298		
Selling expenses, 19X1	3,300	998	30
Increase in general and administrative expenses:			
General and administrative expenses, 19X2	3,191		
General and administrative expenses, 19X1	2,610	581	22
Increase in financing expenses:			
Financing expenses, 19X2	4,916		
Financing expenses, 19X1	4,627	289	6
Increase in estimated federal income taxes:			
Estimated federal income taxes, 19X2.....	4,604		
Estimated federal income taxes, 19X1.....	4,500	104	2
Total of items tending to decrease net income		1,972	
Net increase in net income:			
Net income, 19X2	9,709		
Net income, 19X1	9,207	$ 502	5

QUESTIONS

1. What are the most important elements in the analysis of gross profit?

2. What is the basic principle underlying break-even analysis? What are fixed costs? Variable costs? Semivariable costs?

3. Certain assumptions which underlie break-even computations are often referred to as simplifying assumptions. Name as many of these as you can.

4. In break-even computation what is the "variable cost percentage"? What is its relationship to "contribution margin ratio"?

5. What alternatives to an increase in fixed costs can an enterprise consider when it approaches 100 percent of theoretical capacity?

6. What is operating leverage? Why do leverage and fixed costs go together? What are the analytical implications of operating leverage?

7. Of what analytical significance are (a) the break-even point and (b) the variable cost ratio?

8. What is a useful measure of the adequacy of current provisions for depreciation?

9. To what factors can maintenance and repair costs be meaningfully related?

10. What are the main objectives of an analysis of selling expenses?

11. List some of the reasons why the effective tax rate of one enterprise may vary from that of another enterprise?

8

THE EVALUATION AND PROJECTION OF EARNINGS

OBJECTIVES OF EARNINGS EVALUATION

In the preceding chapters we examined the steps which have to be taken and the understanding which must be brought to bear on the analysis of the operating performance of an enterprise. This chapter will examine the additional considerations involved in the achievement of the major objectives of income statement analysis:

The evaluation of the earnings level and its quality.
Evaluation of the stability and the trend of earnings.
The forecasting of earnings.
The estimation of "earning power."
Monitoring performance and results.

EVALUATION OF EARNINGS LEVEL AND ITS QUALITY

Much of the accounting process of income determination involves a high degree of estimation. The income of an enterprise, as measured by the accounting process, is not a specific amount but can vary depending on the assumptions used and the various principles applied. Complicating these measurements still further is the fact that numerous accounting periods can receive benefits from a single cash outlay and that it may take a number of periods before a transaction results in the collection of all amounts due. For that reason, creditors, in particular, are greatly interested in the cash equivalent of reported earnings.

This distinction between accrual income and the related cash flows has led some of those uninitiated in the income determination process to doubt the validity of all accounting measurements. This, however, is an extreme and unwarranted position because, as any student of accounting should know, the concept of income is the result of a series of complex assumptions and conventions, and exists only as the creation and the approximation of this system of measurement. This system is always subject to reexamination and is, despite its shortcomings, still the most widely accepted method of income determination.

In examining the level of reported income of an enterprise, the analyst must determine the effect of the various assumptions and accounting principles used on that reported income. Beyond that he must be aware of the "accounting risk" as well as the "audit risk" to which these determinations are subject.

Over the years, and especially since the enactment of the Securities Acts of 1933 and 1934, and with improvement in the audit function in this country, the incidence of outright fraud and deliberate misrepresentation in financial statements has diminished markedly. But they have not been completely eliminated and probably never will. Nor can the analyst ever rule out the possibility of spectacular failures in the audit function. While each major audit failure tends to contribute to the improvement of regulation and of auditing, they have not prevented the recurrence of such failures as the security holders of McKesson & Robbins, of Seabord Commercial Corporation, of H. L. Green, of Miami Window, of Yale Express, of BarChris Construction Company, of Continental Vending Company, of Mill Factors Corporation, and Equity Funding Company, well know.

The analyst must always assess the vulnerability to failure and to irregularities of the company under analysis and the character and the propensities of its management, as a means of establishing the degree of risk that it will prove to be the relatively rare exception to the general rule.

The evaluation of the earnings level and of the earnings trend is intimately tied in with the evaluation of management. The evaluation of the management group cannot be separated from the results which they have actually achieved. Whatever other factors may have to be considered, results over a period of time are the acid test of management's ability, and that ability is perhaps the most important intangible (i.e., unquantifiable) factor in the prediction of future results. The analyst must be alert to changes in the management group and must assess its depth, stability, and possible dependence on the talents of one or a few individuals.

The analyst must also realize that not only is it impossible to arrive at a single figure of "net income" but that identical earnings figures may possess different degrees of "quality."

THE CONCEPT OF EARNINGS QUALITY

The concept of earnings quality arose out of a need to provide a basis of comparison among the earnings of different entities as well as from the need to recognize such differences in "quality" for valuation purposes. There is almost no general agreement on definitions of or on assumptions underlying this concept. The elements which comprise the "quality of earnings" can be classified as follows:

a. One type of factor that affects the quality of earnings is the accounting and computational discretion of management and that of the attesting accountants in choosing from among accepted alternative accounting principles. These choices can be liberal, that is, they can assume the most optimistic view of the future, or they can be conservative. Generally, the quality of conservatively determined earnings is higher because they are less likely to prove overstated in the light of future developments than those determined in a "liberal" fashion. They also minimize the possibility of earnings overstatement and avoid retrospective changes. On the other hand, unwarranted or excessive conservatism, while contributing to the temporary "quality" of earnings, actually results in a lack of reporting integrity over the long run and cannot be considered as a desirable factor. Quite apart from the impact which these accounting choices have on the financial statements they also hold important clues to management's propensities and attitudes.

b. The second type of factor affecting the quality of earnings is related to the degree to which adequate provision has been made for the maintenance of assets and for the maintenance and enhancement of present and future earning power. In most enterprises there exists considerable managerial discretion over the size of income streams and particularly over the reported amounts of costs and expenses. Discretionary types of expenses, such as repairs and maintenance, advertising, and research and development costs can be varied for the sole purpose of managing the level of reported net income (or loss) rather than for legitimate operating or business reasons. Here, too, the analyst's task is to identify the results of management practices and to judge its motivations.

c. The third major factor affecting the quality of earnings is not primarily a result of discretionary actions of managements, although skillful management can modify its effects. It is the effect of cyclical and other economic forces on earnings, on the stability of their sources, and particularly on their variability. Variability of earnings is generally an undesirable characteristic and, consequently, the higher the variability the lower the quality of these earnings.

The fairly broad tolerances within which generally accepted accounting principles can be applied have been discussed throughout this work. There follows a consideration of other aspects which affect earnings quality.

Evaluation of discretionary and future-directed costs

Discretionary costs are outlays which managements can vary to some extent from period to period in order to conserve resources and/or to influence reported income. For this reason they deserve the special attention of analysts who are particularly interested in knowing whether the level of expenses is in keeping with past trends and with present and future requirements.

Maintenance and repairs

As was already discussed in the preceding chapter, management has considerable leeway in performing maintenance work and some discretion with respect to repairs. The analyst can relate these costs to the level of activity because they do logically vary with it. Two ratios are particularly useful in comparing the repair and maintenance levels from year to year:

$$\frac{\text{Repairs and Maintenance}}{\text{Sales}}$$

This ratio relates the costs of repairs and maintenance to this most available measure of activity. In the absence of sharp inventory changes, sales are a good indicator of activity. If year-to-year inventory levels change appreciably, an adjustment may be needed whereby ending inventories at approximate selling prices are added to sales and beginning inventories, similarly adjusted, are deducted from them.

The other ratio is:

$$\frac{\text{Repairs and Maintenance}}{\substack{\text{Property, Plant, and Equipment (exclusive of land)} \\ \text{Net of Accumulated Depreciation}}}$$

It measures repair and maintenance costs in relation to the assets for which these costs are incurred. Depending on the amount of information available to the analyst, the ratio of repair and maintenance costs to specific categories of assets can be developed. It should be noted that substandard repairs and maintenance on assets may require revisions in the assumptions of useful lives for depreciation purposes.

The absolute trend in repair and maintenance costs from year to year can be expressed in terms of index numbers and compared to those of related accounts. The basic purpose of all these measurements is to determine whether the repair and maintenance programs of the enterprise have been kept at normal and necessary levels or whether they have been changed in a way that affects the quality of income and its projection into the future.

Advertising

Since a significant portion of advertising outlays has effects beyond the period in which it is incurred, the relationship between advertising outlays and short-term results is a tenuous one. This also means that managements can, in certain cases, cut advertising costs with no commensurate immediate effects on sales, although it can be assumed that over the longer term sales will suffer. Here again, year-to-year variations in the level of advertising expenses must be examined by the analyst with the objective of assessing their impact on future sales and consequently on the quality of reported earnings.

There are a number of ways of assessing the trend in advertising outlays. One is to convert them into trend percentages using a "normal" year as a base. These trend percentages can then be compared to the trend of sales and of gross and net profits. An alternative measure would be the ratio of

$$\frac{\text{Advertising Expenses}}{\text{Sales}}$$

which, when compared over the years, would also indicate shifts in management policy. The ratio of

$$\frac{\text{Advertising}}{\text{Total Selling Costs}}$$

must also be examined so as to detect shifts to and from advertising to other methods of sales promotion.

An analysis of advertising to sales ratios over several years will reveal the degree of dependence of an enterprise on this promotional strategy. Comparison of this ratio with that of other companies in the industry will reveal the degree of market acceptance of products and the relative promotional efforts needed to secure it.

Research and development costs

The significance and the potential value of research and development costs are among the most difficult elements of the financial statements to analyze and interpret. Yet they are important, not only because of their relative size, but even more so because of their significance for the projection of future results.

Research and development costs have gained an aura of glowing potential in security analysis far beyond that warranted by actual experience. Mentioned most frequently are some of the undeniably spectacular and successful commercial applications of industrial research in the post-World War II era in such fields as chemistry, electronics, and photography. Not mentioned are the vast sums spent for endeavors labeled "research" which are expensed or written off while benefits from these fall far short of the original costs.

The analyst must pay careful attention to research and development costs and to the absence of such costs. In many enterprises they represent substantial costs, much of them fixed in nature, and they can represent the key to future success or failure. We must first draw a careful distinction between what can be quantified in this area and, consequently, analyzed in the sense in which we consider analysis in this work, and what cannot be quantified and must consequently be evaluated in qualitative terms.

In the area of research and development costs the qualitative element looms large and important. The definition of what constitutes "research" is subject to wide-ranging interpretations as well as to outright distortion. The label "research" is placed on activities ranging from those of a first-class scientific organization engaged in sophisticated pure and applied research down to superficial and routine product and market testing activities.

Among the many factors to be considered in the evaluation of the quality of the research effort are the caliber of the research staff and organization, the eminence of its leadership, as well as the commercial results of their research efforts. This qualitative evaluation must accompany any other kinds of analysis. Finally, a distinction must be drawn between government or outsider sponsored research and company directed research which is most closely identified with its own objectives. From the foregoing discussion it is clear that research cannot be evaluated on the basis of the amounts spent alone. Research outlays represent an expense or an investment depending on how they are applied. Far from guaranteeing results, they represent highly speculative ventures which depend on the application of extraordinary scientific as well as managerial skills for their success. Thus, spending on research cannot guarantee results and should not be equated with them.

Having considered the all-important qualitative factors on which an evaluation of research and development outlays depends, the analyst should attempt to determine as best he can how much of the current research and development outlays which have been expensed have future utility and potential.

The "future potential" of research and development costs is, from the point of view of the analyst, a most important consideration. Research cost productivity can be measured by relating research and development outlays to:

1. Sales growth
2. New product introductions
3. Acquisition of plant and equipment (to exploit the results of research)
4. Profitability

It must be recognized, however, that often the analyst will not have the adequate information which is necessary for him to check on the judgment of management and their independent accountants in their treatment of research and development outlays.

Another important aspect of research and development outlays is their discretionary nature. It is true that those enterprises which have established research and development departments impart a fixed nature to a segment of these costs. Nevertheless they can be increased or curtailed at the discretion of managements, often with no immediate adverse effects on sales. Thus, from the point of view of assessing the quality of reported income, the analyst must evaluate year-to-year changes in research and development outlays. This he can do by means of trend percentage analysis as well as by years of analysis of ratios such as the ratio of

$$\frac{\text{Research and Development Outlays}}{\text{Sales}}$$

A careful comparison of outlays for research and development over the years will indicate to the analyst whether the effort is a sustained one or one which varies with the ups and downs of operating results. Moreover, "one shot" research efforts lack the predictability or quality of a sustained, well organized longer term research program.

Other future-directed costs

In addition to advertising and research and development, there are other types of future-directed outlays. An example of such outlays are the costs of training operating, sales, and managerial talent. Although these outlays for the development of human resources are usually expensed in the year in which they are incurred, they may have future utility, and the analyst may want to recognize this in his evaluation of current earnings and of future prospects.

BALANCE SHEET ANALYSIS AS A CHECK ON THE VALIDITY AND QUALITY OF REPORTED EARNINGS

The amounts at which the assets and liabilities of an enterprise are stated hold important clues to an assessment of both the validity as well as the quality of its earnings. Thus, the analysis of the balance sheet is an important complement to the other approaches of income analysis discussed in this chapter, and elsewhere in this work.

Importance of carrying amounts of assets

The importance which we attach to the amounts at which assets are carried on the balance sheet is due to the fact that, with few exceptions such as cash, some investments, and land, the cost of most assets enters ultimately the cost stream of the income statement. Thus, we can state the following as a general proposition: Whenever assets are overstated the cumulative income[1] is overstated because it has been relieved of charges needed to bring such assets down to realizable values.

It would appear that the converse of this proposition should also hold true, that is, that to the extent to which assets are understated, cumulative income is also understated. Two accounting conventions qualify this statement importantly. One is the convention of conservatism, which calls for the recognition of gains only as they are actually realized. Although there has been some movement away from a strict interpretation of this convention, in general most assets are carried at original cost even though their current market or realizable value is far in excess of that cost.

The other qualifying convention is that governing the accounting for business combinations. The "pooling of interests" concept allows an acquiring company to carry forward the old book values of the assets of the acquired company even though such values may be far less than current market values or the consideration given for them. Thus, the analyst must be aware of the fact that such an accounting will allow the recording of profits, when the values of such understated assets are realized, which represents nothing more than the

---

[1] The effect on any one period cannot be generalized on.

surfacing of such hitherto understated assets. Since such profits have, in effect, previously been bought and paid for, they cannot be considered as representing either the earning power of the enterprise or an index of the operating performance of its management.

Importance of provisions and liabilities

Continuing our analysis of the effect of balance sheet amounts on the measurement of income, we can enunciate the further proposition that an understatement of provisions and liabilities will result in an overstatement of cumulative income because the latter is relieved of charges required to bring the provision or the liabilities up to their proper amounts. Thus, for example, an understatement of the provision for taxes, for product warranties, or for pensions means that cumulative income is overstated.

Conversely, an overprovision for present and future liabilities or losses results in the understatement of income or in the overstatement of losses. Provisions for future costs and losses which are excessive in amount represent attempts to shift the burden of costs and expenses from future income statements to that of the present.

Bearing in mind the general propositions regarding the effect on income of the amounts at which assets and liabilities are carried in the balance sheet, the critical analysis and evaluation of such amounts represents an important check on the validity of reported income.

Balance sheet analysis and the quality of earnings

There is, however, a further dimension to this kind of analysis in that it also has a bearing on an evaluation of the quality of earnings. This approach is based on the fact that various degrees of risk attach to the probability of the future realization of different types of assets.

Thus, for example, the future realization of accounts receivable has generally a higher degree of probability than has the realization of, say, inventory or unrecovered tools and dies costs. Moreover, the future realization of inventory costs can, generally, be predicted with greater certainty than can the future realization of goodwill or of deferred start-up costs. The analysis of the assets carried in the balance sheet by risk class or risk category holds clues to and is an important measure of the quality of reported income. Stated another way, if the income determination process results in the deferral of outlays and costs which carry a high degree of risk that they may not prove realizable in the future, then that income is of a lower quality than income which does not involve the recording of such high-risk assets.

Effect of valuation of specific assets on the validity and quality of reported income

In order to illustrate the importance of balance sheet analysis to an evaluation of reported income, let us now examine the effect of the valuation of specific assets on the validity and quality of that income.

Accounts receivable. The validity of the sales figure depends on the proper valuation of the accounts receivable which result from it. This valuation must recognize the risk of default in payment as well as the time value of money. On the later score, *APB Opinion No. 21* provides that if the receivable does not arise from transactions with customers or suppliers in the normal course of business under terms not exceeding a year, then, except for some other stated exceptions, it must be valued using the interest rate applicable to similar debt instruments. Thus, if the receivable bears an interest rate of 5 percent while similar receivables would, at the time, be expected to bear an interest rate of 7 percent, both the receivable and the sale from which it arose would be restated at the lower discounted amount.

Inventories. Overstated inventories lead to overstated profits. Overstatements can occur due to errors in quantities, errors in costing and pricing, or errors in the valuation of work in process. The more technical the product and the more dependent the valuation is on internally developed cost records, the more vulnerable are the cost estimates to error and misstatement. The basic problem here arises when costs which should have been written off to expense are retained in the inventory accounts.

An understatement of inventories results from a charge-off to income of costs which possess future utility and which should be inventoried. Such an understatement of inventories results in the understatement of current income and the overstatement of future income.

Deferred charges. Deferred charges such as deferred tooling or start-up and preoperating costs must be scrutinized carefully because their value depends, perhaps more than that of other assets, on estimates of future probabilities and developments. Experience has shown that often such estimates have proven overoptimistic or that they did not contain sufficient provisions for future contingencies. Thus, the risk of failure to attain expectations is relatively higher here than in the case of other assets.

The effect of external factors on the quality of earnings

The concept of earnings quality is so broad that it encompasses many additional factors which, in the eyes of analysts, can make earnings more reliable or more desirable.

In times of rising price levels the inclusion of "inventory profits" or the understatement of expenses such as depreciation lowers in effect the reliability of earnings and hence their quality.

The quality of foreign earnings is affected by factors such as difficulties and uncertainties regarding the repatriation of funds, currency fluctuations, the political and social climate as well as local customs and regulation. With regard to the latter, the inability to dismiss personnel in some countries in effect converts labor costs into fixed costs.

Regulation provides another example of external factors which can affect earnings quality. The "regulatory environment" of a public utility affects the "quality" of its earnings. Thus an unsympathetic or even hostile regulatory environment which causes serious lags in the obtaining of rate relief will detract from earnings quality because of uncertainty about the adequacy of future revenues.

The stability and reliability of earnings sources affect earnings quality. Defense related revenues can be regarded as nonrecurring in time of war and affected by political uncertainties in peace time.

Finally, some analysts regard complexity of operations and difficulties in their analysis (e.g., of conglomerates) as negative factors.

EVALUATION OF EARNINGS STABILITY AND TREND

The analyst will concentrate on identifying those elements in the income and cost streams which show stability, proven relationships, and predictability, and will separate them from those elements which are random, erratic, or nonrecurring and which, consequently, do not possess the elements of stability required for a reasonably reliable forecast or for inclusion in an "earning power" computation. To the intelligent analyst the most desirable income statement is the one containing a maximum of meaningful disclosure which will allow him to do this, rather than one containing built-in interpretations which channel him to specific conclusions.

The analyst must be on his guard against the well-known tendency of managements to practice income smoothing, thus trying to give to the income and expense streams a semblance of stability which in reality they do not possess. This is usually done in the name of "removing distortions" from the results of operations, whereas what is really achieved is the masking of the natural and cyclical irregularities which are part of the reality of the enterprise's experience and with which reality it is the analyst's primary task to come to grips.[2]

---

[2] The dissatisfaction of many managements with SFAS 8 stems in large part from the instability which the current recognition of foreign exchange gains and losses introduces into the income statement. And yet, for the analyst the real question is whether these are not, in fact, a portrayal of underlying realities and risks.

Need to identify erratic elements. In the analysis of the income statement the analyst will strive to identify erratic and unstable factors which will be separated from what may be called the enterprise's stable or basic "earning power." These factors include temporary demand (as was the case with the temporary shortage of color-TV tubes which in the 1960s temporarily increased the fortunes of National Video Company), unusual costs, such as those due to strikes, and items which are genuinely unusual or extraordinary. This analysis will separate results of discontinued operations, restate for accounting changes and assign unusual or extraordinary items to (say, five year) average earnings rather than to the earnings of a single year.

An example of an analytical format which can be used to modify a conventional income statement in order to segregate and highlight special or unusual items bearing on comparability or on income evaluation follows:

	Millions of dollars		
	19X3	19X2	19X1
Net sales	291	283	197
Other income (a)	12	6	7
Total	303	289	204
Cost of sales (b)	198	154	145
Selling, general & adm. (c)	21	16	18
Advertising (c)	12	6	9
Repair & maintenance (b)	5	7	4
Research & development	4	3	1
Interest	5	3	2
	245	189	179
	58	100	25
Income taxes (before items shown below) (d)	26	48	10
Income from continuing operations	32	52	15
Loss form discontinued operations*		(8)	(2)
Equity in associated companies (a)	12	8	6
Investment tax credit (d)	6	7	—
Tax exempt earnings of subsid. (d)		4	
Loss on disposal of oil oper.* (b)			(7)
Gain on patent suit*		12	
Flood loss*			(16)
Net income (loss)	50	75	(4)

* Net of tax.

The keying-letters above (e.g. (a), (b), . . .) indicate where rearranged or highlighted items have been segregated from by the analyst. The analyst will have to decide how to treat these items and whether to include them in a specific year or in the average earnings of a number of years.

The tax information comes from the tax disclosure footnote. Discretionary cost information comes from disclosure required by the SEC.

While this example covers three years, a more valid trend analysis will usually involve a larger number of years.

Determining the trend of income over the years

Having determined the size of a company's basic earnings as well as the factors which require adjustment before those earnings can be used as a basis for forecasts, the analyst will next determine the variability of these earnings, that is, changes in their size over the business cycle and over the longer term.

Evaluation of earnings variability. Earnings which fluctuate up and down with the business cycle are less desirable than earnings which display a larger degree of stability over such a cycle. The basic reason for this is that fluctuating earnings cause fluctuations in market prices. Earnings which display a steady growth trend are of the most desirable type. In his evaluation of earnings, the intelligent analyst realizes the limitations to which the earnings figure of any one year is subject. Therefore, depending on his specific purposes, he will consider the following earnings figures as improvements over the single year figure:

1. *Average earnings* over periods, such as 5 to 10 years, smooth out erratic and even extraordinary factors as well as cyclical influences, thus presenting a better and more reliable measure of "earning power" of an enterprise.
2. *Minimum earnings* are useful in decisions, such as those bearing on credit extension, which are particularly sensitive to risk factors. They indicate the worst that could happen based on recent experience.

The importance of earnings trends. In addition to the use of single, average, or minimum earnings figures, the analyst must be alert to earnings trends. These are best evaluated by means of trend statements such as those presented in Exhibit 7 of Chapter 1. The earnings trend contains important clues to the nature of the enterprise (i.e., cyclical, growth, defensive) and the quality of its management.

Distortions of trends. Analysts must be alert to accounting distortions which affect trends. Among the most important are changes in accounting principles and the effect of business combinations, particularly purchases. These must be adjusted for.

Some of the most common and most pervasive manipulative practices in accounting are designed to affect the presentation of earnings trends. These manipulations are based on the assumptions, generally true, that the trend of income is more important than its absolute size; that retroactive revisions of income already reported in prior periods have little, if any, market effect on security prices[3], and that once a company has incurred a loss, the size of the loss is not as significant as the fact that the loss has been incurred.

These assumptions and the propensities of some managements to use accounting as a means of improving the appearance of the earnings trend has led to techniques which can be broadly described as income smoothing.

Income smoothing. A number of requirements must be met by the income-smoothing process so as to distinguish it from outright falsehoods and distortions.

The income-smoothing process is a rather sophisticated and insidious device. It does not rely on outright or patent falsehoods and distortions but rather uses the wide leeway existing in accounting principles and their interpretation in order to achieve its ends. Thus, income smoothing is performed within the framework of "generally accepted accounting principles." It is a matter of form rather than one of substance. Consequently, it does not involve a real transaction (e.g., postponing an actual sale to another accounting period in order to shift revenue) but only a redistribution of credits or charges among periods. The general objective is to moderate income variability over the years by shifting income from good years to bad years, by shifting future income to the present (in most cases presently reported earnings are more valuable than those reported at some future date), or vice versa. Similarly, income variability can ,be moderated or modified by the shifting of costs, expenses, or losses from one period to another.

Income smoothing may take many forms. Hereunder are listed some forms of smoothing to which the analyst should be particularly alert:

1. The retroactive revision of results already reported, generally with the objective of relieving future income of charges which would have otherwise been made against it. The accounting profession has moved to limit the abuses in this area.
2. Misstatements, by various methods, of inventories as a means of redistributing income among the years. The Londontown Manufacturing Company case provides a classic example of such practices.[4]
3. The offsetting of extraordinary credits by identical or nearly identical extraordinary charges as a means of removing an unusual or

---

[3] This was recognized by *APB Opinion No. 20* which, with but three exceptions, forbids the retroactive restatement of prior year financial statements.

[4] Details can be found in an SEC decision issued October 31, 1963 (41 SEC 676–688).

sudden injection of income which may interfere with the display of a grow.ng earnings trend.

4. The provision of reserves for future costs and losses as a means of increasing the adverse results of what is already a poor year and utilizing such reserves to relieve future years of charges against income which would otherwise be properly chargeable against it. (Abuses in this area have been curtailed by SFAS 5.)

5. The substantial write-downs of operating assets (such as plant and equipment) or of intangibles (such as goodwill) in times of economic slowdown when operating results are already poor. The reason usually given for such write-downs is that carrying the properties at book value cannot be economically justified. (For example, Cudahy Packing Company has effected such a write-down of plant but had to reverse it in a subsequent year.) Particularly unwarranted is the practice of writing down operating assets to the point at which a target return on investment (which management thinks it *should* earn) is realized.

6. Timing the inclusion of revenues and costs in periodic income in such a way as to influence the overall trend of income (or loss) over the years. (Examples are the timing of sales or other disposition of property, incurring and expensing of discretionary costs such as research and development, advertising, maintenance, etc.) This category, unlike most others, entails more than accounting choice in that it may involve the timing of actual business transactions.

EXTRAORDINARY GAINS AND LOSSES

Both the evaluation of current earnings levels and the projection of future earnings rely importantly on the separation of the stable elements of income and expense from those which are random, nonrecurring, and erratic in nature.

Stability and regularity are important characteristics affecting the quality of earnings. Moreover, in making earnings projections the forecaster relies, in addition, on repetitiveness of occurrence. Thus, in order to separate the relatively stable elements of income and expense of an enterprise from those which are random or erratic in nature, it is important, as a first step, to identify those gains and losses which are nonrecurring and unusual as well as those which are truly extraordinary.

This separation is a first step which is mostly preparatory in nature. Following it is a process of judgment and analysis which aims at determining how such nonrecurring, unusual, or truly extraordinary items should be treated in the evaluation of present income, and of management performance as well as in the projection of future results.

Significance of accounting treatment and presentation

The validity of any accounting treatment and presentation is largely dependent on its usefulness to those who make decisions on the basis of financial statements. Unfortunately, particularly in the area of the accounting for, and the presentation of, extraordinary gains and losses, the usefulness of this accounting has been impaired because of the great importance attached to it by those who report the results of operations and who are judged by them.

The accounting for, and the presentation of, extraordinary gains and losses has always been subject to controversy. Whatever the merits of the theoretical debate surrounding this issue, the fact remains that one of the basic reasons for the controversial nature of this topic is reporting management's great interest in it. Managements are almost always concerned with the amount of net results of the enterprise as well as with the manner in which these periodic results are reported. This concern is reinforced by a widespread belief that most investors and traders accept the reported net income figures, as well as the modifying explanations which accompany them, as true indices of performance. Thus, extraordinary gains and losses often become the means by which managements attempt to modify the reported operating results and the means by which they try to explain these results. Quite often these explanations are subjective and are slanted in a way designed to achieve the impact and impression desired by management.

The accounting profession has tacitly, if not openly, recognized the role which the foregoing considerations play in the actual practice of reporting extraordinary gains and losses. Its latest pronouncements on this subject have at least insured a fuller measure of disclosure of extraordinary gains and losses and their inclusion in the income statement. This represents an improvement over prior pronouncements which, in an attempt to arrive at a "true" index of operating performance, sanctioned the exclusion of certain extraordinary gains and losses from the income statement.

Analysis and evaluation

The basic objectives in the identification and evaluation of extraordinary items by the analyst are:

1. To determine whether a particular item is to be considered "extraordinary" for purposes of analysis, that is, whether it is so unusual, nonoperating, and nonrecurring in nature that it requires special adjustment in the evaluation of current earnings levels and of future earning possibilities.
2. To decide what form the adjustment for items which are considered as "extraordinary" in nature should take.

Determining whether an item of gain or loss is extraordinary. The infirmities and shortcomings of present practice as well as the considerations which motivate it lead to the inescapable conclusion that the analyst must arrive at his own evaluation of whether a gain or loss should be considered as extraordinary and, if so, how to adjust for it.

In arriving at this decision it is useful to subdivide items, commonly classified as unusual or extraordinary, into three basic categories:

a. Nonrecurring operating gains or losses. By "operating" we usually identify items connected with the normal and usual operations of the business. The concept of normal operations is more widely used than understood and is far from clear and well defined. Thus, in a company operating a machine shop, operating expenses would be considered as those associated with the work of the machine shop. The proceeds from a sale above cost of marketable securities held by the company as an investment of excess cash would be considered a nonoperating gain. So would the gain (or loss) on the sale of a lathe, even if it were disposed of in order to make room for one that would increase the productivity of the shop.

The concept of recurrence is one of frequency. There are no predetermined generally accepted boundaries dividing the recurring event from the nonrecurring. An event (which in this context embraces a gain or loss) occurring once a year can be definitely classified as "recurring." An event, the occurrence of which is unpredictable and which in the past has either not occurred or occurred very infrequently, may be classified as nonrecurring. On the other hand, an event that occurs infrequently but whose occurrence is predictable raises some question as to its designation. An example of the latter would be the relining of blast furnaces. They last for many years; while their replacement is infrequent, the need for it is predictable. Some companies provide for their replacement by means of a reserve. Casualties do not, however, accrue in similar fashion.

Nonrecurring operating gains or losses are, then, gains or losses connected with or related to operations that recur infrequently and/or unpredictably.

In considering how to treat nonrecurring, operating gains and losses, the analyst would do best to recognize the fact of inherent abnormality and the lack of a recurring annual pattern in business and treat them as belonging to the results of the period in which they are reported.

We must also address ourselves to the question of what should be considered as "normal operations." Thus, it is a bakery's purpose to bake bread, rolls, and cakes, but it is presumably outside its normal purpose to buy and sell marketable securities for gain or loss, or even to sell baking machinery that is to be replaced for the purpose of more efficient baking.

This narrow interpretation of the objectives of a business has undergone considerable revision in modern financial theory. Thus, rather than the "baking bread" or any other specific objective, the main objective and task of management is viewed as that of increasing the capital of the owners, or expressed differently, the enhancing of the value of the common stock. This, according to modern financial theory, can be accomplished by means of the judicious combination of an optimal financing plan and any mix of operations opportunities that may be available to achieve the desired purpose.

The analyst should not be bound by the accountant's concept of "normal operations," and thus he can usefully treat a much wider range of gains and losses as being derived from "operations." This approach reinforces our conclusion that most nonrecurring, *operating* gains and losses should, from the point of view of analysis, be considered part of the operating results of the year in which they occur.

This approach is offered as a general guideline rather than as a mechanical rule. The analyst may, after examination of all attendant circumstance, conclude that some such items require separation from the results of a single year. The relative size of an item could conceivably be a factor requiring such treatment. In this case the best approach is to emphasize *average earnings* experience over, say, five years rather than the result of a single year. This approach of emphasizing average earnings becomes almost imperative in the case of enterprises which have widely fluctuating amounts of nonrecurring and other extraordinary items included in their results. After all, a single year is too short and too arbitrary a period on the basis of which to evaluate the earnings power of an enterprise or the prospects for future results. Moreover, we are all familiar with enterprises which defer expenses and postpone losses and come up periodically with a loss year which cancels out much of the income reported in preceding years.

b. Recurring, nonoperating gains or losses. This category includes items of a nonoperating nature that recur with some frequency. An example would be the recurring amortization of a "bargain purchase credit." Other possible examples are interest income and the rental received from employees who rent company-owned houses.

While items in this category may be classified as "extraordinary" in published financial statements, the narrow definition of "nonoperating" which they involve as well as their recurrent nature are good reasons why they should not be excluded from current results by the analyst. They are, after all, mostly the result of the conscious employment of capital by the enterprise, and their recurrence requires inclusion of these gains or losses in estimates designed to project future results.

c. Nonrecurring, nonoperating gains or losses. Of the three categories, this one possesses the greatest degree of "abnormality." Not only are the events here nonrepetitive and unpredictable, but they do not fall within the sphere of normal operations. In most cases these events are extraneous, unintended, and unplanned. However, they can rarely be said to be totally unexpected. Business is ever subject to the risk of sudden adverse events and to random shocks, be they natural or man-made. In the same manner, business transactions are also subject to unexpected windfalls. One good example in this category is the loss from damage done by the crash of an aircraft on a plant not located in the vicinity of an airport. Other, but less clear-cut, examples in this category may also include:

1. Substantial uninsured casualty losses which are not within the categories of risk to which the enterprise can reasonably be deemed to be subject.
2. The expropriation by a foreign government of an entire operation owned by the enterprise.
3. The seizure or destruction of property as a result of an act of war, insurrection, or civil disorders, in areas where this is totally unexpected.

It can be seen readily that while the above occurrences are, in most cases, of a nonrecurring nature, their relation to the operations of a business varies. All are occurrences in the regular course of business. Even the assets destroyed by acts of God were acquired for operating purposes and thus were subject to all possible risks.

Of the three categories this one comes closest to meeting the criterion of being "extraordinary." Nevertheless, truly unique events are very rare. What looks at the time as unique may, in the light of experience turn out to be the symptom of new sets of circumstances which affect and may continue to affect the earning power as well as the degree of risk to which an enterprise is subject.

The analyst must bear in mind such possibilities, but barring evidence to the contrary, items in this category can be regarded as extraordinary in nature and thus can be omitted from the results of operations of a *single* year. They are, nevertheless, part of the longer term record of results of the enterprise. Thus, they enter the computation of *average earnings,* and the propensity of the enterprise to incur such gains or losses must be considered in the projection of future average earnings.

The foregoing discussion has tried to point out that the intelligent classification of extraordinary items provides a workable solution to their treatment by the analyst. There are, however, other aspects of the evaluation of extraordinary items which must be considered here. One is the effect of extraordinary items on the resources of an enterprise; the other is their effect on the evaluation of management performance.

Effect of extraordinary items on enterprise resources. Every extraordinary gain or loss has a dual aspect. In addition to recording a gain (whether extraordinary or not) a business records an increase in resources. Similarly, a loss results in a reduction of resources. Since return on investment measures the relationship of net income to resources, the incurrence of extraordinary gains and losses will affect this important measure of profitability. The more material the extraordinary item, the more significant that influence will be. In other words if earnings and events are to be used to make estimates about the future, then extraordinary items convey something more than past performance. Thus, if an extraordinary loss results in the destruction of capital on which a certain return is expected, that return may be lost to the future. Conversely, an extraordinary gain will result in an addition of resources on which a future return can be expected.

This means that in projecting profitability and return on investment, the analyst must take into account the effect of recorded "extraordinary" items as well as the likelihood of the occurrence of future events which may cause extraordinary items.

Effect on evaluation of management. One implication frequently associated with the reporting of extraordinary gains and losses is that they have not resulted from a "normal" or "planned" activity of management and that, consequently, they should not be used in the evaluation of management performance. The analyst should seriously question such a conclusion.

What is "normal activity" in relation to management's deliberate actions? Whether we talk about the purchase or sale of securities, of other assets not used in operations, or of divisions and subsidiaries that definitely relate to operations, we talk about actions deliberately taken by management with specific purposes in mind. Such actions require, if anything, more consideration or deliberation than do ordinary everyday operating decisions because they are most often unusual in nature and involve substantial amounts of money. They are true tests of management ability. The results of such activities always qualify or enhance the results of "normal" operations, thus yielding the final net results.

Similarly, management must be aware of the risk of natural or manmade disasters or impediments in the course of business. The decision to engage in foreign operations is made with the knowledge of the special risks which this involves and the decision to insure or not is a normal operating decision. Nothing can really be termed completely unexpected or unforeseeable. Management does not engage, or is at least not supposed to engage, in any activity unconsciously;

hence, whatever it does is clearly within the expected activity of a business. Every type of enterprise is subject to specific risks which are inherent in it, and managements do not enter such ventures blindly.

When it comes to the assesment of results that count and results that build or destroy value, the distinction of what is normal and what is not fades almost into insignificance. Management's beliefs about the quality of its decisions are nearly always related to the normalcy, or lack thereof, of surrounding circumstances. This can be clearly seen in the management report section of many annual reports. Of course, management has to take more time to explain failure or shortcomings than to explain success. Success hardly needs an explanation, unless it involves circumstances not likely to be repeated. Failure often evokes long explanations, and more often than not, unusual or unforeseeable circumstances are blamed for it. If only normal conditions had prevailed, everything would have been much better. But in a competitive economy, normal conditions hardly ever prevail for any length of time. Management is paid to anticipate and expect the unusual. No alibis are permitted. Explanations are never a substitute for performance.

EARNINGS FORECASTING

A major objective of income analysis is the projection of income. The evaluation of the level of earnings is, from an analytical point of view, closely related to their projection. This is so because a valid projection of earnings involves an analysis of each major component of income and a considered estimate of its probable future size. Thus, some of the factors discussed in the preceding section are also applicable to earnings projection.

Projection must be differentiated from extrapolation. The latter is based on an assumption of the continuation of an existing trend and involves, more or less, a mechanical extension of that trend into the uncharted territory of the future.

Projection, on the other hand, is based on a careful analysis of as many individual components of income and expense as is possible and a considered estimate of their future size taking into consideration interrelationships among the components as well as probable future conditions. Thus, forecasting requires as much detail as is possible to obtain. In addition the "stability" of the individual components must be assessed in terms of the likelihood of their future recurrence. This lends particular importance to the analysis of nonrecurring factors and of extraordinary items. Some of the mechanics of earnings forecasting were considered in Chapter 3 as part of the process of projecting short-term fund flows.

Projection requires the use of an earnings record covering a number of periods. Repeated or recurring performance can be projected with a better degree of confidence than can random events.

Projection also requires use of enterprise data by product line or segment wherever different segments of an enterprise are subject to different degrees of risk, possess different degrees of profitability, or have differing growth potentials.

For example, the following tabulation of divisional earnings results indicates the degree to which the results of a component of an enterprise can be masked by the aggregate results:

	Earnings in million dollars			
	19X1	19X2	19X3	19X4
Segment A	1,800	1,700	1,500	1,200
Segment B	600	800	1,100	1,400
Total net income	2,400	2,500	2,600	2,600

Judgment on the earnings potential of the enterprise depends, of course, importantly on the relative importance of, as well as the future prospects of, segment B. The subject of product line reporting is discussed in Chapter 6.

SEC disclosure requirements—aid to forecasting

The "Management's discussion and analysis of the summary of earnings" disclosure requirements of the SEC (see Chapter 6) contain a wealth of information on management's views and attitudes as well as on factors which can influence enterprise operating performance. Consequently, the analyst may find much information in these analyses to aid him in the forecasting process.

Another important SEC disclosure requirement which can identify factors which the analyst should consider in forecasts is found in *ASR 166* (1974) entitled "Disclosure of Unusual Risks and Uncertainties in Financial Reporting." In this release the Commission indicates considerable concern over the number of situations it has noted in which significant and increasing business uncertainties have not been fully reflected in the financial reporting of registrants. It recognizes that investors and others are aware of the large number of estimates required in the preparation of financial statements, but points out that when unusual circumstances arise or there are significant changes in the degree of business uncertainty, a registrant has the responsibility of including comprehensive and specific disclosure of such risks and uncertainties in its financial reports.

The release contains specific examples of unusual risks and uncertainties such as *loans of financial institutions, marketable securities, deferred fuel costs* of public utilities, *crude oil purchase prices* subject to negotiation with foreign governments, and *single major projects* which will significantly affect the *success or failure* of a company. However, the importance of the release to the analyst lies in the principle of disclosure promulgated here. Thus, while these disclosures are not requirements under the Commission's rules, adherence to their spirit and intent by management should provide valuable information to the analyst.

Elements in earnings forecasts

Granted that the decision maker is interested primarily in future prospects, his approach to assessing them must be based primarily on the present as well as on the past. While expected future changes in conditions must be given recognition, the experience of the present and the past form the base to which such adjustments are applied. In doing this the analyst relies on the degree of continuity and perseverance of momentum which is the common experience of the enterprise and the industry of which it is part. Random shocks and sudden changes are always possible, but they can rarely be foreseen with any degree of accuracy.

The importance to the analyst of the underlying continuity of business affairs should not be overemphasized. One should not confuse the basis for the projection of future results, which the past record represents, with the forecast which is the end product. As a final objective the analyst is interested in a projection of net income. Net income is the result of the offset of two big streams: (1) total revenues and (2) total costs.

Considering that net income represents most frequently but a relatively small portion of either stream, one can see how a relatively minor change in either of these large streams can cause a very significant change in net income.

A significant check on the reasonableness of an earnings projection is to test it against the return on invested capital which is implicit in the forecast. If the result is at variance with returns realized in the past the underlying assumptions must be thoroughly examined so that the reasons for such deviations can be pinpointed.

In terms of the framework examined in Chapter 5 the return on investment depends on earnings which are a product of *management* and of *assets* which require funds for their acquisition.

1. Management. That it takes resourceful management to "breathe life" into assets by employing them profitably and causing their optimum utilization is well known. The assumption of stability of relationships and trends implies that there has been no major change in the skill, the depth, and the continuity of the management group or a radical change in the type of business in which their skill has been proven by a record of successful performance.

2. *Assets*. The second essential ingredient to profitable operations is funds or resources with which the assets essential to the successful conduct of business are acquired. No management, no matter how ingenious, can expand operations and have an enterprise grow without an adequate asset base. Thus, continuity of success and the extrapolation of growth must be based on an investigation of the sources of additional funds which the enterprise will need and the effect of the method of financing on net income and earnings per share.

The financial condition of the enterprise, as was seen in Chapters 2 and 4, can have a bearing on the results of operations. A lack of liquidity may inhibit an otherwise skillful management, and a precarious or too risky capital structure may lead to limitations by others on its freedom of action.

The above factors, as well as other economic, industry, and competitive factors, must be taken into account by the analyst when projecting the earnings of an enterprise. Ideally, in projecting earnings, the analyst should add a lot of knowledge about the future to some knowledge of the past. Realistically the analyst must settle for a lot of knowledge about the past and present and only a limited knowledge of the future.

In evaluating earnings trends the analyst relies also on such indicators of future conditions as capital expenditures, order backlogs, as well as demand trends in individual product lines.

It is important to realize that no degree of sophistication in the techniques used in earnings projections can eliminate the inevitable uncertainty to which all forecasts are subject. Even the best and most soundly based projections retain a significant probability of proving widely off the mark because of events and circumstances which cannot be foreseen.

The most effective means by which the analyst and decision maker can counter this irreducible uncertainty is to keep close and constant watch over how closely actual results conform to his projections. This requires a constant monitoring of results and the adjustment and updating of projections in the light of such results. The monitoring of earnings is considered later in this chapter.

Publication of financial forecasts

Recent years have witnessed intensified interest in publication by companies of forecasts of earnings and other financial data. The publication of forecasts in Britain in certain specialized situations as well as a belief that forecasts would be useful to investors were major factors behind this interest. This type of forecasting by insiders (i.e., management) is to be distinguished from forecasts made by financial analysts which are based on all the information which they can obtain.

In early 1977 an advisory committee to the SEC recommended that the agency design procedures to encourage companies to make forecasts of their economic performance.

So far, the commission has not formally encouraged or discouraged forecasting, but in 1975 it put forward rules governing those that do so. These were considered so restrictive, however, that businessmen warned that they would be forced to sharply reduce communications about their companies and the SEC withdrew them.

The SEC did, however, delete in its regulations a reference to predictions of "earnings" as possibly misleading in certain situations. Thus the commission will no longer object to disclosure in filings with it of projections which are made in good faith and have a reasonable basis provided that they are presented in appropriate form and are accompanied by information adequate for investors to make their own judgments.

The issue of forecasts is being considered again in connection with a major study of the agency's disclosure policy. The advisory committee said a so-called safe harbor rule should be adopted to clarify the potential liability of those making voluntary projections. It also said filings should include a cautionary statement about the inherent uncertainty of such data.

The interest in financial forecasts has resulted in a formal consideration of some of the issues by the AICPA which in 1975 issued two statements on the subject.[5]

These statements recommend, among others, that financial forecasts should be presented in a historical financial statement format and that they include regularly a comparison of the forecast with attained results.

Both statements recognize the primary importance which assumptions play in the reliability and creditability of a financial forecast. Consequently, those assumptions which management thinks most crucial or significant to the forecast—or are key factors upon which the financial results of the enterprise depends—should be disclosed to provide the greatest benefit to users of forecasts. There ordinarily should be some indication of the basis or rationale for these assumptions.

Speagle, Clark, and Elgers have categorized assumptions underly-

---

[5] "Guidelines for Systems for the Preparation of Financial Forecasts" and "Presentation and Disclosure of Financial Forecasts," AICPA 1975. (Auditing implication are also being considered.)

ing forecasted financial statements as: (1) "On going assumptions relating to the forecast methodology, company operating characteristics and so on; (2) Standard assumptions bearing upon the continuity in accounting policy, company management, supply sources, etc.; and (3) Transitory assumptions covering events in a particular year such as recapitalizations, labor settlements, new product introductions, facilities expansion, etc.[6]

The validity of any forecasted financial data depends to a high degree on the assumptions, both implicit and explicit, upon which the forecasting technique is based. The financial analyst who uses a management forecast as input to his own projections should pay first and primary attention to the assumptions on which it is based.

Estimating earning power

A culmination of the foregoing analytical and evaluative processes are often the estimation of the earning power of an enterprise. Earning power is a concept of financial analysis, not of accounting. It focuses on stable, and recurring elements and thus aims to arrive at the best possible estimate of repeatable *average* earnings over a span of future years. Accounting, as we have seen, can supply much of the essential information for the computation of earning power. However, the process is one involving knowledge, judgment, experience, a time horizon as well as a specialized investing or lending point of view.

Investors and lenders look ultimately to future cash flows as sources of rewards and safety. Accrual accounting, which underlies income determination, aims to relate sacrifices and benefits to the periods in which they occur. In spite of its known shortcomings, this framework represents the most reliable and relevant indicator of future probabilities of cash inflows and outflows presently known.

In our discussion of the analysis and the prediction of earnings, we recognized that a year represents too short and too arbitrary a time period for purposes of income measurement and evaluation. Because of the length of time required to assess the ultimate workout and the results of many investments and outlays and because of the presence of numerous nonrecurring and extraordinary factors, the determination of the normal earnings level or earning power of an enterprise is best measured by means of average earnings realized over a number of years.

The period of time over which an earnings average should be calculated will vary with the industry of which the enterprise is part

[6] R. E. Speagle, J. J. Clark, and P. Elgers, *Publishing Financial Forecasts: Benefits, Alternatives, Risk* (Laventhol Krekstein Horwath & Horwath, 1974).

and with other special circumstances. However, in general, a from 5- to 10-year earnings average will smooth out many of the distortions and the irregularities which impair the significance of a single year's results.

Monitoring performance and results

The judgments of what the proper financial forecast of an enterprise is or what its earning power is, are based on estimates which hinge on future developments which can never be fully forseen. Consequently, the best course of action is to monitor performance closely and frequently and to compare it with earlier estimates and assumptions. In this way one can constantly revise one's estimates and judgments and incorporate the unfolding reality into earlier judgments and conclusions. One of the best ways of monitoring performance is to follow interim reports closely.

INTERIM FINANCIAL STATEMENTS

The need to follow closely the results achieved by an enterprise requires frequent updatings of such results. Interim financial statements, most frequently issued on a quarterly basis, are designed to fill this need. They are used by decision makers as means of updating current results as well as in the prediction of future results.

If, as we have seen, a year is a relatively short period of time in which to account for results of operations, then trying to confine the measurement of results to a three-month period involves all the more problems and imperfections. For this and other reasons the reporting of interim earnings is subject to serious limitations and distortions. The intelligent use of reported interim results requires that we have a full understanding of these possible problem areas and limitations. The following is a review of some of the basic reasons for these problems and limitations, as well as their effect on the determination of reported interim results.

Year-end adjustments

The determination of the results of operations for a year requires a great many estimates, as well as procedures, such as accruals and the determination of inventory quantities and carrying values. These procedures can be complex, time-consuming, and costly. Examples of procedures requiring a great deal of data collection and estimation include estimation of the percentage of completion of contracts, determination of cost of work in process, the allocation of under- or over-absorbed overhead for the period, and the estimation of year-end inventory levels under the Lifo method. The complex, time-consuming, and expensive nature of these procedures can mean that they are performed much more crudely during interim periods and are often based on records which are less complete than are their year-end counterparts. The result inevitably is a less accurate process of income determination which, in turn, may require year-end adjustments which can modify substantially the interim results already reported.

Seasonality

Many enterprises experience at least some degree of seasonality in their activities. Sales may be unevenly distributed over the year, and so it may be with production and other activities. This tends to distort comparisons among the quarterly results of a single year. It also presents problems in the allocation of many budgeted costs, such as advertising, research and development, and repairs and maintenance. If expenses vary with sales, they should be accrued on the basis of expected sales for the full year. Obviously, the preparer of yearly financial statements has the benefit of hindsight which the preparer of interim statements does not. There are also problems with the allocation of fixed costs among quarters.

ILLUSTRATION 1. A study of the affairs of Mattel, Inc. reveals how company executives came up with targeted earnings quarter by quarter in fiscal years ending January 31, 1971 and 1972 using misleading or blatantly false methods to increase recorded sales or to decrease recorded expenses to reach targets. Mattel used an accounting practice known as "annualization" to match incurred expenses against sales on a year to date basis and these were juggled to achieve preselected results.

ILLUSTRATION 2. The tenuous nature of quarterly gross profit estimates is exemplified by this note by Bristol Products, Inc.: "Results of Fourth Quarter, 1974—As indicated in Note 1, the Company's interim financial statements for 1974 reflected results of operations using estimated gross profit percentages for its wholesale divisions. Physical inventories of these divisions at December 31, 1974 disclosed that the interim gross profit estimates and resultant net income were understated. If fourth quarter, 1974 results were computed using the annual gross profit percentages determined for the wholesale divisions, fourth quarter net income would have amounted to approximately $114,000 or $.10 per share. This compares with fourth quarter net income of $228,645 or $.24 per share computed by substracting interim results reported for the first three quarters of 1974 from results for the year."

ILLUSTRATION 3. The following is an example of adjustments which can result from seasonal variations: "Because of a seasonal production cycle, and in accordance with practices followed by the Company in reporting interim financial statements prior to 19X4, $435,000 of unabsorbed factory overhead has been deferred at July 4, 19X5. Due to uncertainties as to production and sales in 19X4, $487,000 of such unabsorbed overhead was expensed during the first 6 months of 19X4."

APB Opinion No. 28

In its *Opinion No. 28* the APB concluded that interim reports should be prepared in accordance with generally accepted accounting principles used in the preparation of the latest financial statements. Adopting mostly the point of view that a quarterly report is an integral part of a full year rather than a discrete period, it calls for the accrual of revenues and for the spreading of certain costs among the quarters of a year. For example, it sanctions the accrual of such year-end adjustments as inventory shrinkages, quantity discounts, and uncollectible accounts; but it prohibits the accrual of advertising costs on the ground that benefits of such costs cannot be anticipated. Losses cannot, generally, be deferred beyond the interim period in which they occur. Lifo inventory liquidations should be considered on an annual basis. Only permanent declines in inventory values are to be recorded on an interim basis. Moreover, the Opinion calls for the inclusion of extraordinary items in the interim period in which they occur.[7] Income taxes should be accrued on the basis of the effective tax rate expected to apply to the full year.

SEC interim reporting requirements

The SEC took a relatively early and strong interest in interim reporting and as a result brought about very significant improvements in reporting and disclosure in this area. In 1972 it required quarterly reports (on Form 10-Q) and reports on current developments (Form 8-K), disclosure of separate fourth quarter results and details of year-end adjustments.

In 1975 the SEC issued requirements (principally in *ASR 177*) which served to expand substantially the content and the utility of interim reports filed with the Commission. The principal requirements include:

Comparative quarterly and year-to-date abbreviated income statement data—this information may be labelled "unaudited" and

---

[7] SFAS 3 specifies that "If a cumulative effect type accounting change is made in other than the first interim period of an enterprise's fiscal year, no cumulative effect of the change shall be included in net income of the period of change. Instead, financial information for the pre-change interim periods of the fiscal year in which the change is made shall be restated by applying the newly adopted accounting principle to those pre-change interim periods."

must also be included in annual reports to shareholders. (Small companies are exempted).

Year-to-date statements of changes in financial position.

Comparative balance sheets.

Increased pro forma information on business combinations accounted for as purchases.

Conformity with the principles of accounting measurement as set forth in professional pronouncements on interim financial reports.

Increased disclosure of accounting changes with a letter from the registrant's independent public accountant stating whether or not he judges the changes to be preferable.

Management's narrative analysis of the results of operations, explaining the reasons for material changes in the amount of revenue and expense items from one quarter to the next. (See discussion in Chapter 6).

Indications as to whether a Form 8-K was filed during the quarter—reporting either unusual charges or credits to income or a change of auditors.

Signature of the registrant's chief financial officer or chief accounting officer.

In promulgating these expanded disclosure requirements the Commission indicated that it believed that these disclosures will assist investors in understanding the pattern of corporate activities throughout a fiscal period. It maintained that presentation of such quarterly data will supply information about the trend of business operations over segments of time which are sufficiently short to reflect business turning points.

Implications for analysis

While there have been some notable recent improvements in the reporting of interim results, the analyst must remain constantly aware that accuracy of estimation and the objectivity of determinations are and remain problem areas which are inherent in the measurement of results of very short periods. Moreover, the limited association of auditors with interim data, while lending as yet some unspecified degree of assurance, cannot be equated to the degree of assurance which is associated with fully audited financial statements. SEC insistence that the professional pronouncements on interim statements (such as *APB Opinion 28*) be adhered to should offer analysts some additional comfort. However, not all principles promulgated by the APB on the subject of interim financial statements result in presentations useful to the analyst. For example, the inclusion of extraordinary items in the results of the quarter in which they occur will require careful adjustment to render them meaningful for purposes of analysis.

While the normalization of expenses is a reasonable intraperiod accounting procedure, the analyst must be aware of the fact that there are no rigorous standards or rules governing its implementation and that it is, consequently, subject to possible abuse. The shifting of costs between periods is generally easier than the shifting of sales; and, therefore, a close analysis of sales may yield a more realistic clue to a company's true state of affairs for an interim period.

Since the price of the common stock influences the computation of earnings per share the analyst should in his evaluation of per share results be alert to the separation of these market effects from those related to the operating fundamentals of an enterprise.

Some problems of seasonality in interim results of operations can be overcome by considering in the analysis not merely the results of a single quarter, but also the year-to-date cumulative results which incorporate the results of the latest available quarter. This is the most effective way of monitoring the results of an enterprise and bringing to bear on its analysis the latest data on operations that are available.

QUESTIONS

1. Distinguish between income and cash flow. Why is there a distinction between the two?
2. *a.* What is meant by "quality of earnings"? Why do analysts assess it?
   b. On what major elements does the quality of earnings depend?
3. *a.* What are discretionary costs?
   b. Of what significance are discretionary costs to an analysis of the quality of earnings?
4. *a.* Why is the evaluation of research and development costs important to the analysis and projection of income?
   b. What are some of the precautions required in analyzing research and development expenses?
5. *a.* What is the relationship between the carrying amounts of various assets and earnings reported?
   b. What is the relationship between the amounts at which liabilities, including provisions, are carried and earnings reported?
6. Explain briefly the relationship between the quality of earnings and the following balance sheet items:
   a. Accounts receivable.
   b. Inventories.
   c. Deferred charges.
7. In what way is balance sheet analysis a check on the validity as well as the quality of earnings?

8. Comment on the effect which the "risk category" of an asset has on the quality of reported earnings.

9. What is the effect of external factors on the quality of earnings?

10. What is income smoothing? How can it be distinguished from outright falsehoods?

11. Name three forms of income smoothing.

12. Why are managements so greatly interested in the reporting of extraordinary gains and losses?

13. What are the basic objectives of the analyst in the identification and the evaluation of extraordinary items?

14. *a.* Into what categories can items which are described as unusual or extraordinary in the financial statements be usefully subdivided into for purposes of analysis?
    b. Give examples of each such category.
    c. How should the analyst treat items in each category? Is such a treatment indicated under all circumstances? Explain.

15. What are the effects of extraordinary items on—
    a. Enterprise resources?
    b. The evaluation of managements?

16. Comment on the following statement:
    "Extraordinary gains or losses have not resulted from a 'normal' or 'planned' activity of management and, consequently, they should not be used in the evaluation of managerial performance."
    Do you agree?

17. What is the difference between projection and extrapolation of earnings?

18. Cite some of the examples of unusual risks and uncertainties that should be disclosed according to SEC's *ASR No. 166* and their importance to the financial analyst.

19. What are the categories of assumptions underlying forecasted financial statements? Give examples of each category. What is the importance of these assumptions to the financial analyst?

20. *a.* What are interim financial statements used for?
    b. What accounting problems which are peculiar to iterim statements must the analyst be aware of?

21. Why are interim earnings reports particularly useful in the monitoring of earnings trends?

22. Interim financial reporting can be subject to serious limitations and distortions. Discuss some of the reasons for this.

23. What factors (*a*) within the company, and (*b*) within the economy, have and are likely to affect the degree of variability in the earnings per share, dividends per share, and market price per share, of common stock? (C.F.A.)

24. What are the major disclosure requirements by the SEC with regard to interim reports? What are the objectives behind them?

25. What implications do interim reports hold for the financial analyst?

9

COMPREHENSIVE ANALYSIS OF FINANCIAL STATEMENTS

THE METHODOLOGY OF FINANCIAL STATEMENT ANALYSIS

The marshalling, arrangement, and presentation of data for purposes of financial statement analysis can be standardized to some extent in the interest of consistency and organizational efficiency. However, the actual process of analysis must be left to the judgment of the analyst so that he may allow for the great diversity of situations and circumstances which he is likely to encounter in practice, and thus give full reign to his own initiative, originality, and ingenuity. Nevertheless, there are some useful generalizations and guidelines which may be stated as to a general approach to the task of financial statement analysis.

To begin with, financial statement analysis is oriented towards the achievement of definite objectives. In order that the analysis best accomplish these objectives, the first step is to define them carefully. The thinking and clarification leading up to such a definition of objectives is a very important part of the analytical process, for it insures a clear understanding of objectives, that is, of what is pertinent and relevant and what is not, and thus also leads to avoidance of unnecessary work. This clarification of objectives is indispensable to an *effective* as well as to an *efficient* analysis: *effective*, in that, given the specifications, it focuses on the most important and most relevant elements of the financial statements; *efficient*, in that it leads to an analysis with maximum economy of time and effort.

ILLUSTRATION 1. The bank's loan officer, dealing with a request for a short-term loan to finance inventory, may define his objective as assessing the intention and the ability of the borrower to repay the loan on time. Thus, the analyst can concentrate on what is needed to achieve this objective and need not, for instance, address himself to industry conditions which can affect the borrowing entity only over the longer term.

Once the objective of the analysis has been defined, the next step is the formulation of specific questions the answers to which are needed in the achievement of such objectives.

ILLUSTRATION 2. The loan officer in Illustration 1 now needs to define the critical criteria which will affect his decision. For instance, the question of the borrower's *willingness* to repay the short-term loan bears on his character; and financial statement analysis can reveal only the history of past loans granted it. Thus, tools other than financial statement analysis will have to be employed to get complete information on the borrower's character.

Among the other questions on which the loan officer will need information are the following:

1. What is the enterprise's short-term liquidity?
2. What will its sources and uses of cash be during the duration of the loan agreement?

Financial statement analysis can go far towards providing answers to such questions.

Having defined the objective and having translated it into specific questions and criteria which must be resolved, the analyst is ready for the third step in the analysis process. This is to decide which tools and techniques of analysis are the most appropriate, effective, and efficient ones to use in working on the particular decision problem at hand.

ILLUSTRATION 3. Following the sequence developed in Illustrations 1 and 2, the loan officer will now decide which financial statement analysis tools are most appropriate to use in this case. He may choose one or more of the following:

1. Short-term liquidity ratios.
2. Inventory turnover measures.
3. Cash flow projections.
4. Analyses of changes in financial position.

These analyses will have to include estimates and projections of future conditions toward which most, if not all, financial analysis is oriented.

The fourth and final step in analysis is the interpretation of the data and measures assembled as a basis for decision and action. This is the most critical and difficult of the steps, and the one requiring the application of a great deal of judgment, skill, and effort. Interpretation is a process of investigation and evaluation, and of envisaging the reality which lies behind the figures examined. There is, of course, no mechanical substitute for this process of judgment. However, the proper definition of the problem and of the critical questions which must be answered, as well as the skillful selection of the most appropriate tools of analysis available in the circumstances, will go a long way towards a meaningful interpretation of the results of analysis.

ILLUSTRATION 4. Following the sequence of the first three examples above, the collection, by the loan officer, of the data described in Illustration 3 is, of course, not the end result of his analysis. These data must be integrated, evaluated, and interpreted for the purposes of reaching the basic decision of whether to make the loan and, if so, in what amount.

By way of analogy, the weather forecasting function provides an example of the difference between the availability of analytical data and its successful interpretation. Thus, the average listener to weather information does not know how to interpret barometric pressure, relative humidity, or wind velocity. What one needs to know is the weather forecast which results from an interpretation of these data.

The intelligent analyst and interpreter of financial statement data must always bear in mind that a financial statement is at best an abstraction of an underlying reality. Further mathematical manipulation of financial data can result in second, third, and even further levels of abstractions; and the analyst must always keep in mind the business reality behind the figures. No map of the Rocky Mountains can fully convey the grandeur of the terrain. One has to see them in order to appreciate them because maps, like financial statements, are, at best abstractions. That is why security analysts must, at some point, leave the financial statements and visit the companies which they analyze in order to get a full understanding of the phenomena revealed by their analysis. This is particularly true because the static reality portrayed by the abstractions found in the financial statements cannot remain static for very long. Reality is ever changing.

A recognition of the inherent limitations of financial data is needed for intelligent analysis. This does not detract from their importance because financial statements and data are the only means by which the financial realities of an enterprise can be reduced to a common denominator which is quantified and which can be mathematically manipulated and projected in a rational and disciplined way.

SIGNIFICANCE OF THE "BUILDING BLOCK" APPROACH TO FINANCIAL ANALYSIS

The six major "building blocks" of financial analysis which we have examined in this text are:

1. Short-term liquidity.
2. Funds flow.

3. Capital structure and long-term solvency.
4. Return on investment.
5. Asset utilization.
6. Operating performance.

The "building block" approach to financial statement analysis involves:

1. The determination of the major objectives which a particular financial analysis is to achieve.
2. Arriving at a judgment about which of the six major areas of analysis (i.e., our "building blocks") must be evaluated with what degree of emphasis and in what order of priority.

For example, the security analyst, in the evaluation of the investment merit of a particular issue of equity securities, may attach primary importance to the earning capacity and potential of the enterprise. Thus, the first "building block" of the analysis will be the evaluation of "operating performance" and the next, perhaps, "return on investment." A thorough analysis will, of course, require that attention be paid to the other four major areas of analysis, although with perhaps lesser degrees of emphasis, that is, depth. This attention to the other major areas of analysis is necessary in order to detect possible problem areas, that is, areas of potential risk. Thus, further analysis may reveal a liquidity problem arising from a "thin" working capital condition, or it may reveal a situation of inadequate capital funds which may stifle growth and flexibility. It is conceivable that these problem areas may reveal themselves to be so important as to overshadow the question of earning power, thus leading to a change in the relative emphasis which the analyst will accord to the main areas of his particular analysis.

While the subdivision of the analysis into six distinct aspects of a company's financial condition and performance is a useful approach, it must be borne in mind that these areas of analysis are highly interrelated. For example, the operating performance of an enterprise can be affected by the lack of adequate capital funds or by problems of short-term liquidity. Similarly, a credit evaluation cannot stop at the point where a satisfactory short-term liquidity position has been determined because existing or incipient problems in the "operating performance" area may result in serious drains of funds due to losses. Such drains can quickly reverse the satisfactory liquidity position which may prevail at a given point in time.

At the start of his analysis the analyst will tentatively determine the relative importance of the areas which he will examine and the order in which they will be examined. This order of emphasis and priority may subsequently change in the light of his findings and as the analysis progresses.

THE EARMARKS OF GOOD FINANCIAL ANALYSIS

As we have noted, the foundation of any good analysis is a thorough understanding of the objectives to be achieved and the uses to which it is going to be put. Such understanding leads to economy of effort as well as to a useful and most relevant focus on the points that need to be clarified and the estimates and projections that are required.

In practice, rarely can all the facts surrounding a particular analysis be obtained, so that most analyses are undertaken on the basis of incomplete and inadequate facts and data. The process of financial analysis is basically one of reducing the areas of uncertainty—which can, however, never be completely eliminated.

A written analysis and report is not only a significant medium of communication to the reader but it also serves importantly to organize the thinking of the analyst as well as to allow him or her to check the flow and the logic of the presentation. The process of writing reinforces our thinking and vice versa. As we revise our words, we also refine our thoughts—and improvements in style lead, in turn, to the sharpening and improvement in the thinking process itself.

A good analysis separates clearly for the reader the interpretations and conclusions of the analysis from the facts and data upon which they are based. This not only separates fact from opinion and estimate, but also enables the reader to follow the rationale of the analyst's conclusions and allows him to modify them as his judgment dictates. To this end the analysis should contain distinct sections devoted to:

1. General background material on the enterprise analyzed, the industry of which it is a part, and the economic environment in which it operates.
2. Financial and other data used in the analysis as well as ratios, trends, and other analytical measures which have been developed from them.
3. Assumptions as to the general economic environment and as to other conditions on which estimates and projections are based.
4. A listing of positive and negative factors, quantitative and qualitative, by important areas of analysis.
5. Projections, estimates, interpretations, and conclusions based on the aforementioned data.(Some analyses list only the positive and negative factors developed by the analysis and leave further interpretations to the reader.)

A good analysis should start with a brief "Summary and Conclusion" section as well as a table of contents to help the busy reader decide how much of the report he wants to read and on which parts of it to concentrate.

The writer of an analytical report must guard against the all-too-common tendency to include irrelevant matter. For example, the reader need not know the century-old details of the humble beginnings of the enterprise under analysis nor should he be taken on a "journey" along all the fruitless byways and missteps which the analyst inevitably encountered in his process of ferreting out and separating the important from the insignificant. Irrelevant bulk or "roughage" can only serve to confuse and distract the reader of a report.

Ambiguities and equivocations which are employed to avoid responsibility or to hedge conclusions do not belong in a good analytical report. Finally, the writers of such reports must recognize that we are all judged on the basis of small details. Consequently, the presence of mistakes in grammar or of obvious errors of fact in a report can plant doubt in the reader's mind as to the competence of the author and the validity of the analysis.

SPECIAL INDUSTRY OR ENVIRONMENTAL CHARACTERISTICS

In this text, the analysis of the various segments of financial statements was treated from the point of view of the regular commercial or industrial enterprise. The financial analyst must, however, recognize that there are industries with distinct accounting treatments which arise either from their specialized nature or from the special conditions, such as governmental regulation, to which they are subject. The analysis of the financial statements of such enterprise requires a thorough understanding of the accounting peculiarities to which they are subject, and the analyst must, accordingly, prepare himself for his task by the study and the understanding of the specialized areas of accounting which affect his particular analysis.

Thus, for example, the analysis of a company in the Oil and Gas Industry requires a thorough knowledge of such accounting concepts peculiar to that industry such as the determination of "cost centers," prediscovery costs, discovery costs, and the disposition of capitalized costs. There are particular problems in the treatment of exploratory, development, and other expenditures as well as in amortization and depletion practices.

Life insurance accounting, to cite another example, also requires specialized knowledge which arises from the peculiarities of this industry and from the regulation to which it is subject. There are special problems in the area of recognition of premium revenues, the accounting for acquisition costs of new business, and the determination of policy reserves.

Public utility regulation has resulted in specialized accounting concepts and problems of which every utility analyst must be aware. There are tax allocation problems resulting in differences among companies which "normalize" taxes versus those which "flow" them through. Then there are problems related to the adequacy of provisions for depreciation, and problems concerning the utility's "rate base" and the method by which it is computed.

As in any field of endeavor specialized areas of inquiry require that specialized knowledge be brought to bear upon them. Financial analysis is, of course, no exception.

ILLUSTRATION OF A COMPREHENSIVE ANALYSIS OF FINANCIAL STATEMENTS—MARINE SUPPLY CORPORATION

The following analysis of the financial statements and other data of the Marine Supply Corporation will serve as an illustration of this process.

Introduction

The Marine Supply Corporation, a leader in the outboard motor industry, was incorporated some 40 years ago. While outboard motor engines and related marine products still account for the bulk of the company's sales, other products are gaining in importance and growing at a rate much faster than the primary products (see Exhibit 9–1, sales breakdown).

Snow vehicle production was launched in fiscal year 19X4. Its growth rate looks dramatic because it starts from an extremely low

EXHIBIT 9–1

MARINE SUPPLY CORPORATION
Sales Breakdown
(in millions of dollars)

Product	19X5		19Y0		Sales increase 19X5– 19Y0	Annual growth rates*
	Sales	%	Sales	%	%	%
Marine products	135.0	74.5	217.3	71.0	+ 61	10
Lawn care equipment	16.2	9.0	30.5	10.0	+ 88	13
Vehicles	14.1	7.8	19.6	6.4	+ 39	7
Chain saws	9.4	5.2	9.5	3.1	+ 1	0
Snow vehicles	5.1	2.8	23.4	7.7	+359	36
Miscellaneous.............	.9	.7	4.2	1.8	+367	36
Total	180.7	100.0	304.5	100.0	+ 69	11.2

* Five-year period, compounded annually.

base. Outboard motors can be regarded as the primary base of the company's growth, and outboard engines contribute an even larger portion of corporate profits.

While most of Marine Supply Corporation's products have some commercial applications, they are sold primarily for recreation or leisure-time purposes. Being generally big-ticket items, the company's sales are greatly subject to swings in consumer buying cycles.

The use of outboard motors and the majority of the company's other products is largely confined to the warmer months of late spring, summer, and early fall. This means peak retail demand for these items is seasonal; dealer buying tends to be concentrated in this period as well. As a result, the first quarter of the company's fiscal year (ending December) frequently produces a nominal deficit while the June quarter generates 40 percent or more of annual profits.

Marine Supply is one of the world's largest manufacturers of outboard motors; its twin lines command something more than one half the U.S.-Canadian market (by far the most important), and the company estimates a similar proportion overseas. Competition in the industry is keen but is generally centered on performance (racing) results rather than price. Marine Supply's principal advantages are:

1. A highly efficient sales-distribution-repair network (currently about 8,000 dealers) in North America.
2. Exceptional brand loyalty.
3. Almost total domination of the lower horsepower ranges where the vast majority of engines are still sold.

Marine Supply's position in golf carts is also dominant, but its degree of domination is less pronounced. While an important factor in snow vehicles, lawn care, and chain saws, these are highly fragmented markets with many competitors. Still, the company's marketing strategy is the same as in outboards: build a quality product with a strong dealer organization, use intensive advertising, and maintain a premium price structure. This approach has been successful in lawn mowers where Lawn King is a strong competitor despite tremendous product similarity among all brands. In snow vehicles—a comparatively new product to which Marine Supply was a comparative late comer—the company has not yet been totally successful in building its market share.

Financial statements

The financial statements of Marine Supply Corporation are presented in Exhibits 9–2, 9–3, and 9–4 below.

The auditor's opinion on the financial statements has been unqualified for the past six years.

Additional information

Marine Supply has a good, if very cyclical, historic operating performance record. In 19W4, for example, sales were only $73 million as against $304.5 million in 19Y0, more than 300 percent increase. Over the same span net income grew from $5.5 million to $13.4 million, an increase of 144 percent. The slower gain in net income, reflecting sharply reduced operating margins due largely to Federal Trade Commission action in the mid 19W0s, has meant erosion of the company's return on investment from an exceptional 25 percent (on net worth) in the 19W4–W6 period to just over 11 percent for the last three years.

EXHIBIT 9-2

MARINE SUPPLY CORPORATION
Balance Sheets
As of September 30 for Years 19X5–Y0
(in millions of dollars)

	19X5	19X6	19X7	19X8	19X9	19Y0
Assets						
Current Assets:						
Cash and equivalents	15.00	24.30	12.10	17.40	19.50	17.48
Receivables	22.50	24.50	31.40	35.40	46.50	53.70
Inventories	49.50	57.60	64.70	78.90	100.80	97.32
Other current assets	—	.00	.0	.10	.0	.00
Total Current Assets	87.00	106.40	108.20	131.80	166.80	168.50
Gross plant	85.20	88.60	98.70	114.70	129.70	137.90
Accumulated depreciation	(45.20)	(48.70)	(52.50)	(56.10)	(60.80)	(65.88)
Net plant......................	40.00	39.90	46.20	58.60	68.90	72.02
Intangibles and other assets	7.00	6.40	10.70	11.90	12.70	15.45
Total Assets	134.00	152.70	165.10	202.30	248.40	255.97
Liabilities and Capital						
Current Liabilities:						
Accounts payable	1.10	1.10	7.00	15.20	24.60	24.53
Other current liabilities	15.80	24.90	23.50	26.90	35.00	36.75
Total Current Liabilities...	16.90	26.00	30.50	42.10	59.60	61.28
Long-term debt	14.50	13.50	12.40	28.70	45.70	46.04
Deferred taxes and investment credits	1.94	2.19	2.57	4.58	5.38	7.14
Other liabilities	2.39	2.57	2.03	1.52	2.57	1.05
Total Liabilities	35.73	44.26	47.50	76.90	113.25	115.51
Net worth	98.27	108.44	117.60	125.40	135.15	140.46
Total Liabilities and Capital	134.00	152.70	165.10	202.30	248.40	255.97

EXHIBIT 9-3

MARINE SUPPLY CORPORATION
Income Statements
For Years Ending September 30
(in millions of dollars)

	19X5	19X6	19X7	19X8	19X9	19Y0
Net sales	180.70	212.50	233.40	280.20	327.10	304.48
Other income	—	—	—	—	—	.19
Total revenue	180.70	212.50	233.40	280.20	327.10	304.67
Cost of goods sold*						
(excluding depreciation)	113.35	130.95	145.03	180.16	209.52	190.58
Depreciation	4.28	4.26	4.40	4.75	5.59	6.25
Gross profit	63.07	77.29	83.97	95.29	111.99	107.84
Selling, general, and administrative						
expenses	41.98	47.04	54.04	61.99	71.44	72.99
Operating income	21.09	30.25	29.93	33.30	40.55	34.85
Fixed interest charges	.70	1.05	1.23	2.10	4.73	6.60
Other expenses	.62	.54	.62	1.05	1.54	—
Net income before tax	19.77	28.66	28.08	30.15	34.28	28.25
Income taxes:						
Deferred	.47	.26	.38	.37	.80	1.75
Current	8.66	12.73	12.47	14.12	16.40	13.11
Net income	10.64	15.67	15.23	15.66	17.08	13.39
Common dividends	5.13	6.35	6.37	7.98	8.06	8.08
Retained earnings	5.51	9.32	8.86	7.68	9.02	5.31
* Includes:						
Research and development costs	11.8	11.2	13.4	12.1	12.4	12.8
Maintenance and repairs	10.3	10.4	11.6	12.4	12.7	11.5

Exhibit 9-5, fifteen-year growth rates—annually compounded, compares various growth rates, first using single years, then a three-year span.

Note that with the exception of sales per share, the growth rates are still higher for the single year comparisons. This is attributable to the very low 19W4 base and the tremendous gains from 19W4 through 19W6—a three-year span in which sales, net income, dividends, and book value each increased from 75 percent to 133 percent.

Exhibit 9-6, five-year growth rates—annually compounded, indicates the most recent five-year performance, first on a single-year basis, then using three-year "smoothed" base. On either basis, the company's record looks better in recent years than over the long pull.

Two noteworthy points should be made about this record:

1. The gains represent almost solely internal growth. Acquisitions have been few, their relative size quite small, and their profit contributions have often been negative.

EXHIBIT 9-4

MARINE SUPPLY CORPORATION
Statement of Changes in Financial Position
For Years Ending September 30
(in thousands of dollars)

	19X5	19X6	19X7	19X8	19X9	19Y0	Total %	Total Amount
Source:								
From operations:								
Net earnings	10,642	15,666	15,375	15,662	17,078	13,390	46.5	87,813
Depreciation	4,284	4,264	4,448	4,747	5,587	6,254	15.7	29,584
Amortization of tooling	—	3,360	2,755	4,595	6,484	6,637	12.6	23,831
Other—principally provision for deferred income taxes	755	527	493	372	800	1,753	2.5	4,700
Total from operations	15,681	23,817	23,071	25,376	29,949	28,034	77.3	145,928
Proceeds from sale of:								
Long-term borrowings	174	—	—	17,030	18,202	1,391	19.4	36,623
Plant and equipment (net)	52	662	326	146	347	112	.9	1,767
Common stock	—	859	294	317	732	—	1.2	2,254
Other items, net	—	—	45	1,808	413	—	1.2	2,266
Total sources	15,907	25,338	23,736	44,677	49,643	29,537	100.0	188,838
Application:								
Additions to plant and equipment	2,964	4,739	11,177	16,639	16,109	9,461	32.3	61,089
Tooling expenditures	—	2,565	7,635	6,430	6,825	7,398	16.3	30,853
Long-term debt maturing currently	1,136	1,073	1,126	1,035	1,142	1,073	3.6	6,585
Dividends paid	5,128	6,351	6,369	7,981	8,060	8,080	22.2	41,969
Other items, net	408	355	—	1,199	—	3,526	2.9	5,488
Total applications	9,636	15,083	26,307	33,284	32,136	29,538	77.3	145,984
Working capital increase (decrease)	6,271	10,255	(2,571)	11,393	17,507	(1)	22.7	42,854

2. No adjustments need be made for dilution. The company has no convertible securities outstanding; stock options are also insignificant.

Exhibits 9–7 through 9–10 are based on the financial statements of Marine Supply Corporation.

EXHIBIT 9-5

MARINE SUPPLY CORPORATION
Fifteen-Year Growth Rates
(annually compounded)

Per share	19W4–Y0	19W4–W6 to 19X8–Y0
Sales	8.0%	8.0%
Net income	4.6	3.3
Dividends	10.0	7.4
Book value	11.0	7.4

EXHIBIT 9-6

MARINE SUPPLY CORPORATION
Five-Year Growth Rates
(annually compounded)

Per share	19X5–Y0	19X4–X6 to 19X8–Y0
Sales	10.5%	9.7%
Net income	4.2	5.7
Dividends	9.0	9.6
Book value	7.0	5.7

EXHIBIT 9-7

MARINE SUPPLY CORPORATION
Common-Size Balance Sheets

	19X5	19X6	19X7	19X8	19X9	19Y0
Assets						
Current Assets:						
Cash and equivalents	11%	16%	7%	9%	8%	7%
Receivables	17	16	19	17	18	21
Inventories	37	38	39	39	41	38
Total current assets	65	70	65	65	67	66
Land, plant, and equipment, net	30	26	28	29	28	28
Intangibles and other assets	5	4	7	6	5	6
Total Assets	100	100	100	100	100	100
Liabilities and Equity						
Current liabilities	13	17	18	21	24	24
Long-term debt	11	9	8	14	18	18
Deferred taxes and investment credits	1	1	2	2	2	3
Other liabilities	2	2	1	1	1	—
Total Liabilities	27	29	29	38	45	45
Net worth	73	71	71	62	55	55
Total Liabilities and Equity	100	100	100	100	100	100

EXHIBIT 9-8

MARINE SUPPLY CORPORATION
Common-Size Income Statements

Item	19X5	19X6	19X7	19X8	19X9	19Y0	Industry composite 19Y0
Net sales	100.0%	100.0%	100.0%	100.0%	100.0%	100.0%	100.0%
Cost of goods sold* (excluding depreciation)..............	62.7	61.6	62.1	64.3	64.1	62.6	64.6
Depreciation	2.4	2.0	1.9	1.7	1.7	2.0	2.8
Gross profit	34.9	36.4	36.0	34.0	34.2	35.4	32.6
Selling, general, and administrative expenses	23.2	22.2	23.2	22.1	21.8	24.0	21.0
Operating income	11.7	14.2	12.8	11.9	12.4	11.4	11.6
Interest expense.............	.4	.5	.5	.8	1.4	2.2	0.8
Other income (expense)......	(.3)	(.2)	(.3)	(.4)	(.5)	.1	0.2
Net income before tax	11.0	13.5	12.0	10.7	10.5	9.3	11.0
Deferred taxes	.3	.1	.2	.1	.3	.6	.3
Income taxes................	4.8	6.0	5.3	5.0	5.0	4.3	4.9
Net income	5.9	7.4	6.5	5.6	5.2	4.4	5.8
* Including: Research and development..	6.5	5.2	5.7	4.3	3.8	4.2	5.4
Maintenance and repairs	5.7	4.9	5.0	4.4	3.9	3.8	6.2

EXHIBIT 9-9

MARINE SUPPLY CORPORATION
Trend Index of Selected Accounts
(19X5 = 100)

Account	19X6	19X7	19X8	19X9	19Y0
Cash.................................	162	81	116	130	117
Accounts receivable	109	140	157	207	239
Inventory	116	131	159	204	197
Total current assets	122	124	151	192	194
Total current liabilities.................	154	180	249	353	363
Working capital	115	111	128	153	153
Fixed assets	100	116	147	172	180
Other assets	94	157	175	187	227
Long-term debt.......................	93	86	198	315	318
Total liabilities	124	133	215	317	323
Equity capital	110	120	128	138	143
Net sales.............................	118	129	155	181	169
Cost of goods sold	116	128	159	185	168
Gross profit	123	133	151	178	171
Selling, general, and administrative expenses	112	132	148	170	174
Interest expense	150	176	300	676	945
Total expenses	114	128	155	182	172
Operating income	143	142	158	192	165
Profit before taxes	145	142	153	173	143
Net income	147	143	147	161	126

EXHIBIT 9–10

MARINE SUPPLY CORPORATION
Selected per Share Results

Item	19X5	19X6	19X7	19X8	19X9	19Y0
Sales	$22.90	$26.71	$29.28	$34.85	$40.48	$37.68
Net income	1.35	1.97	1.91	1.95	2.11	1.66
Dividends	.65	.80	.80	1.00	1.00	1.00
Book value	12.43	13.63	14.76	15.60	16.73	17.38

While the economy in general was slow in 19Y0, 19X8 and 19X9 were good years for boat sales; and responses at boat shows across the country were strong in those years. Compared to automobiles, revolutionary model changes are rare in the boating industry.

The company's contract with the union expired at the end of 19Y0, and the company was not sure during 19Y0 whether it could avoid a strike.

After careful analysis, we conclude that about one half of deferred taxes and investment credits account balances will be reversed in the future; however, the possibility of reversal in the foreseeable future for the remaining one half is very remote. "Other liabilities" represent various debts having the characteristic of long-term debt. "Other current liabilities" represent amounts owing to various banks under revolving credit agreement.

The company is nearing its production capacity limits, necessitating new construction. For example, in 19X8 and 19X9, the company was forced to utilize some aging facilities on a multishift basis.

The period 19X5–Y0 has been by far the most prosperous in Marine Supply's history. Sales and earnings have each reached peak levels, although the last six years have not been as profitable as mid 19W0s.

Based on the foregoing data and information we are to analyze the financial statements of Marine Supply Corporation with the following alternative points of view (objectives) in mind:

1. That of a bank to extend to the company a short-term loan of $15 million.
2. That of an insurance company to whom the company wants to sell privately $30 million of 25-year bonds.
3. That of an investor considering a substantial investment in the company.

These diverse and broad points of view require that we analyze all major aspects of the company's financial condition and results of operations, that is:

1. Short-term liquidity.
2. Funds flow.

3. Capital structure and long-term solvency.
4. Return on investment.
5. Asset utilization.
6. Operating performance.

The following assumptions will be used in the projection of operating results and of fund flows for 19Y1:

It is expected that the annual growth rate by product line will continue except that snow vehicles and miscellaneous are expected to grow at a rate of 29 percent and 30 percent respectively. Improvements in production facilities will lower the cost of goods (exclusive of depreciation) to 60 percent of sales. The composite depreciation rate (depreciation expense as a percent of ending net plant) is expected to be 10 percent. Amortization of tooling costs included in cost of goods sold will be 10 percent higher than in 19Y0. Selling expenses, which amount to one fourth of the selling, general, and administrative group of expenses are expected to go up by 10 percent in 19Y1. The other three fourths of this category will remain unchanged. Taxes will average 53 percent of income before taxes, and the amount of deferred taxes will amount to the same proportion of the total tax accrual as in 19Y0. Dividend payout is expected to amount to 50 percent of net income.

In order to retire $15 million in revolving credit notes (shown under current liabilities) and to finance a major plant expansion and modernization program just starting, the company expects to sell at par, early in 19Y1, $30 million in 30-year 7 percent sinking fund bonds. That will leave $20 million in revolving credit notes outstanding. Interest expenses in 19Y1 are estimated at $5,810,000. The maturities and sinking fund requirements of long-term debt are as follows:

Million $

19Y1	1.0
19Y2	2.3
19Y3	4.4
19Y4	8.6
19Y5	12.2

Research and development outlays are expected to amount to $3 million in 19Y1, and outlays for tooling are planned at $13 million.

The company plans to spend $30 million in 19Y1 on plant and equipment. Sales of equipment are expected to bring in $200,000 after tax. The chain-saw division which has a book value of $5 million is expected to be disposed of for $2 million, net of tax.

The problem of obtaining a meaningful and valid standard of external comparison for this analysis has been a difficult one. Two major sources of such data are industry statistics, such as those compiled by

Robert Morris Associates, Standard & Poor's, or Dun & Bradstreet, or comparative data derived from companies of similar size and in similar lines of business. In this case comparative data was developed from the published reports of companies in lines of business similar to those of Marine Supply Company.

Analysis of short-term liquidity

Exhibit 9–11 presents some important liquidity measures of Marine Supply Corporation over the last six years. Both the current ratio and the acid test ratio have been declining over this period. However, they are still at sound levels in 19Y0 on an absolute basis and also when compared to industry averages. The downward trend in these measures must be interpreted in the light of management's possible policy and intent. It is quite conceivable, particularly in view of the lower levels of the comparable industry ratios, that the current position in earlier years was unnecessarily strong and represented a wasteful tying up of resources which did not earn an acceptable return for the company. A glance at the common-size analysis in Exhibit 9–7 reveals the changes which have occurred in the composition of working capital elements over the past six years; the proportion of cash and cash equivalents among the current assets has dropped by almost half even though the absolute amount of cash and equivalents has not diminished on average. There has been a significant increase in current liabilities; they now represent almost a quarter of the funds invested in the enterprise whereas in 19X5 they represented 13 percent of the total. This is confirmed in the trend index analysis (Exhibit 9–9) which shows that since 19X5 current liabilities have increased 3.63 times while cash increased 1.17 times, receivables 2.39 times, and inventories only 1.97 times. That the increase in current liabilities was out of proportion to that of sales is seen by the fact that during the same period sales increased only 1.69 times. That means that Marine Supply Corporation was somehow able to secure short-term credit from suppliers and banks at a rate twice as fast as that warranted by growth in sales. This, in turn, is importantly responsible for the steady decline in the current and the acid-test ratios.

A more serious problem area is the quality of the two important elements of current assets: accounts receivable and inventories. The accounts receivable turnover has undergone constant decline over the past six years, reaching a low point of 5.67 in 19Y0. In that year it compared unfavorably as to 8.2 turnover in the industry. The alternative measure of "days' sales in accounts receivable" presents a similar picture with an increasing number of "days' sales" tied up in receivables. The 19Y0 figure of 63.5 days compares to an industry experi-

EXHIBIT 9–11

MARINE SUPPLY CORPORATION
Short-Term Liquidity Analysis

	Units	19X5	19X6	19X7	19X8	19X9	19Y0	Industry composite 19Y0
Current ratio	Ratio	5.15	4.09	3.55	3.13	2.80	2.75	2.40
Acid-test ratio	Ratio	2.22	1.88	1.43	1.26	1.11	1.16	.90
Accounts receivable turnover	Times	8.03	8.67	7.43	7.92	7.03	5.67	8.20
Inventory turnover	Times	2.29	2.27	2.24	2.28	2.08	1.96	2.30
Days sales in receivables	Days	44.8	41.5	48.5	45.5	51.2	63.5	43.9
Days to sell inventory	Days	157.2	158.6	160.7	157.9	173.1	183.7	156.5
Conversion period	Days	202.0	200.1	209.2	203.4	224.3	247.2	200.4
Cash to current assets	%	17.24	22.84	11.18	13.20	11.69	10.37	9.80
Cash to current liabilities	%	88.76	93.46	39.67	41.33	32.72	28.52	29.60
Working capital	$(MM)	70.10	80.40	77.70	89.70	107.20	107.22	—
Liquidity index	#	127	118	139	134	150	163	—

ence of 44.0 days. It also compares unfavorably to the company's most common terms of sales of net 30 days. Thus, it is possible that the collectibility and the liquidity of accounts receivable have deteriorated.

Inventory turnover has also decreased over the past six years, although the deterioration has not been as marked as has been the case with receivables. A number of factors could account for this, including a larger number and variety of outboard motors, lawn mowers, and snow vehicles models which must be stocked, the larger variety of spare parts that these require, as well as a possible accumulation of raw materials in anticipation of a strike at suppliers. It is also possible that Marine Supply Corporation overestimated sales for 19Y0, while sales dropped 7 percent from the 19X9 level, inventories dropped by only 3 percent, thus contributing to the turnover slowdown. The 19Y0 turnover of Marine Supply Corporation of 1.96 compares unfavorably with the 2.3 industry average. In 19Y0 it took 183.7 days to sell the average inventory compared to an industry average of 156.2 days. The comparable figure for the company in 19X5 was 157.2 days.

The deterioration in the liquidity of the principal operating assets of the current asset group, accounts receivable, and inventories is also seen in the period of days it takes to convert inventories into cash. It grew from 202 days in 19X5 to 247.2 days in 19Y0 and compares to an industry average of only 200.2 days in the latter year.

The liquidity index at 163 in 19Y0 up from 127 in 19X5, also corroborates the deterioration in the liquidity of the current assets which we have already determined in the analysis of individual components of working capita.

It is conceivable that further analysis and inquiry from management will reveal that the slowdown in the turnover of accounts receivable and inventories does not affect their ultimate realization even if that would take a longer time. In that case the repercussions of such a slowdown lie in the area of liquidity and funds flow as well as in the area of asset utilization which will be examined later in this analysis.

Analysis of funds flow

This analysis has two main objectives:

1. To supplement the static measures used to assess short-term liquidity by means of a short-term funds flow forecast.
2. To analyze the statement of changes in financial position in order to assess its implications on the longer term flow of funds (i.e., long-term solvency).

Our first step will be to build a funds flow forecast for Marine Supply Corporation in 19Y1. Since sources of funds from operations are an important element of funds and a projection of earnings will be necessary anyway, we start with such a projection for 19Y1, using the data and the supplementary information provided (see Exhibit 9–12).

EXHIBIT 9–12

MARINE SUPPLY CORPORATION
Projected Income Statement for 19Y1
(millions of dollars)

	19Y0 sales level	Incre- ment factor	19Y1 esti- mated amount	Total	%
Net sales:					
Marine products	217.3 ×	1.10	239.03		
Lawn care equipment	30.5 ×	1.13	34.47		
Vehicles	19.6 ×	1.07	20.97		
Snow vehicles	23.4 ×	1.29	30.19		
Miscellaneous	4.2 ×	1.30	5.46	330.12	100.0
Cost of goods sold (exclusive of depreciation)			198.07		60.0
Depreciation (1)			8.70		2.6
				206.77	62.6
Gross profit				123.35	37.4
Selling, general, and administrative expenses:					
General and administrative (2)			54.74		
Selling (3)			20.08		
Amortization of deferred startup costs			1.00	75.82	23.0
				47.53	14.4
Interest expenses				5.81	1.8
Income before taxes				41.72	12.6
Income taxes:					
Current			19.24		
Deferred (4)			2.88	22.12	6.7
				19.60	5.9
Loss on disposal of chain-saw division (net of tax)				3.00	0.9
Net income				16.60	5.0

(1) Beginning net plant plus half of 19Y1 additions times 10%: (72.2 + 15.0) × 10%. It is assumed that the plant additions were in use, on average, half of the year.
(2) Three fourths of 72.99 (last year selling, general, and administrative).
(3) Selling expenses at 10% above the 19Y0 level (72.99 − 54.74) × 1.10.
(4) Deferred taxes at 13% of the total provision for the year which amounts to 53% of pretax income.

Having established the estimated net income for 19Y1 we can now proceed, using the data and the additional information we now have, to construct an estimated statements of sources and uses of working capital (funds) for 19Y1.

Exhibit 9–13 projects an increase in working capital of about $16 million. If this forecast proves reasonably accurate, the current ratio should improve to about 3:1. As is true of all forecasts, their reliability depends on the validity of the assumptions on which they are based.

EXHIBIT 9–13

MARINE SUPPLY CORPORATION
Projected Statement of Sources and Uses of Funds for 19Y1
(in millions of dollars)

Sources of funds:
From operations:

Net income	16.60	
Add: Items not requiring current funds:		
Depreciation	8.70	
Amortization of tooling costs	7.30	
Deferred income taxes	2.88	
Amortization of startup costs	1.00	
Loss on sale of chain-saw division	3.00	
Total from operations		39.48
Proceeds from sale of 7% sinking fund bonds		30.00
Sale of chain-saw division		2.00
Sale of equipment		0.20
Total sources		71.68
Uses of funds:		
Additions to plant and equipment	30.00	
Outlays for tooling	13.00	
Outlays for research and development	3.00	
Long-term debt maturities	1.00	
Dividends declared	8.30	
Total uses		55.30
Increase in working capital		16.38

The assumption that Marine Supply Corporation can sell $30 million in 7 percent sinking fund bonds appears reasonable in the light of the company's present capital structure. Its failure to do so would require either the abandonment or deferral of expansion and modernization plans or it will result in a deterioration of the current ratio to about 2.5

The projected net income of $16.6 million for 19Y1 appears reasonable because it is based on the assumption of a continuation of present sales trends and a reduction in the growth rate of two product line categories. However, it is more vulnerable on the expense side. The increase in the gross margin is predicated on increases in productivity which are envisaged but which are yet to be realized. Moreover, any program of expansion and modernization is subject to the risk of delays, misjudgments, and short falls which may delay, postpone, or completely undermine the realization of improvements and economies.

On the other hand, the increases in fixed costs which such a program entails are a reality with which the enterprise must live for a long time.

Any degree of failure to realize savings and improvements will also affect the short-term flow of funds. Thus, for example, continuing the assumption that 50 percent of the net income will be distributed as dividends, a 5 percent increase in cost of goods sold (exclusive of depreciation) will lower the inflow of funds as follows:

	Millions of dollars (approximately)
Increase in cost of goods sold (exclusive of depreciation)—5% of $198 million...................	9.90
Less tax effect at 53%	5.25
	4.65
Less: Dividend reduction (50%).......................	2.32
	2.33
Less: Deferred taxes (13% of 5.25)	0.68
Reduction in funds available from operations	1.65

A similar computation can, of course, be made for any other change in assumptions. The likelihood of any of the above assumptions materializing and the probability attached to them is, ultimately, a matter of judgment.

The longer range funds flow picture is subject to a great many uncertainties. Examination of the company's historical pattern of fund flows over the 19X5 to 19Y0 period (see Exhibit 9–4) is revealing. Funds from operations provided 77 percent of all funds inflows while long-term borrowing provided most of the rest. Such borrowing occurred mostly in 19X8 and 19X9. Equity financing was negligible.

Additions to plant and equipment used about 32 percent of all funds available. These outlays were, however, twice as high as the provision for depreciation. With the company bumping against the ceiling of its practical capacity in many lines this trend is likely to continue. Already in 19Y1 capital expenditures are planned at three times the 19Y0 level and long-term debt will be incurred to finance this as well as the working capital needs of an expanding business. As will be discussed further under "capital structure" there is, of course, a limit to the company's debt capacity, and equity financing will be required. This may explain the company's relatively generous dividend policy over the recent years.

In spite of relatively heavy long-term borrowing in 19X8 and 19X9 long-term debt maturities and sinking fund requirements are low. These will, however, increase sharply from $1 million in 19Y1 to $12 million in 19Y5. The proposed $30 million bond issue in 19Y1 will undoubtedly add to these maturities.

The longer term fund flow outlook of Marine Supply Corporation is one of increasing demand for funds due to accelerating outlays for plant equipment and tooling as well as sharply rising debt service outlays. While funds from operations have been significant and are growing, they will have to continue to do so to meet increasing demands. Since funds from operations represented 77 percent of all sources of funds in the past six years, the company's fund flow is particularly vulnerable to any reduction in net income. Working capital needs will also increase along with the expected increase in sales volume.

It should be borne in mind that focusing on *net* working capital does not tell the whole story of Marine Supply Corporation's borrowing. Included in current liabilities are $35 million in revolving credit notes. The company may well want to convert this short-term interest sensitive debt into a longer term type of obligation. A beginning towards this goal is expected to be made in 19Y1. That too will require using up some of the company's shrinking capacity to finance by means of long-term debt.

Analysis of capital structure and long-term solvency

Having just examined the funds aspect of Marine Supply Corporation's long-term solvency we now turn to an examination of its capital structure and the risk inherent in it. The change in the company's capital structure can be gauged by means of a number of measurements and comparisons.

Looking at Exhibit 9–7 we see that the contribution of equity capital to the total funds invested in the enterprise has shrunk from 73 percent in 19X5 to 55 percent in 19Y0. With the expected issuance of $30 million on additional bonds, this proportion can be expected to dip below 50 percent. The long-term debt portion of the total funds invested in the enterprise increased from 11 percent in 19X5 to 18 percent in 19Y0 and is headed considerably higher in 19Y1.

In Exhibit 9–9 we can see the relative change in debt, equity, and other related elements in the financial statements. On a basis of 19X5 = 100 long-term debt rose to 318 while equity capital increased only to 143. In the same period net sales rose only to 169, net income to 126, while interest costs soared to 945. Quite clearly the company decided to finance its needs by means of debt, both short and long term. Reasons for this could be an unwillingness to dilute the equity or a desire to incur monetary liabilities in times of inflation. Whatever the reason, the leverage and hence the risk in the capital structure increased substantially. This is particularly true because Marine Supply Corporation is in a relatively cyclical industry and relies on a share of the consumer's discretionary dollar.

The capital structure and long-term solvency ratios in Exhibit 9–14 bear out these conclusions. Equity to total debt stands at 1.29 in 19Y0 compared to 2.86 in 19X5, and compares to an industry composite of 1.4. Similarly, equity to long-term debt stands at 2.84 in 19Y0 compared to an industry composite of 3.1. The times interest earned ratio plummeted from 29.24 in 19X5 to 5.28 in 19Y0 and compares with an industry composite of 8.6. The income projections as well as the borrowing plans for 19Y1 would result in an improved interest coverage ratio of 8.2 as a consequence of the refinancing of high-interest short-term debt and also because the 7 percent bonds will be outstanding for only part of the year. This improvement in the coverage ratio may, however, prove to be only temporary in nature.

EXHIBIT 9–14

MARINE SUPPLY CORPORATION
Capital Structure and Long-Term Solvency Ratios

	19X5	19X6	19X7	19X8	19X9	19Y0	19Y0 industry composite
Equity to total debt	99.24* / 34.76 = 2.86	109.54 / 43.16 = 2.54	118.89 / 46.21 = 2.57	127.69 / 74.61 = 1.71	137.84 / 110.56 = 1.25	144.03 / 111.94 = 1.29	1.4
Equity to long-term debt	99.24 / 17.86* = 5.56	109.54 / 17.16 = 6.38	118.89 / 15.71 = 7.57	127.69 / 32.51 = 3.93	137.84 / 50.96 = 2.70	144.03 / 50.66 = 2.84	3.1
Equity to net fixed assets	2.48	2.75	2.57	2.18	2.00	2.00	2.2
Times interest earned	29.24	28.30	23.83	15.36	8.25	5.28	8.6

* Computed as following:

One half of deferred income taxes	0.97
Net worth shown	98.27
Adjusted net worth	99.24
Total liabilities shown	35.73
Less: One half of deferred income taxes	0.97
Adjusted total liabilities	34.76
Less: Total current liabilities	16.90
Adjusted long-term debt	17.86

As we saw from the longer term funds flow analysis, the company is now entering a period of increasing capital investment needs and of increasingly heavy debt service schedules. It does this at a time when its debt is high in relation to its equity capital and when shrinking interest coverage ratios exert downward pressure on its credit rating. Moreover, the increasing fixed charges which stem from recent substantial additions to plant and equipment make operating results more vulnerable to cyclical downturn with the result that sources of funds from operations are similarly vulnerable.

Analysis of return on investment

The return which the company realizes on total assets, Exhibit 9–15, has been on the decline in recent years, having declined from 10.6 percent in 19X6 (which was the best year in this respect) to 6.4 percent in 19Y0. Even if we regard 19X6 as an unusually good year, the decline from the prior year return levels is quite significant. In comparison with an industry return on total assets in 19Y0 of 9.3 percent, the company's 6.4 percent return is also significantly worse. This negative trend over the past six years is reason for concern and requires further investigation. The two major elements which make up the return on total assets, that is, net profit margin and asset turnover, will be examined later in this analysis.

EXHIBIT 9–15

MARINE SUPPLY CORPORATION
Return on Investment Ratios

	19X5	19X6	19X7	19X8	19X9	19Y0	19Y0 industry composite
Return on total assets	8.2% (1)	10.6%	9.6%	8.3%	7.8%	6.4%	9.3%
Return on equity capital...............	10.8% (2)	14.5% ,	13.0%	12.5%	12.6%	9.5%	12.8%
Return on long-term liabilities and equity	9.4% (3)	12.8%	11.8%	10.5%	10.3%	8.5%	10.6%
Financial leverage index.................	1.32 (4)	1.37	1.23	1.27	1.32	1.33	1.38
Equity growth rate	5.6 (5)	8.6	7.5	6.1	6.7	3.88	—

Notes:

(1) $\dfrac{\text{Net income} + \text{Interest expense} (1 - \text{Tax rate})}{\text{Total assets}} = \dfrac{10.64 + .7(1 - .46)}{134}$

(2) $\dfrac{\text{Net income}}{\text{Net worth}} = \dfrac{10.64}{98.27}$

(3) $\dfrac{\text{Net income} + \text{Interest expense} (1 - \text{Tax rate})}{\text{Long-term liabilities} + \text{Equity}} = \dfrac{11.018}{134.0 - 16.90}$

(4) $\dfrac{\text{Return on equity capital}}{\text{Return on total assets}} = \dfrac{10.8}{8.2}$

(5) $\dfrac{\text{Net income—Payout}}{\text{Common shareholders' equity}} = \dfrac{\text{Amount retained}}{\text{Common shareholders' equity}} = \dfrac{5.51}{98.27}$

In comparison with the return on total assets, the decline in the return on equity has not been quite as significant. This is mainly due to the relatively advantageous use of short-term and long-term credit. The financial leverage index (Exhibit 9–15) which in 19Y0 stands at 1.33 is practically unchanged from its 19X5 level. It must be noted, however, that the company cannot expand its debt much more from the present level since over the past six years debt has expanded very significantly. Thus, in the immediate future an adequate return on equity will be dependent primarily on improvements in profitability and in asset utilization. As can be seen from Exhibit 9–15, the equity growth rate from earnings retention has shrunk in 19Y0 to 3.8 percent from over 6 percent in the two years before that and from 8.6 percent in 19X6. This is largely due to the maintenance of a generous dividend policy in the face of shrinking earnings. This shrinkage in the internal equity growth rate comes at a time when the company is increasingly in need of additional equity capital. Conceivably, however, a liberal dividend record can facilitate in the future the raising of equity capital.

Analysis of asset utilization

Exhibit 9–16 indicates that in most categories the asset utilization ratios have been declining over the past six years. The sales to total assets ratio is down to 1.2 in 19Y0 from the 1.4 level in 19X8 and compares to an industry average 1.5 times. The impact of this change can be assessed as follows:

EXHIBIT 9–16

MARINE SUPPLY CORPORATION
Asset Utilization Ratios

	19X5	19X6	19X7	19X8	19X9	19Y0	19Y0 industry composite
Sales to cash and equivalents	12.0	8.7	19.3	16.1	16.8	17.4	9.1
Sales to receivables	8.0	8.7	7.4	7.9	7.0	5.7	10.6
Sales to inventories	3.7	3.7	3.6	3.6	3.2	3.1	4.1
Sales to working capital	2.6	2.6	3.0	3.1	3.1	2.8	4.0
Sales to fixed assets	4.5	5.3	5.1	4.8	4.7	4.2	6.4
Sales to other assets	25.8	33.2	21.8	23.4	25.8	19.7	22.3
Sales to total assets	1.3	1.4	1.4	1.4	1.3	1.2	1.5
Sales to short-term liabilities	10.7	8.2	7.7	6.7	5.5	5.0	—

Given the company's net income to sales ratio in 19Y0 of 4.4 percent and a net of tax interest expense of about 1.1 percent (Exhibit 9–8) a total asset turnover of 1.4 (the 19X8 rate) would have yielded a return on total assets of 7.7 percent $[(4.4 + 1.1) \times 1.4]$ rather than the 6.4 percent return actually realized in 19Y0. At a rate of turnover of 1.5 (industry average) the present profit rate would yield a return on investment of about 8.2 percent $[(4.4 + 1.1) \times 1.5]$.

The asset categories where the turnover rate has dropped most sharply over the six years are "other assets" and "receivables." Only cash showed an increase in turnover (utilization). Judging by the fact that there were significant fixed asset additions in 19X8 and 19X9 (see Exhibit 9–9), the drop in the fixed asset turnover rate was moderate. It must be borne in mind that it takes time before fixed asset additions become sufficiently productive to generate an expected volume of sales. In addition, certain types of fixed asset outlays represent improvements in production facilities which lead to efficiencies and savings rather than to expansion of productive capacity. Such outlays, consequently, do not lead to greater sales but rather to savings in variable costs and result in improvements in profit margins. Exhibit 9–8 indicates that while profit margins are below the 19X6–X7 levels, they have been in an improving trend in the last three years. The drop over the six-year span in the turnover of the "other assets" group reflects growth in deferred charges, particularly tooling.

Analysis of operating performance

Exhibit 9–8 presents common-size income statements of the company for the six years, 19X5–Y0.

The gross profit of Marine Supply Corporation has held within a relatively narrow range over the last six years. In 19Y0 at 35.3 percent the gross profit margin is higher than in the preceding two years but is below the levels reached in 19X6 and 19X7. It does compare favorably to the industry gross margin of 32.6 percent. However, the research and development costs as well as the repair and maintenance costs included in the cost of goods sold figure are lower, as a percentage of sales than the industry composite. This aspect of the quality of earnings will be further discussed below.

In 19Y0 the percentage relationship between depreciation expense and sales was 2.1 percent up from 1.7 percent the year before. The disparity between this percentage and the industry composite of 2.8 percent is noteworthy because it may affect the quality of Marine Supply Corporation's earnings. It would appear that an inadequate amount of depreciation is recorded by Marine Supply Corporation. Before a definite judgment can be made, additional information would be required. The company is now approaching the limit of practical capacity in many of its product lines. Competitors may have more reserve capacity available and that may express itself in a relatively higher composite depreciation rate. It is also possible that Marine Supply Corporation's equipment is, on average, of an older vintage, and hence lower cost, than its competitors'. On the other hand, a lower composite depreciation rate than necessary is a factor which lowers the quality of the company's earnings.

We have two more measures available to judge the size of the yearly depreciation charge:

	19X5	19X6	19X7	19X8	19X9	19Y0
Accumulated depreciation as a percentage of gross plant	53	55	53	49	47	48
Annual depreciation expense as a percentage of gross plant	5.0	4.8	4.4	4.2	4.3	4.5

The decline in the percentage of accumulated depreciation in relation to gross plant most likely reflects the substantial additions of new equipment in recent years. The decline of depreciation expense as a percentage of gross plant is, however, indicative of a less conservative depreciation policy in the more recent years.

Selling, general, and administrative expenses as a percentage of sales have, generally, been on the rise. In 19Y0 they stood at 24 percent which compares to an industry composite figure of only 21 percent. Thus, by the time we reach operating income, the advantage which the company held over the industry because of larger gross margin has now been neutralized. Operating income for Marine Supply Corporation represents 11.4 percent of sales, and that compares with 11.6 percent for the industry. Further inquiries should be made to determine whether the selling expense component or the general and administrative part are responsible for the increase in this category.

Interest expenses have shown by far the steepest increase over the past six years. On the basis of 19X5 = 100 they have grown to 945 (almost tenfold) by 19Y0 (Exhibit 9–9). This is due, of course, primarily to the sharp expansion of debt. Moreover, the short-term revolving debt is interest sensitive and thus introduces a measure of uncertainty in the forecasting of future interest charges.

Two other aspects of the quality of Marine Supply Corporation's earnings should be noted.

Research and development costs as a percentage of sales have been in a declining trend having reached 4.2 percent in 19Y0 down from 6.5 percent in 19X5 (Exhibit 9–3). This raises a question about the effect on future sales and profits of the decline in the research and development cost outlays in relation to sales. Similarly, the percentage of sales devoted to reparis and maintenance has declined from 5.7 percent in 19X5 to 3.8 percent in 19Y0, a matter of concern particularly in the light of the fact that Marine Supply Corporation's facilities are, on average, older now than in 19X5. In the latter year the percentage of repair and maintenance expense in relation to gross plant was 12.1 percent. In 19Y0 that relationship dropped to 8.3 percent. This *prima facie* evidence of a deterioration in the quality of Marine Supply Corporation's earnings merits further investigation.

The total effective tax rate of Marine Supply Corporation in 19Y0 is 52 percent which compare to industry composite effective rate of 47 percent. The net income to sales of Marine Supply Corporation is 4.4 percent for 19Y0 significantly below the industry composite of 5.8 percent for that year. However, since 19Y0 was a year of labor trouble and recession for the company, the percentages of net income to sales prevailing in the prior years, which are closer to the industry average, may be taken as more representative of the company's earning power.

Exhibit 9-17 analyzes the change occurring in net income between the 19X5-X7 period and the 19X8-Y0 period. Sales increased by 46 percent, but due largely to greater increases in the cost of good sold (49 percent) and interest expenses (353 percent) the increase in net income was held to only 11 percent.

EXHIBIT 9-17

MARINE SUPPLY CORPORATION
Statement Accounting for Variations in Net Income
Three-Year Period 19X5-X7 (average) Compared to
Three-Year Period 19X8-Y0 (average)
(in millions of dollars)

Items tending to increase net income:				
Increase in net sales:				
Net sales, 19X8-Y0	303.93			
Net sales, 19X5-X7	208.87	95.06		46%
Deduct increase in cost of goods sold:				
Cost of goods sold, 19X8-Y0	193.42			
Cost of goods sold, 19X5-X7	129.78	63.64		49
Net increase in gross margin			31.42	
Items tending to decrease in net income:				
Increase in depreciation:				
Depreciation, 19X8-Y0	5.53			
Depreciation, 19X5-X7	4.31	1.22		28
Increase in selling, general, and administrative expenses:				
S.G.A., 19X8-Y0	68.81			
S.G.A., 19X5-X7	47.69	21.12		44
Increase in interest expense:				
Interest expense, 19X8-Y0	4.48			
Interest expense, 19X5-X7	.99	3.49		353
Increase in other income and expense:				
Other income and expense, 19X8-Y0	.80			
Other income and expense, 19X5-X7	.59	.21		36
Net increase in expenses			26.04	
Net increase in profit before taxes			5.38	21
Increase in income taxes:				
Income taxes, 19X8-Y0	15.52			
Income taxes, 19X5-X7	11.66		3.86	33
Net increase in net income			1.52	11

Summary and conclusions

This analysis has examined all facets of Marine Supply Corporation's record of results of operations and financial position and has estimated the projected results and fund flows for one year. An analysis such as this is an indispensable step in arriving at a decision on the three questions posed. Nevertheless, essential as the data and information developed by this analysis is, it is not sufficient in most cases to arrive at a final conclusion. This is so because qualitative and other factors can have an important bearing on the final conclusion. Only when all the factors, those developed by the analysis as well as the others, have been assembled can a decision be reached by the application of judgment.

For example, the *bank* which is asked to extend short-term credit must take into consideration the character of the management, past loan experience, as well as the ongoing relationship with the loan applicant.

In addition to the foregoing intangibles, the long-term lender will focus on such matters as security arrangements and provisions which safeguard the solvency of the recipient of the loan.

The *equity investor* is, of course, interested in earning power and in earnings per share, but many considerations and judgments must be joined with these data before an investment decision is made. Thus, for instance, what earnings are, and what they are likely to be, is the product of financial analysis. At what price-earnings ratio they should be capitalized is a question for investment judgment. Similarly, the risk inherent in an enterprise, the volatility of its earnings, and the breadth and quality of the market for its securities are factors which must also be considered. They determine whether an investment fits into the investor's portfolio and whether it is compatible with his investment objectives.

Since the ultimate conclusions regarding problems, such as the lending and investing decision which we consider in this case, is based on more than the data and facts brought out by financial analysis alone, it follows that the most useful way to present the results of financial analysis is to summarize them by listing the most relevant and salient points which were developed by the analysis and which the decision maker should consider. This we shall do in this case.

The following are the main points which have been developed by our analysis of Marine Supply Corporation.

Short-term liquidity. The current ratio is in a downtrend but still stands at a relatively sound level. The downtrend may, in part, represent a correction of former excessive levels in the ratio.

The current assets are, as a whole, less liquid than in former years.

The slower turnover in accounts receivable indicates a possible deterioration in collectibility. The decline in inventory turnover may be due to diversity of product line rather than to unsaleable or obsolete items in stock.

Current liabilities have risen sharply in recent years, and they now represent one fourth of all funds available to the enterprise.

The decline in liquidity is evidenced by a rise in the liquidity index.

Fund projections for 19Y1 indicate a projected increase in working capital of $16 million by the end of that year. This assumes, however, the successful sale of $30 million in bonds and that expense projections which incorporate benefits of efficiencies will be realized. There is a moderate amount of risk that these projections may not be realized.

Capital structure and long-term solvency. In 19Y0 equity capital represented 55 percent of total funds invested in the enterprise down from 73 percent in 19X5. In recent years (see Exhibit 9–9) long-term debt increased drastically (3.18 times), out of proportion to such measures as growth in sales (1.69 times) or in equity (1.43 times).

The reduction of equity capital relative to debt and all funds invested in the company is not a favorable development in view of the fact that Marine Supply Corporation is in a cyclical industry. The company may be nearing the limit of its debt capacity.

Times interest earned is down to 5.28 in 19Y0 (from 29.24 to 19X5). If a portion of rentals would be included as fixed charges, the coverage ratio would drop lower still. Next year, assuming the $30 million in long-term bonds are sold, this ratio is slated to improve to 8.2 times.

Over the last six years 77 percent of all funds inflows were funds generated by operations. Thus, a very substantial source of funds is vulnerable to changes in operating results. Over the longer term, demand for funds is expected to increase significantly. Long-term debt maturities are slated to increase sharply even excluding those from the $30 million bond issue which is expected to be sold in 19Y1. There will be a growing need of funds for plant and equipment. Provisions for depreciation were consistently below fixed-asset additions in recent years.

Return on investment and asset utilization. The return on investment is in a declining trend. In 19Y0 the return on total assets was 6.4 percent compared with an industry composite of 9.3 percent in 19Y0 where the disparity with the industry composite of 12.8 percent is less marked.

The decline in return on total assets is due to the twin effects of declining asset utilization rates as well as a decline in profitability per dollar of sales.

Operating performance. The company's gross profit percentage has held relatively steady over the past six years. Other costs have neutralized Marine Supply Corporation's higher gross margin compared to the industry. Interest expenses have risen sharply over recent years. Both research and development expenses and repair and maintenance outlays have declined as a percentage of sales in recent years.

The significant decline in net income as a percentage of sales to 4.4 percent in 19Y0 (industry composite 5.8 percent) is due to the particularly adverse labor and economic conditions of that year. In prior years the company's net as a percentage of sales, compared more favorably to industry experience.

Projected income for 19Y1, based on the assumptions stated in the analysis, is $16.6 million after a loss of $3 million on disposal of the chain-saw division. On a per share basis the net income per share is expected to be $2.06 per share compared to earnings per share in 19Y0 of $1.66 and in 19X9 of $2.11. In 19Y0 income per share before the loss on the chain-saw division is projected at $2.43.

USES OF FINANCIAL STATEMENT ANALYSIS

The foregoing analysis of the financial statements of Marine Supply Corporation consists of two major parts: (1) the detailed analysis and (2) the summary and conclusions. As was mentioned earlier, in a formal analytical report the summary and conclusions section may precede the detailed analysis so that the reader is presented with material in the order of its importance to him.

The *bank* loan officer who has to decide on the short-term loan application by the company will normally give primary attention to short-term liquidity analysis and to the funds flow projection and secondarily to capital structure and operating results.

The investment committee of the *insurance company* may, in taking a longer term point of view, pay attention first to capital structure and long-term solvency and then to operating performance, return on investment, asset utilization, and short-term liquidity, and in that order of emphasis.

The *potential investor* in Marine Supply Corporation's shares will, of course, be interested in all the aspects of our analysis. His emphasis may, however, be different again and take the following order of priority: results of operations, return on investment, capital structure, and long-term solvency and short-term liquidity.

An adequate financial statement analysis will, as the Marine Supply Corporation analysis illustrates, contain in addition to the analysis of the data, enough information and detail so as to allow the decision maker to follow the rationale behind the analyst's conclusions as well as allow him to expand it into areas not covered by the analysis.

QUESTIONS

1. What kind of processes should normally precede an analysis of financial statements?
2. What are the analytical implications of the fact that financial statements are, at best, an abstraction of underlying reality?
3. Name the six major "building blocks" of financial analysis. What does the "building block" approach involve?
4. What are some of the earmarks of a good analysis? Into what distinct sections should a well-organized analysis be divided?
5. What additional knowledge and analytical skills must an analyst bring to bear upon the analysis of enterprises in specialized or regulated industries?

Appendix

EARNINGS PER SHARE—
COMPUTATION AND EVALUATION

The determination of the earnings level of an enterprise which is relevant to the purposes of the analyst is a complex analytical process. This earnings figure can be converted into an earnings per share (EPS) amount which is useful in the evaluation of the price of the common stock, in the evaluation of dividend coverage and dividend paying ability, as well as for other purposes. The analyst must, consequently, have a thorough understanding of the principles which govern the computation of EPS.

The intelligent analyst will never overemphasize the importance of, or place exclusive reliance on, any one figure, be it the widely used and popular EPS figure or any other statistic. In using the EPS figure he should always be alert to the composition of the "net income" figure used in its computation.

In the mid-1960s, when a wave of mergers brought with it the widespread use of convertible securities as financing devices, the attention of analysts and of accountants turned also to the denominator of the EPS computation, that is, the number of shares of common stock by which the earnings should be divided. It became obvious that the prior practice of considering only the common shares actually outstanding without a consideration of the future potential dilution which is inherent in convertible securities, had often led to an overstatement of EPS.

The managements of merger-minded companies had discovered that it was possible to buy the earnings of a company by compensating its owners with low-yield convertible securities which in effect represented a deferred equity interest. Since the acquired earnings were immediately included in the combined income of the merged enterprise while the dilutive effect of the issuance of convertible securities was ignored, an illusory increase in EPS was thus achieved. Such growth in EPS increased the value of the securities, thus enabling the merger-minded company to carry this value enhancing process even further by using its attractive securities to effect business combination at increasingly advantageous terms for its existing stockholders.

ILLUSTRATION 1. Merging Company A, which pays no dividend and whose stock sells at $35, issued to merged Company B, which is earning $3 per share, $1 convertible preferred, on a share-for-share basis which allows for conversion into Company A's common at $40 per share. Because of the dividend advantage there is no prospect of an early conversion of the convertible preferred into common. Thus, prior to *APB Opinion No. 15*, Company A realized "instant earnings" by getting a $3 per share earnings boost in return for a $1 preferred dividend requirement. It is obvious that the $1 convertible preferred derives most of its value from the conversion feature rather than from its meager dividend provision.

MAJOR PROVISIONS OF *APB OPINION NO. 15*

APB Opinion No. 15, issued in 1969, put an end to this unrealistic disregard of the potential dilutive effect of securities convertible into common stock. The *Opinion* looks to the substance of a securities issue rather than merely to its legalistic form.

Simple capital structure

If a corporation has a simple capital structure which consists only of common stock and nonconvertible senior securities and does not include potentially dilutive securities, then most of the provisions of the *Opinion* do not apply. In that case a single presentation of EPS is called for and is computed as follows:

$$\frac{\text{Net Income less claims of senior securities}}{\text{Weighted Average Number of Common Shares Outstanding during the period after adjustments for stock splits and dividends (including those effected after balance sheet date due before completion of financial statements)}}$$

In the above computation dividends of cumulative senior securities, whether earned or not, should be deducted from net income or added to net loss.

Computation of weighted average of common shares outstanding

The theoretically correct weighted average number of shares is the sum of shares outstanding each day divided by the number of days in the period. Less precise averaging methods, such as on a monthly or quarterly basis, where there is little change in the number of shares outstanding, is also permissible.

In the computation

1. Reacquired shares should be excluded from date of acquisition.
2. Previously reported EPS data should be adjusted retroactively for changes in outstanding shares resulting from stock splits or stock dividends.

Example of computation or weighted average number of shares outstanding

19X1	Transactions in common stock	Number of shares
January 1	Outstanding	1,200
February 2	Stock options exercised	200
April 15	Issued as 5% stock dividend	70
August 16	Issued in pooling of interests	400
September 2	Sale for cash	300
October 18	Repurchase of treasury shares	(100)
		2,070

Computation of weighted average number of shares

		Shares outstanding		Product:
		Number	Days	Share—days
Date of change:				
January 1		1,200		
Retroactive adjustment:				
For stock dividend (5%)		60		
Issued in pooling		400		
January 1—adjusted		1,660	32	53,120
February 2—stock option	200			
+5% stock dividend	10	210		
		1,870	212	396,440
September 2—sale for cash		300		
		2,170	46	99,820
October 18—repurchase		(100)		
		2,070	75	155,250
			365	704,630

19X1 weighted average number of shares $\dfrac{704,630}{365} = 1,930$ shares

As can be seen in the illustrations above, shares issued in a pooling of interests are included in the computation of EPS as of the beginning of all periods presented. This is so because under the pooling of interests concept the merged companies are assumed to have been combined since their respective inceptions. In the case of purchases the EPS reflect new shares issued only from date of acquisition.

Example of computation

Pooling of interests

Assumptions: On July 1, 19X2 Company A and B merged to form Company C. The transaction was accounted for as a *pooling of interests*.

	Company A	Company B
Net income January 1 to June 30, 19X2	$100,000	$150,000
Outstanding shares of common stock at June 30, 19X2 ...	20,000	8,000
Shares sold to public April 1, 19X2	10,000	

		Company C
Net income July 1 to December 31, 19X2		$325,000
Common shares issued for acquisition of:		
Company A		200,000
Company B		400,000
Computation:		
Net income ($100,000 + $150,000 + $325,000)		575,000
Average shares outstanding during year, using equivalent shares for pooled companies:		
Company A:		
$100,000 \times 3$ months	300,000	
$200,000 \times 3$ months	600,000	
Company B:		
$400,000 \times 6$	2,400,000	
Company C:		
$600,000 \times 6$	3,600,000	
	6,900,000	
Average	575,000	

Net income per weighted average number of shares of common stock outstanding during the year (equivalent shares used for pooled companies) $1.00

Purchase

Assumptions: Company X has outstanding at December 31, 19X2, 120,000 shares of common stock. During the year (October 1) Company X issued 30,000 shares of its own common stock for another company. This transaction was accounted for as purchase. Net income for 19X2 was $292,500.

Computation:
9 months × 90,000 shares outstanding   810,000
3 months × 120,000 shares outstanding   360,000
                                                                      1,170,000

$$\text{Average shares} \frac{1,170,000}{12} = 97,500$$

Net income per weighted average number of shares of common

$$\text{stock outstanding during the year} \frac{\$292,500}{97,500} = \$3.00$$

COMPLEX CAPITAL STRUCTURE

A company is deemed to have a complex capital structure if it has outstanding potentially dilutive securities such as convertible securities, options, warrants, or other stock issue agreements.

By dilution is meant a reduction in EPS (or increase in net loss per share) resulting from the assumption that convertible securities have been converted into common stock, or that options and warrants have been exercised, or that shares have been issued in compliance with certain contracts.

A company having a complex capital structure has to give a dual presentation of EPS if the aggregate dilutive effect of convertible and other securities is more than 3 percent. Such dual presentation is to be effected with equal prominence on the income statement and show: (1) primary EPS and (2) fully diluted EPS.

Primary EPS

Primary EPS is the amount of earnings attributable to each share of common stock outstanding plus dilutive common stock equivalents.

Definition of common stock equivalents (CSE). The concept of CSE is basic to the approach adopted in the *APB Opinion No. 15.* It denotes a security which derives the major portion of its value from its common stock characteristics or conversion privileges. Thus, a CSE is a security which, because of its terms or the circumstances under which it was issued, is in substance equivalent to common stock. The following are examples of CSE.

1. *Convertible debt and convertible preferred stocks* are CSE only if at the time of issuance they have a cash yield (based on market price) of less than 66⅔ percent of the then current bank prime interest rate. If a convertible security is issued which is a CSE and that same security was previously issued when it was not a CSE at time of issuance, the earlier issued shares or debt should be considered a CSE *from the date of issuance of the later shares or*

debt. Prior periods EPS should not be restated. Similarly, any subsequent issuance of shares or debt with the same terms as previously issued shares or debt classified as a CSE should be classified as a CSE at its time of issuance even though the later issue of shares or debt would not be a CSE under the yield test at the later date of issue. This requirement can be overcome by a change in a term having economic significance which is expected to affect prices in the securities market.

2. *Stock options and warrants (including stock purchase contracts)* are always to be considered as CSE.

3. *Participating securities and two-class common stocks* are CSE if their participation features enable their holders to share in the earnings potential of the issuing corporation, on substantially the same basis as common stock, even though the securities may not give the holder the right to exchange his shares for common stock.

4. *Contingent shares*—if shares are to be issued in the future upon the mere passage of time, they should be considered as outstanding for purposes of computing EPS. If additional shares of stock are issuable for little or no consideration upon the satisfaction of certain conditions, they should be considered as outstanding when the conditions are met.

5. *Securities of subsidiaries* may be considered common stock equivalents and conversion or exercise assumed for computing consolidated or parent company EPS when—

   a. As to the subsidiary

   (1) Certain of the subsidiaries' securities are CSE in relation to its own common stock.

   (2) Other of the subsidiary's convertible securities, although not CSE in relation to its own common stock, would enter into the computation of its fully diluted earnings per share.

   b. As to the parent

   (1) The subsidiary's securities are convertible into the parent company's common stock.

   (2) The subsidiary issues options and warrants to purchase the parent company's common stock.

Computation of primary EPS. If CSE with a dilutive effect are present, then primary EPS should be based on the weighted average number of shares of common stock and CSE. The computation is also based on the assumption that convertible securities which are CSE were converted at the beginning of the period (or at time of issuance, if later), and that requires adding back to net income any deductions for interest or dividends, net of tax effect, related to such securities.

Use of treasury stock method for options, warrants, and other securities requiring "boot" for conversion.   The *treasury stock* method recognizes the use of proceeds that would be obtained upon exercise of options and warrants in computing EPS. It assumes that any proceeds would be used to purchase common stock at current market prices. For options and warrants the treasury stock method of computing the dilution to be reflected in EPS should be used (except for two exceptions to be explained). Under the treasury stock method:

1. EPS data are computed as if the options and warrants were exercised at the beginning of the period (or at time of issuance, if later) and as if the funds obtained thereby were used to purchase common stock at the average market price during the period.
2. But the assumption of exercise is not reflected in EPS data until the market price of the common stock obtainable has been in excess of the exercise price for substantially all of three consecutive months ending with the last month of the period to which EPS relate.[1]

> Example of treasury stock method
> *Assumptions:*
>   1,000,000 common shares outstanding (no change during year)
> $80 average market price for the common stock for the year
>   100,000 warrants outstanding exercisable at $48
> *Computation:*
>   *Shares*
>   100,000   shares issuable on exercise of warrants (proceeds $4,800,000)
>   (60,000) shares acquirable with $4,800,000 proceeds (at $80 per share)
>   ——————
>   40,000 CSE
>   1,000,000 common shares
>   ——————
>   1,040,000 shares used for computing primary EPS

First exception to treasury stock method.   Warrants or debt indentures may permit or require certain uses of funds with exercise of warrants. Examples:

1. Debt is permitted or required to be tendered towards exercise price.
2. Proceeds of exercise are required to retire debt.
3. Convertible securities require cash payments upon conversion.

---

[1] The following formula will yield the number of incremental shares which will result from applying the treasury stock method to options or warrants (*Y*);

$$Y = \frac{M - E}{M}(N)$$

where *M* is the market price per share, *E* is the exercise price of option or warrant per common share and *N* is the total number of shares obtainable on exercise.

In these cases, an "if converted" method, which assumes conversion on exercise at the beginning of the period should be applied as if retirement or conversion of the securities had occurred and as if the excess proceeds, if any, had been applied to the purchase of common stock under the treasury stock method.

Second exception to treasury stock method. If the number of shares of common stock obtainable upon exercise of outstanding options and warrants in the aggregate exceeds 20 percent of the number of common shares outstanding at the end of the period for which the computation is being made, the treasury stock method should be modified. In these circumstances all the options and warrants should be assumed to have been exercised and the aggregate proceeds therefrom to have been applied in two steps:

1. As if the funds obtained were first applied to the repurchase of outstanding common shares at the average market price during the period (treasury stock method) but not to exceed 20 percent of the outstanding shares; and then
2. As if the balance of the funds were applied first to reduce any short-term or long-term borrowings and any remaining funds were invested in U.S. government securities or commercial paper, with appropriate recognition of any income tax effect.
3. The results of steps 1 and 2 of the computation (whether dilutive or antidilutive) should be aggregated, and if the net effect is dilutive, it should enter into the EPS computation.

Example of second exception of treasury stock method

	Case 1	Case 2
Assumptions:		
Net income for year	$ 4,000,000	$ 3,000,000
Common shares outstanding (no change during year)	3,000,000	3,000,000
Options and warrants outstanding to purchase equivalent shares	1,000,000	1,000,000
20% limitation on assumed repurchase	600,000	600,000
Exercise price per share	$15	$15
Average market value per common share to be used	$20	$14*
Interest rate on borrowings	6%	6%
Computations:		
Application of assumed proceeds ($15 × 1,000,000 shares) toward repurchase of outstanding common shares at applicable market value (600,000 × $20) and (600,000 × $14)	$12,000,000	$ 8,400,000
Reduction of debt	3,000,000	6,600,000
	$15,000,000	$15,000,000

Adjustment of net income:		
Actual net income	$ 4,000,000	$ 3,000,000
Interest reduction on debt (6%) less 50%		
tax effect......................................	90,000	198,000
Adjusted net income (A)	$ 4,090,000	$ 3,198,000
Adjustment of shares outstanding:		
Actual number outstanding	3,000,000	3,000,000
Net additional shares issuable		
(1,000,000–600,000)	400,000	400,000
Adjusted shares outstanding (B)	3,400,000	3,400,000
Primary EPS:		
Before adjustment	$1.33	$1.00
After adjustment (A ÷ B)	$1.20	$0.94

* The three consecutive months test has previously been met.

Provisions concerning antidilution. Antidilution is an increase in EPS resulting from the assumption that convertible securities have been converted or that options and warrants have been exercised or other shares have been issued upon the fulfillment of certain conditions. For example, although stock options and warrants (and their equivalents) and stock purchase contracts should always be considered CSE, they should not enter into EPS calculations until the average market price of the common stock exceeds the exercise price of the option or warrant for preferably three consecutive months before the reporting period.

Computations of primary EPS should not give effect to CSE or other contingent issuance for any period in which their inclusion would have the effect of increasing the EPS amount or decreasing the loss per share amount otherwise computed.

Fully diluted EPS

Definition of fully diluted EPS. Fully diluted EPS is designed to show the maximum potential dilution of current EPS on a prospective basis. Fully diluted EPS is the amount of current EPS reflecting the maximum dilution that would have resulted from conversions, exercises, and other contingent issuances that individually would have decreased EPS and in the aggregate would have had a dilutive effect. All such issuances are assumed to have taken place at the beginning of the period (or at the time the event or contingency arose, if later).

When required. Fully diluted EPS data are required for each period presented if shares of common stock (1) were issued during the period on conversions, exercise, etc., or (2) were contingently issuable at the close of any period presented and if primary EPS for such period would have been affected (dilutively or incrementally) had such actual issuances taken place at the beginning of the period or would have been reduced had such contingent issuances taken place at the beginning of the period.

Computation of fully diluted EPS. The computation should be based on the assumption that all such issued and issuable shares were outstanding from the beginning of the period (or from the time the contingency arose, if after the beginning of the period). Interest charges applicable to convertible securities and nondiscretionary adjustments that would have been made to items based on net income or income before taxes—such as profit-sharing expense, certain royalties, and investment credit—or preferred dividends applicable to the convertible securities should be taken into account in determining the balance of income applicable to common stock.

Use ending market price for treasury stock method. The treasury stock method (with the two exceptions) should be used to compute fully diluted EPS if dilution results from outstanding options and warrants; however, in order to reflect maximum potential dilution, the market price at the close of the period reported upon should be used to determine the number of shares which would be assumed to be repurchased (under the treasury stock method) if such market price is higher than the average price used in computing primary EPS.

Example of computation of fully diluted EPS. Assume that there are 1,000,000 shares of Class A preferred stock and 1,500,000 shares of Class B preferred stock outstanding, both issues convertible into common on a share-for-share basis. Two million shares of common are outstanding. Class A preferred is a CSE with a $1.80 dividend; Class B is a nonCSE preferred with a $1 dividend. Net income before either preferred dividend was $7,300,000.

Computation

	Shares	Net income	EPS
Net income		$7,300,000	
Shares outstanding	2,000,000		
$1.80 preferred dividend.....................		(1,800,000)	
$1.00 preferred dividend.....................		(1,500,000)	
($2 per share)	2,000,000	4,000,000	
Assume conversion of CSE Class A preferred ..	1,000,000	1,800,000	
	3,000,000	5,800,000	
Primary EPS			$1.93
Assume conversion of nonCSE Class B preferred	1,500,000	1,500,000	
	4,500,000	$7,300,000	
Fully diluted EPS (beginning with primary EPS			$1.62

Since the intention in presenting fully diluted EPS is to show the *maximum* dilution possible, an alternative computation is possible in this case which would yield a lower figure of fully diluted EPS. This computation has as a starting point the outstanding common shares and income after preferred dividends rather than the primary EPS.

Computation

	Shares	*Net income*	*EPS*
Shares outstanding and income after dividends	2,000,000	$4,000,000	
Assume conversion of nonCSE Class B preferred	1,500,000	1,500,000	
	3,500,000	$5,500,000	
Fully diluted EPS–beginning with outstanding shares and income after preferred dividends			$1.57

The reason why the alternative computation yields a lower fully diluted EPS is that while the $1.80 preferred issue is dilutive for purposes of computing primary EPS, it is antidilutive for purposes of computing the fully diluted EPS.

Provisions regarding antidilution.   As with primary EPS, no antidilution should be recognized. Consequently, computations should exclude those securities whose conversion, exercise, or other contingent issuance would have the effect of increasing the EPS amount or decreasing the loss per share amount for each period.

Requirements for additional disclosures in conjunction with the presentation of EPS data

Complex capital structures require additional disclosures either on the balance sheet or in notes. Financial statements should include a description sufficient to explain the pertinent rights and privileges of the various securities outstanding.

With regard to EPS data, disclosure is required for—

1. The bases upon which both primary and fully diluted EPS are calculated, identifying the securities entering into computations.
2. All assumptions and any resulting adjustments used in computations.
3. The number of shares issued upon conversion, exercise, etc. during at least the most recent year.

Supplementary EPS data should be disclosed (preferably in a note) if

1. Conversions during the period would have affected primary EPS (either dilutive *or* incremental effect) if they had taken place at the beginning of the period, or
2. Similar conversions occur after the close of the period but before completion of the financial report.

This supplementary information should show what primary EPS would have been if such conversions had taken place at the *beginning* of the period or date of issuance of security if within the period.

It should be understood that the designation of securities as CSE is done solely for the purpose of determining primary EPS. No changes from present practices in the accounting for such securities or in their presentation within the financial statements are required.

Elections at the time EPS opinion became effective

APB Opinion No. 15 became effective for fiscal periods beginning after December 31, 1968, for *all* EPS data (primary, fully diluted, and supplementary) regardless of when the securities entering into computations of EPS were issued. In addition, an election was available as of May 31, 1969, for all securities whose time of issuance had been prior to June 1, 1969. This election is only for purposes of computing primary EPS. Under this election a computation is made by either:

1. Determining the classifications of all such securities under *APB Opinion No. 15* or,
2. Determining the classification under *APB Opinion No. 9* regardless of how they would be classified under *APB Opinion No. 15*. This election in effect "freezes" securities as previously classified.

This means that in determining EPS for reporting after May 31, 1969, certain securities can be classified as CSE under either the old rules or the new. Regardless of the election made, computations of EPS should be based on the guidelines set forth in *APB Opinion No. 15*.

COMPREHENSIVE ILLUSTRATION OF COMPUTATION OF EPS

The following illustration of the computation of EPS shows the application of many of the provisions included in the foregoing discussion of *APB Opinion No. 15*. To facilitate comprehension the illustration is organized as follows:

Schedules

	Facts and data
I	EPS: Computation
II	EPS: Summary of share computations
A	Weighted average common shares outstanding
B	Share computations—5% subordinated debentures
C	Share computations—5% convertible preferred stock
D	Share computations—warrants
E	Share computations—options
F	Share computations—contingently issuable—purchase

Facts and data

The Multiplex Corporation has the following capital structure, with special factors as noted:

5% subordinated debentures, convertible into common stock at $50 per share:

Issued 4/1/X1	$1,000,000 } Not a CSE at
Issued 4/1/X2	1,000,000 } time of issue
Issued 8/1/X2 (bank prime rate 8½%)	1,000,000
Converted 12/1/X2 into 30,000 shares of common	(1,500,000)
Outstanding 12/31/X2 convertible into 30,000 shares of common	1,500,000

7% prior preference stock, authorized, issued, and outstanding:

December 31, 19X1 and 19X2	100,000
Annual dividends	$ 700,000

$5 convertible preferred stock, convertible into common stock at $50 (2 shares for 1), authorized 1,000,000 shares, issuable in series:

Series A—issued 2/1/X1 in a pooling of interests	100,000 } A CSE since time of issue
Series B—issued 6/1/X2 in a purchase (bank prime rate, 7½%; market value at issuance was $100)	100,000
Converted 11/1/X2 into 25,000 shares of common—	
Series A	(12,500)
Outstanding, 12/31/X2:	
Series A	87,500
Series B	100,000
Total (convertible into 375,000 shares of common)	187,500

Warrants to purchase common stock at $50 per share—issued with Series A preferred:

Total number	100,000
Exercised 12/1/X2	(20,000)
Outstanding 12/31/X2	80,000

Options granted under executives stock option plans at market value on date of grant:

Plan B—granted 3/1/X1 at $30 per share	8,000
Exercised 7/1/X2	(8,000)
Plan C—granted 12/1/X2 at $60 per share, none exercised	5,000

Shares contingently issuable in connection with 6/1/X2 purchase: If acquired net earnings for the three years 19X2–19X4 are at least equal to certain amounts, a total number of additional shares will then be issued, as shown:

$1,500,000	10,000 shares
2,250,000	20,000
3,000,000	40,000

Net earnings of the purchased company for 19X2 were $520,000.

Other relevant hypothetical facts about the hypothetical corporation are as follows:

1. On April 1, 19X2 the corporation completed a public offering of 200,000 common shares.
2. On October 1, 19X2 the corporation purchased 60,000 common shares for its treasury.
3. Market prices of the company's common stock during 19X2 were:

	First	Average	Quarterly	19X2 average
January	40	34		
February	30	30	32	
March	30	32		
April	35	35		
May	40	43	42	
June	45	48		
July	50	47		
August	40	38	43	
September	35	44		
October	55	51		
November	50	54	55	
December	60	60		43

The closing market price on December 31 was 65.

4. For the year 19X2, the corporation's earnings, in condensed form, were:

Income before extraordinary items	$5,000,000
Extraordinary credits, net of taxes	1,000,000
Net income	$6,000,000

5. Included in the above is pretax interest on the subordinated debentures, as follows:

January 1–March 31	$12,500
April 1–July 31	33,333
August 1–December 1	50,000
December 1–December 31	6,250

6. Not included are total preferred dividends (paid quarterly, March 1, June 1, September 1, and December 1) as follows:

7% prior preference stock	$700,000
Series A	484,375
Series B	250,000

SCHEDULE I

EPS: Computations

	Income before extra- ordinary item	Extra- ordinary item	Net income
Amounts before adjustment	$5,000,000	$1,000,000	$6,000,000
Less: Dividend on 7% prior preference stock	(700,000)		(700,000)
Amounts after preferred dividends	$4,300,000	$1,000,000	$5,300,000
Adjustments for computing primary EPS: Interest on 5% convertible subordinated debentures, net of tax effect (assumed 50% rate)	28,125		28,125
Income for primary EPS	$4,328,125	$1,000,000	$5,328,125
Adjustments for computing fully diluted EPS: Interest on 5% convertible subordinated debentures, net of tax effect (assumed 50% rate)	$ 22,916		$ 22,916
Income for fully diluted EPS	$4,351,041	$1,000,000	$5,351,041
Adjustments for computing supplementary EPS: Income for primary EPS, as above	$4,328,125	$1,000,000	$5,328,125
Add: Additional interest on 5% convertible subordinated debentures (net of assumed 50% tax effect)	18,750		18,750
Income for supplementary EPS	$4,346,875	$1,000,000	$5,346,875

Note: Interest is eliminated (*a*) for primary EPS, for period after 8/1/X2 (date on which entire issue be-came a CSE), and (*b*) for fully diluted EPS, for all earlier months. For supplementary EPS, interest eliminated for primary EPS is increased to reflect the assumption that the actual conversion of debentures took place as of the beginning of the year (or date of issuance).

Weighted average common and common equiv- alent shares (from Schedule II)	1,490,900	1,490,900	1,490,900
Related income, as above	$4,328,125	$1,000,000	$5,328,125
Earnings per common share and common equivalent share	$2.90	$.67	$3.57
Weighted average shares adjusted for full dilution (from Schedule II)	1,529,649	1,529,649	1,529,649
Related income, as above	$4,351,041	$1,000,000	$5,351,041
Earnings per common share, assuming full dilution	$2.84	$.66	$3.50

Note: Dilution is less than 3%, and could therefore be considered immaterial.

Supplementary data:

Weighted average common and common equiv- alent shares adjusted to give pro forma effect to actual conversions as though made at the beginning of the year (from Schedule II)	1,505,900	1,505,900	1,505,900
Related income, as above	$4,346,875	$1,000,000	$5,346,875
Supplementary earnings per common and common equivalent share, giving pro forma effect to conversions	$2.89	$.66	$3.55

Note: Effect on primary EPS is clearly immaterial, and disclosure would probably be confined to noting that that is the case.

SCHEDULE II
EPS: Summary of share computations

Shares

Weighted average common shares outstanding (Schedule A)	1,147,333
Weighted average CSE:	
5% subordinated debentures (Schedule B)	22,500
$5 convertible preferred (Schedule C)	312,500
Warrants (Schedule D)	1,977
Options (Schedule E)	757
Contingently issuable—purchase (Schedule F)	5,833
Weighted average common and common equivalent shares (Used to compute primary EPS)	1,490,000 *(To Sch. I)*
Adjustments for full dilution:	
5% subordinated debentures (Schedule B)	18,333
$5 convertible preferred (Schedule C)	—
Warrants (Schedule D)	19,541
Options (Schedule E)	875
Contingently issuable—purchase (Schedule F)	—
	38,749
Weighted average shares adjusted for full dilution	1,529,649 *(To Sch. I)*
(Used to compute fully diluted EPS)	
Weighted average common and common equivalent shares, as above	1,490,900
Adjustment for supplementary purposes:	
5% subordinated debentures (Schedule B)	15,000
Weighted average shares giving pro forma effect to conversions of debentures as though made at beginning of year (or date of issue)	1,505,900 *(To Sch. I)*

(Used to compute supplementary EPS)

SCHEDULE A
Weighted average common shares outstanding

Number of shares

Date	Source	Increase (decrease)	Total	Months	Weighted product
Jan. 1	Balance		1,000,000	3	3,000,000
Apr. 1	Public offering	200,000	1,200,000	3	3,600,000
July 1	Stock options exercised	8,000	1,208,000	3	3,624,000
Oct. 1	Treasury stock	(60,000)	1,148,000	1	1,148,000
Nov. 1	Conversion—Series A preferred	25,000	1,173,000	1	1,173,000
Dec. 1	Conversion—debentures	30,000 }	1,223,000	1	1,223,000
	Exercise of warrants	20,000 }			
				12	13,768,000
	Weighted average common shares outstanding				1,147,333

SCHEDULE B
5% subordinated debentures

	Total shares	Weight	Weighted average shares
CSE for primary EPS:			
Equivalent shares—issue of 4/1/X1	20,000	5/12	
Equivalent shares—issue of 4/1/X2	20,000	5/12	25,000
Equivalent shares—issue of 8/1/X2	20,000	5/12	
Less: Shares issued on conversion 12/1/X2 and included in shares outstanding	(30,000)	1/12	(2,500)
Weighted CSE—debentures— primary EPS			22,500

Note: Issue of 8/1/X2 was a CSE at time of issuance because cash yield was less than two thirds of the bank prime rate. Accordingly, earlier issues of this security with same terms acquired CSE status at that time.

	Total shares	Weight	Weighted average shares
Fully diluted EPS:			
Equivalent shares—issue of 4/1/X1	20,000	12/12	20,000
Equivalent shares—issue of 4/1/X2	20,000	9/12	15,000
Equivalent shares—issue of 8/1/X2	20,000	5/12	8,333
			43,333
Less: Shares issued on conversion 12/1/X2 and included in shares outstanding (as above)			(2,500)
Share equivalents included in CSE above			(22,500)
Net additional shares—debentures— fully diluted EPS			18,333

Note: For fully diluted EPS, convertibility before acquiring CSE status relates to entire period during which issues were outstanding.

	Total shares	Weight	Weighted average shares
Supplementary EPS:			
Equivalent shares—actual conversions as though made at beginning of year (or date of later issuance):			
Issue of 4/1/X1 (entire)	20,000	12/12	20,000
Issue of 4/1/X2 (part)	10,000	9/12	7,500
Equivalent shares—not converted:			
Issue of 4/1/X2 (remainder)	10,000	5/12	4,167
Issue of 8/1/X2	20,000	5/12	8,333
			40,000
Less: Shares and CSE reflected in primary EPS (as above)			(25,000)
Net additional shares—debentures— supplementary EPS			15,000

SCHEDULE C
$5 convertible preferred stock

	Total shares	Weight	Weighted average shares
CSE for primary EPS:			
Series A—equivalent shares	200,000	12/12	200,000
Less: Shares issued on conversion 11/1/X2 and included in shares outstanding	(25,000)	2/12	(4,167)
			195,833
Series B—equivalent shares—issue of 6/1/X2	200,000	7/12	116,667
Weighted CSE—preferred—primary EPS			312,500

Note: The cash yield of Series B at time of issuance was *not* less than two thirds the prime rate. This security, which thus would not have been a CSE, assumes that status because Series A—an outstanding security with the same terms—was a CSE. (Because the issuance involved a *purchase*, Series B is a CSE only from 6/1/X2.)

Fully diluted EPS:
   No additional effect: convertible preferred was a CSE during entire period outstanding.

Supplementary EPS:
   Had the conversion of Series A taken place at the beginning of the year, primary EPS would not have been affected, because the issue was a CSE during the entire period. Accordingly, this conversion does not call for supplementary EPS disclosure.

SCHEDULE D
Warrants

		Total shares	Weight	Weighted average shares
CSE for primary EPS:				
As to warrants exercised Dec. 1:				
Number of shares................		20,000		
Exercise price—proceeds	$1,000,000			
Average market price, 4th quarter, prior to exercise	$52.50			
Treasury stock shares		(19,048)		
Net shares added in respect of period before exercise		952	2/12*	159
As to warrants outstanding Dec. 31:				
Number of shares................		80,000		
Exercise price—proceeds	$4,000,000			
Average market price, 4th quarter........................	$55			
Treasury stock shares		(72,727)		
Net shares added in respect of outstanding		7,273	3/12	1,818
Weighted CSE—warrants— primary EPS				1,977

Note:Average quarterly market prices were *anti*dilutive during the 1st, 2d, and 3d quarters, and *dilutive* during the 4th quarter. Accordingly the first three quarters are ignored in the computation, which is based on the average market price during the 4th quarter. For warrants exercised, the average price used is that for the portion of the 4th quarter prior to exercise.

		Total shares	Weight	Weighted average shares
Fully diluted EPS:				
As to warrants exercised Dec. 1:				
Number of shares................		20,000		
Exercise price—proceeds	$1,000,000			
Market price at date of exercise........................	$60			
Treasury stock shares		(16,667)		
Shares added in respect of period before exercise		3,333	11/12*	3,056
As to warrants outstanding Dec. 31:				
Number of shares................		80,000		
Exercise price—proceeds	$4,000,000			
Market price at December 31	$65			
Treasury stock shares		(61,538)		
Shares added in respect of outstanding		18,462	12/12	18,462
Total shares added.................				21,518
Less: CSE added (as above)				(1,977)
Weighted average additional shares—warrants, for fully diluted EPS				19,541

Note: For fully diluted EPS, market prices at *date of exercise* and *year-end* as appropriate, are used rather than *averages*.

* The exercised warrants enter the computation of primary EPS only for the two months preceding their exercise because only during this period was the average market price of the common stock above the exercise price. For fully diluted EPS the end of period coincides with date of exercise on which date the market price was $60 per common share.

SCHEDULE E
Options

	Total shares	Weight	Weighted average shares
CSE for primary EPS:			
Plan B: Shares optioned at beginning of year	8,000		
Exercise price—proceeds $240,000			
Average market price during the 6-month period before exercise $37			
Treasury stock shares	(6,486)		
Shares added (to date of exercise)	1,514	6/12	757
Plan C: Shares optioned December 1	5,000		
Exercise price $60			
Average market price, December $60			
No effect			
Weighted CSE—options— primary EPS			757
Fully diluted EPS:			
Plan B: Prior to exercise	8,000		
Exercise price—proceeds $240,000			
Market price at date of exercise $50			
Treasury stock shares	(4,800)		
Shares added to date of exercise	3,200	6/12	1,600
Less: CSE added (as above)			(757)
Net shares added—Plan B			843
Plan C:	5,000		
Exercise price—proceeds $300,000			
Market price at December 31 ...... $65			
Treasury stock shares	(4,615)		
Shares added—Plan C	385	1/12	32
Weighted average shares— options—fully diluted EPS			875

Note: For fully diluted EPS, market prices at *date of exercise* and *year-end*, as appropriate, are used rather than *averages*.

SCHEDULE F
Contingently issuable—purchase

	Total shares	Weight	Weighted average shares
CSE for primary EPS:			
If total earnings for 19X2–X4 of the acquired company are $1,500,000, an additional 10,000 shares will be issued. This is equivalent to annual earnings of $500,000 for each of these three years; since this level has been attained, the entire 10,000 shares are regarded *as though issued,* for primary EPS:			
Shares (weighted from date of purchase	10,000	7/12	5,833

Fully diluted EPS:
Both of the other earnings levels (i.e., $750,000 and $1,000,000 average annual) specified as a basis for additional share issuances are above that currently attained. In no case would these enter primary EPS; they would, however, enter fully diluted EPS *if dilutive.* Neither of the increased-earnings contingencies is dilutive, and therefore neither enters the computation of fully diluted EPS. (The fact that neither is dilutive is readily seen by reference to the *incremental* factors: the *increment* of $250,000 in earnings will result in an *increment* of 10,000 shares—representing $25 per *incremental* share; *incremental* earnings of $500,000 will result in an *increment* of 30,000 shares—representing $16.67 per *incremental* share.)

IMPLICATIONS FOR ANALYSIS

APB Opinion No. 15 has been criticized, particularly by accountants, because it covers areas outside the realm of accountancy, relies on pro forma presentations which are influenced in large measure by market fluctuations, and because it deals with areas properly belonging to financial analysis.

Whatever the merit of these criticisms, and they do have merit, the financial analyst must welcome this initiative by the accounting profession. It does provide specific and workable guidelines for a meaningful recognition of the dilutive effects, present and prospective, of securities which are the equivalents of common stock. The elements entering the consistent computation of primary EPS and fully diluted EPS are so many and varied and require so many internal data that it is best that the accounting profession has assumed the responsibility for their computation rather than choosing the alternative of disclosing the information and leaving it to outsiders to make their own computations. The financial analyst must, however, have a thorough understanding of the bases on which EPS are computed.

APB Opinion No. 15 has a number of flaws and inconsistencies which the analyst must consider in his interpretations of EPS data:

1. There is a basic inconsistency in treating certain securities as the equivalent of common stock for purposes of computing EPS while not considering them as part of the stockholders equity in the

balance sheet. Consequently the analyst will have difficulty in interrelating reported EPS with the debt-leverage position pertaining to the same earnings.

2. There are a number of arbitrary benchmarks in the Opinion, such as the 20 percent treasury stock repurchase assumption limitation and the 66⅔ percent of prime rate test. The latter is particularly vulnerable to criticism because it does not differentiate among the types of securities issued, their credit standing, or between short-term and long-term interest rates. The prime rate is basically a short-term rate, whereas an interest rate placed on convertibles is mostly a long-term rate.[2] Normally short-term rates are lower than long-term rates. The effect of this is that many low coupon convertibles can be issued which would nevertheless not qualify as CSE under the Opinion.

3. Generally EPS are considered to be a factor influencing stock prices. The Opinion considers options and warrants to be CSE at all times, and whether they are dilutive or not depends on the price of the common stock. Thus, we can get a circular effect in that the reporting of EPS may influence the market price, which, in turn, influences EPS. Also, under these rules earnings may depend on market prices of the stock rather than only on economic factors within the enterprise.

Under these rules the projection of future EPS requires not only the projection of earnings levels but also the projection of future market prices.

4. Since the determination of whether a security is a CSE or not is made only at the time of issuance, it is quite possible that a security which was not originally a CSE is later so recognized in the marketplace. Nevertheless, the status of the security in the computation of EPS cannot be changed to recognize the new reality.

Despite these limitations, primary EPS and fully diluted EPS computed under the provisions of APB *Opinion No. 15* are more valid measurements of EPS than those which were obtained under the rules which were previously in effect.

Statement accounting for changes in earnings per share

When analyzing or projecting EPS the analyst can focus on changes in income on a per share basis. Table A–1 presents an analysis of the changes in the EPS of a large chemical company for 19X4.

---

[2] When *APB Opinion 15* was issued short- and long-term rates were unusually close to each other. Since then the spread between them has widened thus making comparisons with the prime rate less meaningful.

TABLE A–1
Analysis of changes in earnings per share

		Earnings per share	
Year 19X3 earnings			$2.77
Additional earnings resulting from:			
Higher sales volume		$1.20	
Manufacturing cost savings		0.37	
Lower raw material prices		0.06	
		$1.63	
Reductions in earnings caused by:			
Lower selling prices	$0.25		
Higher selling, administrative research, development, and other expenses	0.49	0.74	
Increase in operating results			0.89
			$3.66
Nonoperating items:			
Lower income taxes, due primarily to difference in tax rate		$0.12	
Higher investment tax credit on property additions		0.12	
Other income and charges–net		0.03	
Unusual write-offs:			
Obsolescence	$(.06)		
Self-insurance reserve	(.07)		
Other	.03	(.10)	
Effect on earnings of shares issued during the year........................		(.11)	0.06
Year 19X4 earnings			$3.72
Increase in EPS			$0.95

This published analysis is noteworthy particularly because it contains details such as those pertaining to changes due to sales volume and selling prices, which are normally available only to those with access to internal management records. This information, whenever available, can be of great help to the analyst in the evaluation and prediction of earnings and EPS.

INDEX